The Economics of Interdependence:
Economic Policy in the Atlantic Community

Published volumes in
"The Atlantic Policy Studies"

H. A. KISSINGER
The Troubled Partnership:
A Re-appraisal of the Atlantic Alliance

Z. BRZEZINSKI
Alternative to Partition:
For a Broader Conception of America's Role in Europe

J. COPPOCK
Atlantic Agricultural Unity:
Is It Possible?

M. CAMPS
European Unification in the Sixties:
From the Veto to the Crisis

H. CLEVELAND
The Atlantic Idea and Its European Rivals

T. GEIGER
The Conflicted Relationship:
The West and the Transformation of Asia,
Africa and Latin America

J. PINCUS
Trade, Aid and Development:
The Rich and Poor Nations

B. BALASSA
Trade Liberalization among Industrial Countries:
Objectives and Alternatives

S. HOFFMANN
Gulliver's Troubles, Or the Setting
of American Foreign Policy

The Economics
of Interdependence:
Economic Policy
in the
Atlantic Community

RICHARD N. COOPER

A volume in the series
"The Atlantic Policy Studies"

Published for the Council on Foreign Relations by
McGRAW-HILL BOOK COMPANY
New York   Toronto   London   Sydney

HF
1411
.C587
1968 / *51,611*

The Economics of Interdependence

Copyright © 1968 by Council on Foreign Relations, Inc.
All Rights Reserved.
Printed in the United States of America.
This book, or parts thereof, may not be reproduced
in any form without permission of the publishers.

Library of Congress Catalog Card Number: 68-20053

07-012920-7
07-012921-5

3456   VBVB   787654

To my parents

The Atlantic Policy Studies

The Atlantic Policy Studies is a series of major works on the future of the Atlantic Community. The project was undertaken by the Council on Foreign Relations assisted by a generous grant from the Ford Foundation. Mr. Cooper's book, the tenth to be published in the series, is an analysis of the growing economic interdependence among the members of the Atlantic Community. It poses the problem of how nations may enjoy the many benefits of international commerce while preserving considerable freedom to set and pursue successfully their own economic objectives, and makes the case for close international cooperation to prevent the uncontrolled use of restrictions from negating the principal benefits from trade.

Undertaken out of a conviction that a re-examination of U.S. relations with and policies toward Western Europe is urgently needed, the Atlantic Policy Studies are an attempt to come to grips with basic questions about the future of America's Atlantic relations.

The studies are policy-oriented, seeking not only to describe and forecast but also to prescribe. Each of the ten studies is the responsibility of its author, but considers its special problems in the light of the general aim of the program as a whole. The program is under the guidance of a Steering Committee, of which Charles M. Spofford is chairman.

The Atlantic Policy Studies are divided into four broad categories, dealing respectively with the broad strategic problems of the Atlantic Alliance; with economic relations among the Atlantic countries and between them and less-developed countries; with the external environment of the West; and with Atlantic political relations.

Mr. Cooper's book is the last of the four studies dealing with economic problems. The first, *Atlantic Agricultural Unity: Is It Possible?* by John O. Coppock, was published in 1966. John Pincus' volume

Trade, Aid and Development: The Rich and Poor Nations, and Bela Balassa's *Trade Liberalization among Industrial Countries: Objectives and Alternatives,* were published in 1967.

Two studies of the Atlantic world's external environment have been made: *Alternative to Partition* by Zbigniew K. Brzezinski of Columbia University was published by McGraw-Hill in May 1965. A study by Theodore Geiger of the National Planning Association, *The Conflicted Relationship: The West and the Transformation of Asia, Africa, and Latin America,* examines the nature of the great transition now going on throughout the three continents in which development is hoped for—not always realistically. The implications of the changes in these areas for the future of political relations with the Western world are also explored.

Atlantic military problems are considered in their political context in Henry A. Kissinger's *The Troubled Partnership: A Re-appraisal of the Atlantic Alliance,* which McGraw-Hill published in April 1965.

Political relations among the Atlantic nations are the subject of three studies. Miriam Camps of Chatham House and the Council on Foreign Relations wrote a volume on the future of European unity, *European Unification in the Sixties: From the Veto to the Crisis,* published in 1966. In the spring of 1965 Stanley Hoffmann of Harvard University gave at the Council a series of lectures that reviewed the principal constraints, particularly the domestic constraints, on U.S. action in Atlantic affairs; the lectures were published in 1968 under the title *Gulliver's Troubles, Or the Setting of American Foreign Policy.* A third political volume, by the Director of the Atlantic Policy Studies, *The Atlantic Idea and Its European Rivals,* published late in 1966, addresses the question of the future shape of political relations among the Atlantic countries.

HAROLD VAN B. CLEVELAND
Director, Atlantic Policy Studies
Council on Foreign Relations

Preface

This book was conceived while I was working on international economic problems for the Council of Economic Advisers in 1962–63. I was troubled by the absence of acceptable methods for correcting imbalances in international payments. Even though unemployment was nearly 6 per cent of the labor force and wholesale prices had been stable for more than four years, both Europeans and some of its own citizens were urging the United States to stop "inflating," for balance-of-payments reasons. This advice seemed to me then, and still seems to me, to get everything backward, to put cart before horse. Yet devaluation of the dollar against other currencies, while advocated by a number of academic economists, seemed out of the question, not least because of clear indications that America's major trading partners would quickly move to counteract, through devaluation or other means, the sharp worsening in their trade positions that devaluation of the dollar would entail.

If not that, what? Over the course of time, the United States adopted a number of expedients—such as tying government procurement to American goods, taxing and otherwise limiting capital outflows, even restricting foreign travel—which amounted to partial devaluations of the dollar. Other countries in payments difficulties have also resorted to a miscellany of *ad hoc* devices to cut their payments to foreigners, or in some cases to raise their foreign exchange receipts. And the actions of one country have often partially or completely offset those of another.

Two questions are raised by these events of the past decade: Were the actions desirable for all countries, or even for the major industrial countries, taken as a group? Can the existing payments system, under its present conventions, be expected to work any better than it has? Official preoccupation with the question of "international liquidity," which is important in its own right, has diverted attention from other weaknesses in the international monetary system.

This book addresses these questions only indirectly. It does so by considering alternative payments arrangements and the economic—and political—preconditions for making them work. Some of the deficiencies in existing arrangements arise from flaws in the basic plan of the present system, laid down at Bretton Woods in 1944. Others arise from the rapid changes in the world economy in the past two decades—in particular, goods and services, capital, technology, and even labor have become far more mobile internationally. Arrangements that were quite workable in past circumstances have become outdated. Failure to adapt institutional arrangements to these changes in economic structure threatens the attainment of national and international economic objectives. Without successful efforts to coordinate them, restrictions on international payments may be expected to remain a prominent feature of the international economic environment, and one that, like air or water pollution, is ultimately costly to all.

The book consists of three parts. Hurried readers will find the principal strand of argument in Chapters 1, 6, and 10. Chapters 3–5 describe and analyze the consequences for economic policy of changes in the structure of international economic intercourse among industrial countries. Chapter 2 describes the present international payments system and its evolution since the mid-1940s, while Chapters 7–9 consider alternative payments arrangements. Chapter 6 was published previously in *The Yale Law Journal.*

The book was drafted in the summer of 1965. Completion was interrupted by my return to government service, this time to the State Department. The rapid pace of events in international finance has dated some of the illustrations, but it has also, I think, made more urgent the need for improvements in cooperative arrangements for handling balance-of-payments problems.

In writing a book one inevitably incurred many debts, which can be only partially and inadequately acknowledged in a preface. First, Harold van B. Cleveland invited my participation in the Atlantic Policy Studies, and he shepherded the manuscript gently and helpfully from beginning to end. I am greatly indebted to him for his patience and his insights. As is customary at the Council on Foreign Relations, a study group was formed, under the able chairmanship of Gardner Patterson. The members of this group were: Henry G. Aubrey, Bela Balassa, Harold van B. Cleveland, Benjamin Cohen, William B. Dale, William Diebold, Jr., Isaiah Frank, Dillon Glendinning, Michael Hoffman, James C. Ingram, Norris Johnson, Peter B. Kenen, Hal Lary, John Pincus, Judd Polk, John Renner, Walter Salant, Frank W. Schiff, Frank A. Southard, Jr., and Robert Triffin. The group held several sessions which were most helpful to me, and a number of its members offered valuable comments on the manuscript. I am particularly indebted to Peter Kenen, Walter Salant, and Ton de Vries, all of whom commented in detail on an early draft of the manuscript; and to Robert Triffin, with whom I have had many stimulating conversations on the topics covered in this book. None of these individuals is, of course, responsible for the opinions expressed here.

I am also grateful to Robert Dickler for valuable research assistance, to Joyce Blakeslee for unstinted typing and for patiently undertaking the miscellany of tasks always associated with writing a book, to the staff of the Council on Foreign Relations for guiding the manuscript through publication, and to the Economic Growth Center of Yale University for providing time and research facilities for carrying out the work.

R.N.C.

New Haven, Connecticut
February 1968

Contents

                                                                          xiii

LIST OF TABLES AND FIGURES

PART I

Introduction

CHAPTER ONE

The Central Problem

The members of the Atlantic Community have become much more interdependent over the years. While political dissension among the Communist countries seems to offer greater scope for divergent diplomacy among the Western countries, divergent economic policy has become less possible. Most national economic policy-makers have always been aware of the influence of foreign economic developments on their own problems, but they are made increasingly aware too of the impact of their own decisions on others. At the same time, the large and relatively self-contained United States is discovering that its policies not only influence others but also must be influenced by what happens abroad. The postwar quip that when America sneezes Europe catches pneumonia is perhaps less true than it once was, but there is now a larger grain of truth in its converse.

The sources of this growing interdependence are not hard to find. Since 1950, international commodity trade has grown at the extraordinary rate of more than 7 per cent a year, substantially faster than the growth in world output, itself high by historical standards. International travel has increased nearly as rapidly. In 1966 an estimated 128 million foreign visitors were recorded. Large numbers of people reside outside their countries of citizenship—nearly a million American forces and their dependents in Europe, over a million Italian, Greek, Turkish, and Spanish workers in West Germany and other northern European countries, over a million Canadian students, professionals, and other workers in the United States. Capital moves much more freely among nations than it has for many decades, and American firms alone now start over five hundred new operations in Western Europe each year.

People in different countries are much closer to one another than they have ever been. They see one another's goods in the stores, travel to one another's cities (or know people who have), read about one another extensively in the newspapers, or see one another on television. As a result of communications satellites, people all over the world can hear a Presidential address—or watch a world championship boxing match—as it is happening.

Many observers hail these developments as wholesome and urge that they be encouraged in every way possible. They are viewed as paving the path to various grand designs for international comity, of which perhaps the most important was the vague but powerfully attractive Atlantic Partnership fostered by President Kennedy and favored by leading citizens on both sides of the Atlantic.

The Central Problem

Like other forms of international contact, international economic intercourse both enlarges and confines the freedom of countries to act according to their own lights. It enlarges their freedom by permitting a more economical use of limited resources; it confines their freedom by embedding each country in a matrix of constraints which it can influence only slightly, often only indirectly, and without certainty of effect. Like the competitive firm, the small country must accept the international environment and adjust its own behavior accordingly; even the large country can change that environment only slowly and with much effort. The competitive firm, if it finds the environment too constraining, can go out of business; the nation does not even have that option. And it can abandon unilaterally the tacit international code of good behavior only if it is prepared to accept the adverse reaction of other countries.

As with marriage, the benefits of close international economic relations can be enjoyed only at the expense of giving up a certain amount of national independence, or autonomy, in setting and pursuing economic objectives. National *autonomy,* as used here to mean the ability to frame and carry out objectives of domestic economic policy which may diverge widely from those of other countries, should not be confused with the notion of *sovereignty,* which represents the formal ability of countries or other political units to make their own decisions—and to renounce decisions previously made—but not necessarily to achieve their objectives. It will become clear later that autonomy may at times be increased by yielding some "sovereignty" in the freedom to formulate economic policy with apparent (but often illusory) independence of other nations' actions. The central problem of international economic cooperation—and of this book—is *how to keep the manifold benefits of extensive international economic intercourse free of crippling restrictions while at the same time preserving a maximum degree of freedom for each nation to pursue its legitimate economic objectives.*

Extensive international economic intercourse threatens national autonomy in two ways. The first, and at present by far the more important, is through each country's balance of international payments. If the citizens of each country can decide freely what to buy, where to travel, and how to invest their savings, a country may find that its citizens are paying out to foreigners more than they are taking in, producing a deficit in its balance of payments which must somehow be financed or eliminated. Except in rare circumstances, financing for imbalances in international payments is available in only limited amounts; therefore, countries in deficit must take steps to bring their international payments and receipts into line.

Yet the methods at hand for bringing about the adjustment in international payments are few. Past experience indicates that certain methods of eliminating imbalances in international payments can be profoundly destructive of international commerce, eliminating not only the imbalance but also many of the benefits which attend foreign trade. Ruling out by common consent these modes of adjustment, however, throws the burden of adjustment to other means. As methods of adjustment are increasingly circumscribed by international rule or convention, countries find growing difficulty in maintaining international balance without compromising some of their own, more strictly domestic objectives. This is how international commerce and the need to maintain some kind of international balance come to intrude upon such seemingly domestic economic policies as government expenditures, the manner in which government expenditures are financed, the level and structure of taxation, and the regulation of business.

Exigencies of the balance of payments thus may force countries to take domestic actions which they would otherwise find objectionable. The larger and more frequent the pressures on the balance of payments, relative to the means available to finance payments deficits, the greater will be the pressure on domestic policies to bring about balance-of-payments adjustment. These pressures will increase with the degree of international economic exposure. The benefits of international commerce thus entail some costs in terms of loss of domestic autonomy.

A second way in which international economic intercourse threatens national autonomy is in the ability of each country to regulate and tax business and banking. The laws of different countries reflect different judgments about the extent to which corporate financial structure, disclosure of information, working conditions, relationships among competing firms, and the like should be subject to public regulation. So long as such regulations are in force over an area as large as the area considered by firms in deciding where to incorporate and where to locate, the regulatory intent can be accomplished. But if firms become highly mobile and international commerce is relatively free from restriction, they may evade national regulations—which are often inconvenient and sometimes raise costs—by locating abroad. In Chapter 4 the *decision-making domain* of a business enterprise is defined and compared with the *jurisdiction* of the government which wants to regulate it. If business domains exceed governmental jurisdictions, effective regulation is greatly weakened, and to satisfy a country's economic objectives it is necessary either to extend the jurisdiction in certain dimensions or to reduce the international mobility of firms.

This threat to autonomy has not yet become acute at the international level—although it is well known to local governments within countries—and our attention will be directed primarily to pressures on domestic policies which arise from the balance of payments. But it will be necessary to look occasionally at the influence of the internationalization of corporate enterprise on public regulation of business, for it is a facet of national policy which will become more threatened as the process of economic integration continues.

Focus on the Atlantic Community

The pressures which increasing international commerce exert on national policy are not confined to any small circle of nations. But the discussion that follows is limited primarily to the industrial countries of North America and Western Europe—and for some purposes Japan should be treated as a member of these regions.

There are two reasons for focussing attention on the members of the Atlantic Community. One is pragmatic and political, the other structural and economic.

Since World War II a major aim of American foreign policy has been to prevent the recrudescence of latent intra-European animosities from ever again embroiling the world in war. Implementation of this policy led the United States to encourage a high degree of cooperation among the Europeans, leading eventually to integration of various functions and perhaps ultimately to full unification. The threat of Soviet political infiltration and military invasion produced the first vehicles for greater European cooperation: in 1948 the Organization for European Economic Cooperation (OEEC) was formed to allocate Marshall Plan aid from the United States, and in 1949 the North Atlantic Treaty Organization (NATO) was established to provide for a common defense. The United States has encouraged the forces for European integration, partly to permit the economic and political recovery (and rearmament) of Germany within an acceptable framework, partly to permit Europe to pool its economic resources to bear some of the responsibility for maintaining security and fostering economic development in the rest of the world. Official American statements abound in references to an Atlantic Partnership of co-equals —the United States on one side and a United Europe on the other.

In short, focussing a discussion of economic cooperation on the "Atlantic" is justified by an historical and continuing political interest in Europe arising from its industrial might (when taken collectively), its political influence, its diplomatic astuteness, and its military potentiality for good or harm.[1]

There is a second, and for our purposes more powerful, reason for directing attention to the Atlantic countries. There has been a marked convergence in the economic systems and economic objectives of these countries.[2] Despite occasional ideological claims to the contrary, they all involve a refined mixture of free enterprise and government

[1] Postwar involvement of the United States in European affairs—and European willingness to accept this involvement—derives, of course, in large measure from the existence of a common threat to security. That the "Atlantic economic community" is largely derivative from the "Atlantic security community" has been emphasized by Harold van B. Cleveland, *The Atlantic Idea and Its European Rivals* (New York: McGraw-Hill Book Co., for the Council on Foreign Relations, 1966), pp. 158–59. But it does not follow from this historical fact that strong mutual interest in economic issues will diminish if the common threat to security diminishes, as will be indicated below.

[2] Same, p. 156.

activity. The mixture varies from country to country, but the narrowness of variation stands in marked contrast to the polarized laissez-faire and corporate state systems of the interwar period. They all espouse national objectives of growth, full employment, and price stability; and they all have accepted the principle that national governments both can successfully and should gear their policies to these objectives. All have accepted some public responsibility for welfare of the indigent and the aged, and most undertake some regulation of business and the conditions of competition. Thus, these industrial countries face a common and interrelated set of problems.

That they share common problems would be reason enough for a high degree of interest in each others' economies and policies; but that the problems are interdependent compels such interest. These countries are closely and increasingly linked by ties of trade, technology, and capital. Knowledge of each others' institutions and practices has increased enormously, and the level of mutual confidence in national economic policies has risen to the point of greatly reducing psychological barriers to the movements of capital and the location of production. In short, the major industrial countries are becoming more closely "integrated."

Defining an Integrated Area

To be sure, the term "integrated area" has many meanings—legal, psychological, economic—depending on the focus of attention and purpose of analysis. Integration has recently become popularly associated with the establishment of certain institutions of government, such as the Commission of the European Economic Community, which sets out rules and regulations governing the entire area under its jurisdiction. Under this legal view of integration, most *nations* must be considered integrated areas, and integration in this sense has barely begun to extend beyond national boundaries. But this is too narrow a view to take of the term.

An integrated area can be defined in behavioral rather than legal terms. An area might be said to be integrated, for example, when political pressure groups follow predominantly functional rather than regional lines. Texan plumbers would speak primarily as plumbers, not as Texans. A closely related psychological definition would look at attitudes, or public opinion, on various nonlocal issues. In an integrated area one would expect these attitudes to show little relationship with the region of birth or residence. By these standards, of course, even nations, which meet the legal definition of integrated areas, may reflect great regional diffuseness and lack of integration. This can be seen in Canada and Italy, for example, or in the relationship between England and Scotland and between the northern and southern United States. Certainly, national identification in the Atlantic Community has not yet been overtaken by functional identification,[3] and few political pressure groups have been formed across national boundaries—although the close affiliation of the Christian Democratic parties in several European countries represents a move in this direction.[4]

[3] We have little direct evidence on this point. But the results of surveys by the U.S. Information Agency perhaps indicate something along these lines. In 1961, for example, typically less than half the population of Britain, France, Germany, and Italy would trust the other major European countries as allies in time of war. Interestingly enough, trust in the United States was much higher.

The percentage of respondents in June 1961 who felt that in time of war they could trust country X as an ally "a great deal" was as follows:

Country of Respondent	Country X				
	France	*Germany*	*Italy*	*U.K.*	*U.S.*
France	—	21	11	32	45
Germany	20	—	7	27	65
Italy	14	19	—	16	52
United Kingdom	25	17	6	—	63

These percentages had generally declined from those of the responses to identical questions asked in the early and mid-1950s, except for a sharp rise in French-German mutual trust. See Donald J. Puchala, "Western European Attitudes on International Problems, 1952–1961," Research Memorandum No. 1, Yale Research Memoranda in Political Science, January 1964, pp. 10–11.

[4] To the extent that regional identifications do continue to exist—as they certainly do within most countries—integration requires that preservation of the union of regions must outweigh all regional issues as a social and political objective. This criterion comes close to that of Deutsch and his collaborators, who define "integration" as "the attainment, within a territory, of a 'sense of community' and of institutions and practices strong enough and widespread enough to assure, for a 'long' time, dependable expectations of 'peaceful change' among its population" and "sense of community" represents "a belief on the part of individuals in a group that they have come to agreement on at least this one point: that common social problems must and can be resolved

Even economic integration can be defined in many ways. An area is defined as integrated if it is characterized (*a*) "by the absence of various forms of discrimination between national economies," [5] (*b*) "by the optimum of international economic cooperation," [6] or (*c*) "by factor price equalization—uniform wages (except for differences in skills, etc.), common interest rates on comparable financial assets, and equal profits on comparable investments." [7] Many areas which meet the first test of integration come nowhere near to meeting the third; indeed, the third test may be represented as a kind of limiting case against which actual areas may be compared. It requires a high degree of factor mobility within the area.[8] The Atlantic economic community does not meet any of these economic tests of integration, although the European Economic Community (EEC) and the European Free Trade Association (EFTA) are moving toward meeting the first.

But to focus exclusively on tests of integration would miss the importance of a process which is taking place and which, if it is not to be reversed, will compel a higher degree of economic cooperation. This process involves the increasing *sensitivity* of economic events in one country to what is happening in its trading partners. The structural changes in the economic relations among industrial countries which

---

by processes of 'peaceful change.' " See Karl W. Deutsch *et al., Political Community and the North Atlantic Area* (Princeton: Princeton University Press, 1957), p. 5.

[5] Bela Balassa, *The Theory of Economic Integration* (Homewood, Ill.: Richard D. Irwin, 1961), p. 1.

[6] J. Tinbergen, *International Economic Integration* (Amsterdam: Elsevier, 1954), p. 30.

[7] C. P. Kindleberger, "European Integration and the International Corporation," *Columbia Journal of World Business,* Winter 1966, p. 1.

[8] It is not necessary, of course, that *all* factors migrate or even be willing to migrate. One of the principal lessons of economic analysis is that economic phenomena are determined largely by a relatively few decisions—decisions by the "marginal" units, be they businessmen, workers, or consumers. But to achieve integration labor and capital must migrate in sufficient quantity significantly to influence factor prices—wages, interest, and profits—in the country or region of origin or destination. An occasional migrant or investment abroad is not enough to achieve integration.

The celebrated "factor-price-equalization theorem" of economic theory, whereby factor prices can be brought to equality through foreign trade alone, is too restricted in its assumptions to be of practical importance here.

give rise to this increased sensitivity will be considered in Chapters 3, 4, and 5. There it is argued that the steady lowering of tariffs and transport costs, the increasing similarity of comparative cost structures, and the extension of decision-making domains of banks and businesses across national boundaries will increasingly limit the effectiveness of tested instruments of policy.

There is no hard and fast line between the countries which have been affected by this process and those which have not. It is a question of more or less, not all or none. Analysis of increasing interdependence could be applied with only minimal change to regions outside the Atlantic Community, or indeed to regions within a country. Moreover, the group of countries which need to cooperate closely in economic policy must be a flexible one, for the whole of commerce and finance is changing rapidly. Preconceived notions about membership in a cooperative international enterprise may lead to slippages which vitiate the combined effort. Thus, for purposes of economic cooperation, it may be more appropriate to include in the Atlantic Community Italy and Japan, whose shores are not touched by the Atlantic Ocean, than Iceland and Portugal, which are completely or largely surrounded by it. Economic cooperation must derive from the need for cooperation, not from geography alone.

There is little question, however, that at present the need for economic cooperation in the areas of regulation and of macro-economic policy is higher among the major industrial countries—where private capital moves in great volume in response to small differences in yield, and where trade is highly competitive—than between these countries and the rest of the world. Yet, any distinction among countries is bound to be somewhat arbitrary, since some countries will barely qualify to be included and will be hardly distinguishable from some which are left outside. This is an argument for flexibility of membership in cooperative ventures, not for no regional arrangements at all.

The architects of the postwar agreements to guide and govern international trade and finance made virtually no allowance for regional cooperation on common economic problems. Their view was global, and each country was treated on a par with every other country as far as the rules of behavior were concerned. Such regional arrangements as did exist, notably the British Imperial Preference System and the colonial areas of Belgium, France, and the Netherlands, produced bitter resentment in many Americans. But the links between major industrial countries often create common problems and require special talents and techniques for dealing with them. Many countries outside this group do not share these problems, and their presence in all the discussions of attempts to resolve them might actually impede mutually acceptable solutions by reducing the candor of discussion, introducing irrelevancy, and lowering the probability of confidentiality.

However, nonparticipating countries often have a direct interest in the outcome of any economic and financial arrangements among major industrial countries because of their intimate dependence on the latter for markets and for crucial imports, especially capital goods. It is important, therefore, to keep this interest in mind and to provide forums where it can be voiced effectively.

In addition, it must be recognized that the "causation" does not run in only one direction, from close economic ties and common economic problems to institutional arrangements. On the contrary, it is more usual to emphasize the opposite direction: common institutions are often urged for the sake of building greater political cohesion and economic integration. There is a continual interaction between the two aspects. Institution-building neither wholly precedes nor wholly follows economic integration and psychological identification between two or more areas.[9]

Because of this two-way interaction, international economic cooperation is not merely a technical matter, the form and scope of which can be determined purely on technical grounds. It is also a political question. It is not sufficient simply to examine trade and capital flows, ties of ownership, and the limits of labor migration among regions or countries to determine an "optimal" jurisdiction for government in the realm of economic policy-making. Political weights must be at-

---

[9] An illustration of this interaction between attitudes and institutions is provided by the eruption of heavy criticism of the European Coal and Steel Community (ECSC) by German businessmen in 1954, after the French rejection of the European Defense Community. Many businessmen had apparently suppressed their irritations in the interests of "community-building"; but when construction of a European-wide defense community faltered, many suppressed criticisms of the mode of operation of the ECSC came out into the open, and various parties reasserted their shorter run self-interest. See Gabriel A. Almond, "The Politics of German Business," in Hans Speier and W. Phillips Davison (eds.), *West German Leadership and Foreign Policy* (Evanston, Ill.: Row, Peterson, and Co., 1957), pp. 234–35.

tached to the various alternative arrangements, recognizing that these arrangements will *build* close ties as well as *reflect* them. This consideration has been dominant in the focus of American foreign policy both on European unification and on an Atlantic partnership.

Coping with Imbalances in International Payments

It was argued above that the increased interdependence among nations shows up principally in the balance of payments. A country's balance of payments quickly reflects economic changes at home or abroad which influence levels of income, competitiveness, and yields on assets.

Measures for dealing with a prospective, or *ex ante,* payments deficit [10] can be grouped in various ways; the most useful distinction here is between external and internal methods.

External methods of adjustment rely on measures which differentiate between transactions with foreigners and domestic transactions. Tariffs, export subsidies of all kinds, import quotas with licensing, taxes or restrictions on international capital flows, and exchange controls or multiple exchange rates fall into this category. Internal methods of adjustment are those which do not rely on such differentiation, but which nonetheless affect the balance on international transactions by influencing the level of incomes, prices, interest rates, and asset values. These include changes in monetary or fiscal policy, increases in interest rates and reductions in the availability of funds, and changes in the structure of taxation in ways designed indirectly to improve the trade balance or to attract foreign capital.

To the extent that measures within these two broad categories are not taken, a country in prospective deficit will have an actual (*ex post*) deficit which will require some sort of financing. Such financing

[10] The terms *"Ex ante* deficit" or *"ex ante* surplus" will be used throughout to indicate the payments deficit or surplus which would have resulted if no policy action were taken specifically to influence the balance of payments. Thus it signifies what the balance-of-payments position would be if the economic authorities used the measures at their disposal to influence their other domestic and foreign objectives, without regard to the balance of payments.

An *ex ante* deficit is to be contrasted with an *ex post* deficit, which is the balance-of-payments deficit actually observed *after* the authorities have taken what measures they deem necessary to affect the deficit; similarly for an *ex post* surplus.

often takes the form of drawing down gold and foreign-exchange reserves; but it can also involve compensatory official capital movements from abroad, special borrowing through private markets or commercial banks, or even compensatory sales of goods and services —all motivated by the imbalance in international payments.

The observed deficit in international payments will often be only an imperfect measure of the *ex ante* disequilibrium, for a country may have been compelled by limited financing to take measures to reduce the deficit. Countries in surplus are rarely constrained to adopt really repugnant measures, although on occasion they may be pressured by the deficit countries into doing so. Sometimes, of course, measures to reduce imbalances may themselves be desirable on other grounds, as when a surplus country with unemployment adopts an expansionary program. But happy coincidences such as this usually become policy conflicts before both internal and external equilibrium are restored.

We have thus far not mentioned changes in exchange rates as a means of coping with imbalances, although they can be used two ways: as a system of fixed exchange-rate parities which are changed from time to time (the "adjustable peg"); and a system of flexible rates, in which exchange rates are determined from day to day in the exchange market. The first has the well-known disadvantage of inviting large movements of speculative funds whenever a change in parities is thought to be imminent. It can, however, be grouped with other external measures, representing an extreme case in which, in one stroke, the prices or profitability of all external transactions are adjusted relative to purely domestic transactions.

A system of floating exchange rates has the apparent virtue of solving the balance-of-payments problem, since exchange rates always adjust themselves to maintain balance at all times.[11] The implications of somewhat greater flexibility in exchange rates is considered briefly in Chapter 9. But the analysis that follows assumes a system of fixed exchange parities. This reflects partly the pragmatic judgment that yet

---

[11] The literature on this question is voluminous. Probably the source most often quoted is Milton Friedman, "The Case for Flexible Exchange Rates," in his *Essays in Positive Economics* (Chicago: University of Chicago Press, 1953), pp. 157–203; a more recent statement is James E. Meade, "The Future of International Payments," in U.S. Congress, Joint Economic Committee, *Factors Affecting the United States Balance of Payments*, 87th Cong., 2nd sess. (Washington: GPO, 1962), pp. 241–52.

another call for flexible rates will fall on official ears as deaf as those to which all previous calls have been directed. Whatever the merits of flexible rates, such a system is ruled out by those who consider greater economic integration between North America and Western Europe as a desirable objective in itself. Flexible exchange rates, it is thought, would disrupt international transactions and would impede the process of integration.[12]

More fundamentally, however, a system of fixed rates is assumed because establishing a system of flexible rates would presume that one of the central analytical questions of international economic cooperation has been solved: namely, what are the relevant geographic areas over which exchange rates should be *fixed* in a regime of flexible rates?

Why is the nation the logical limit? Why not a larger area or a smaller one? Some of the problems of West Virginia might be more easily overcome if there were a flexible exchange rate between the

---

[12] Moreover, occasional adjustments in *fixed* exchange rates also seem to have been downgraded in practice, even though they are a central feature of the system of international payments based on the Bretton Woods Agreement of 1944. A recent report by officials of the Group of Ten, for example, lists six areas of economic policy which members may have to use to "counteract" a sustained deficit or a "sustained surplus on their over-all balance of payments" without including changes in exchange rates among them. "Ministerial Statement of the Group of Ten and Annex Prepared by Deputies," August 1964, p. 5. The statement goes on to declare: "Such instruments must be employed with proper regard for obligations in the field of international trade and for the IMF obligation to maintain stable exchange parities which are subject to change only in cases of fundamental disequilibrium." This is the only mention of changes in exchange rates in the statement, which apparently draws a distinction between "sustained" and "fundamental" disequilibrium but without specifying what this distinction is or how it can be identified in practice.

A more recent official statement, however, concedes that there are some occasions when revaluation or devaluation may be preferable to their alternatives. A Report by Working Party No. 3 of the Economic Policy Committee of the Organization for Economic Cooperation and Development, *The Balance of Payments Adjustment Process* (Paris: OECD, August 1966), para. 46.

Of course, changes in exchange-rate parities have occurred from time to time, usually under the pressure of heavy speculation, as when the French franc was devalued in 1958 or the British pound in 1967. Each such experience reinforces officials in their view that exchange-rate changes are strongly disruptive in the short run, and hence are undesirable.

U.S. dollar and the West Virginia dollar. But despite the advantages which flexible rates might offer, the citizens of West Virginia undoubtedly consider it to their net advantage to have a fixed relationship between their currency and that of the United States. When should several countries tie their currencies to one another, but allow them to float relative to other currencies? In other words, what is the "optimal currency area"? [13]

Answers to these questions are not easy to give. They depend largely on the degree of factor mobility between the regions in question, the extent of their dependence on foreign trade, and the sensitivity of their residents to movements in the cost of living. The greater the mobility of labor and capital out of a region, the larger its dependence on trade; and the higher the sensitivity of its residents to changes in the cost of living, the less desirable it is for the exchange rates of the region to vary relative to those of its trading partners.

The reason for this can be seen by considering a very small region closely integrated economically with the surrounding area. If its exchange rate fluctuated frequently and substantially, there would be sizable fluctuations in the cost of living. Residents sensitive to such changes could respond by bidding up wages and other prices (to maintain real income when import prices rose) and by sending liquid savings abroad to stabilize the value of those assets in terms of import prices. The first response would partially vitiate the equilibrating effects of the change in exchange rate, and the second would deprive the region of some of its savings. Moreover, if labor and capital are highly mobile between regions, relatively smooth balance-of-payments adjustment can take place in a regime of fixed rates, since a decline in demand evokes outward migration, and rate fluctuations thus become unnecessary.

In summary, even if a system of flexible exchange rates were politically acceptable, there would be some difficulty in defining the areas

[13] This question has been tentatively examined by Robert A. Mundell in "A Theory of Optimum Currency Areas," *American Economic Review,* LI, September 1961, pp. 657–65. Mundell emphasizes the importance of labor mobility. See also Ronald I. McKinnon, "Optimum Currency Areas," *American Economic Review,* LIII, September 1963, pp. 717–25; and same, "Optimum World Monetary Arrangements and the Dual Currency System," *Banca Nazionale del Lavoro Quarterly Review,* XVI, December 1963, pp. 366–96. McKinnon emphasizes the influence of import price fluctuations on the disposition of liquid assets.

between which rates should be flexible. If a single currency area is too large, one of the important claims made for flexible rates—that they permit maintenance of internal balance—will not be met for all its regions. Some would have to inflate and others would have to deflate to maintain balance. If currency areas are too small, they will experience a steady outflow of savings and possibly even destabilizing wage settlements. There is no guarantee, moreover, that the appropriate region coincides with the jurisdiction of national monetary authorities, which usually determine the single currency region.[14]

Since we live in a world of fixed and only infrequently changed exchange parities, it is of considerable interest to trace through the consequences of rapidly growing trade and increasing factor mobility for economic policy under a regime of fixed exchange rates, and that will be the assumption adopted here. In certain circumstances, of course, changing an exchange parity may offer the only reasonable solution for a country in balance-of-payments difficulties.

The three broad categories for coping with imbalances under fixed exchange rates—internal measures, external measures, and financing—can be illustrated diagrammatically as a triangle, as in Figure 1–1. Each point in the triangle represents some combination of the three types of measure for handling a given *ex ante* imbalance in the international payments of any country or region during a specified period of time.[15] The three vertices of the triangle represent exclusive use of measures in each of the three categories, and the closer a point is to a vertex, the greater the reliance on measures of that type. Thus, point G in Figure 1–1 represents the textbook gold standard, which relies primarily on domestic deflation to reduce a payments deficit and on

[14] Many exceptions are found, precisely for the reasons discussed above. Liechtenstein has formed a monetary union with Switzerland, Luxembourg with Belgium, Eire (*de facto*) with the United Kingdom, and so on.

[15] In a triangular coordinate system each point is associated with three fractions adding to unity. We can regard these numbers here as the percentage of a given *ex ante* imbalance which is covered by each of the three categories of measures—adding to 100 per cent. Geometrically, for example, the point L in Figure 1–1 indicates that of a given *ex ante* deficit represented by the length of the side of the triangle, MN was eliminated through the use of internal measures, the distance from N to the lower right-hand corner was eliminated by use of external measures, and the distance from M to the lower left-hand corner was the *ex post* deficit that had to be financed. For further discussion, see Richard N. Cooper, "The Relevance of International Liquidity to Developed Countries," *American Economic Review*, LVIII, May 1968.

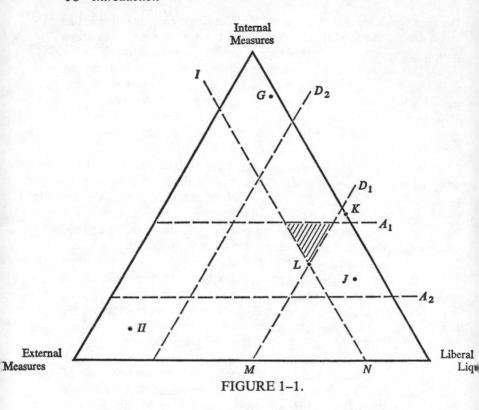

FIGURE 1–1.

domestic expansion or inflation to reduce a payments surplus. Temporary financing for deficit countries was often arranged by borrowing, and modest exchange rate flexibility within the gold points can be regarded as a minor external measure. But principal reliance is on adjustments in the domestic economy. By contrast, point *H* represents heavy reliance on external measures such as exchange control and changes in import quotas. Point *J* represents a country which has ample ability to finance deficits. Some Europeans claim that the United States is in this position by virtue of its role as a reserve currency country, since foreign countries simply accumulate the excess dollars arising from U.S. deficits.

Point *K* might represent a state within the United States. External measures are totally ruled out—no state can impede interstate commerce or impair contracts made by its residents in U.S. dollars. On the other hand, it acquires liberal financing through many cushioning features of a federal system. A drop in income and employment as a result of a fall in exports reduces tax payments to "foreigners" and increases receipts from "foreigners" in the form of unemployment compensation—both through the federal fiscal system. Moreover, a state can, up to a point, sell financial claims in the national capital market, and it can draw down its stock of cash.

This characterization is extremely rough; there are many variants of each type of measure, and in some instances the differences between various types of external measure may be far greater than between certain external and certain internal or financing measures. Moreover, the time dimensions and the size of the deficit are important. Virtually all regions have ample sources of finance to cover short-lived deficits of modest size. But if a deficit persists, they must arrange extraordinary financing or resort to other solutions. It will be most useful, then, to consider the position of regions with reference to some considerable length of time, say, two to four years. Finally, the pressures on a surplus country are considerably less than those on a deficit country. A surplus country can, if necessary, finance its surpluses indefinitely—or, if it is taking gold or other international reserves, at least until the deficit countries exhaust their reserves. Thus, it is most instructive to consider the position of a country with respect to payments *deficits.*

The choice among the three methods for coping with prospective imbalances touches on matters of high national importance. Nations are, therefore, far from indifferent about which types of measure are used.

Figure 1–1 can be used to illustrate the relationship among different objectives for the international payments system, and to indicate the relationship between balance-of-payments adjustment and international liquidity. Most observers want to avoid extreme forms of each of the three categories of action. Many bankers, for example, speak of the need for the "discipline" of the balance of payments; they wish to restrict the means to finance deficits. Liberal economists and those favoring international integration object to trade quotas and exchange controls and generally dislike autarkic measures which interfere with trade and payments. Other observers emphasize the need to preserve domestic autonomy in economic policy-making and, in particular, the need to maintain full employment or stability in the level of domestic prices.

The three objectives can be represented on Figure 1–1 by boundaries beyond which various observers do not want to venture. Thus the line D_1 may represent the limits of financing which those in favor of maintaining balance-of-payments discipline are willing to permit. They do not want to see the country closer than that to the vertex representing liberal liquidity. Similarly, the line I represents the greatest reliance on external measures which integrationists are willing to countenance. Finally, the line A_1 can represent the greatest intrusion on domestic policies which those predominantly concerned with domestic autonomy are willing to permit. With these three constraints, potential imbalances can be handled only by combinations of measures in the shaded area.

The diagram makes clear what is not always clear in public discussion—that we cannot generally forswear extensive use of external measures, internal measures, and liberal financing simultaneously. Prospective balance-of-payments deficits must be handled in some combination of the three ways, and if we set our standards too high, one or more of them will have to give way. For instance, if those urging discipline insist on no greater financing than that permitted by line D_2, and if those wanting to preserve domestic autonomy in economic policy set a limit of line A_2, the country or region would have conflicting objectives and one or more of them would have to yield. No point can satisfy the limits set by the lines I, D_1, and A_2. Given a high degree of international agreement to avoid external measures and a strong desire for balance-of-payments discipline, for example, our ability to pursue domestic economic objectives without regard to the balance of payments is sharply limited.

Those who argue that the mechanism of balance-of-payments adjustment is defective under the constraint of fixed exchange rates argue in effect that we do not have enough balance-of-payments discipline under the present international payments system. (It is precisely to escape this implication that many academic economists urge flexible exchange rates as a preferable system.) Some of those who think that more liquidity is needed feel that the discipline is too severe, that domestic economic policies are already too threatened by balance-of-

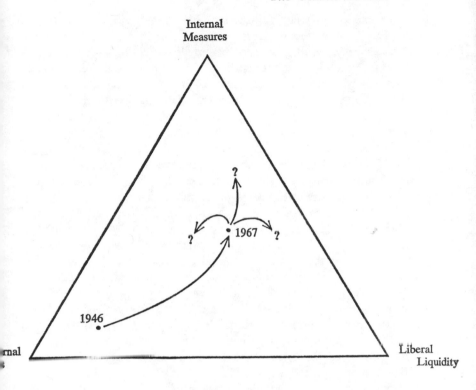

FIGURE 1–2.

payments considerations, and that the adjustment which does take place is apt to involve *ad hoc,* and for the most part undesirable, restrictions over international payments.[16]

The postwar evolution of the international payments system, at least as it affects the typical industrial country, can be characterized as a steady movement away from reliance on external measures, such as import quotas and exchange controls, to greater reliance on international financing of deficits (as with the Marshall Plan grants after

---

[16] Some advocates of new arrangements for international liquidity, however, are primarily concerned with matters other than the degree of balance-of-payments discipline exerted by the payments system. See Chapter 8.

1948) and on internal adjustment (Figure 1-2). The question we now face is where to go from here. Growth in the world economy will, over time, result in greatly increased transactions—and prospective imbalances—among countries. Therefore, more frequent and more extensive use must be made of internal policies, or liquidity must increase sufficiently to accommodate the larger imbalances. Otherwise, freedom of trade and capital movements will have to be restricted.

The choice of a "mix" of measures for adjustment and financing is basically a political choice, not an economic one. Certain economic considerations can be brought to bear on the choice. These are considered in Chapters 7, 8, and 9. Some mixes involve greater losses in output than others, for example, and the magnitude of the loss will vary with the economic circumstances of the country. But whether a country can follow what seems to be the best mix depends to a very great extent on the degree of mutual confidence which it and other governments have developed in the ability of each to manage its affairs sensibly, and on the extent to which the residents of neighboring countries take seriously the economic problems of their neighbors. Mutual support depends on something like national empathy. If this is missing, the range of possibilities is correspondingly restricted. To anticipate a judgment reached below, the present degree of empathy falls far short of what is required for an efficiently functioning Atlantic economic community under a regime of fixed exchange rates. Despite the marked improvement since the interwar period, one of the tasks of those favoring further integration is to establish an environment and a set of conventions in which this empathy can be increased.

The remainder of the book discusses the problems created by growing economic interdependence and explores some of the possible ways for solving these problems.

Chapter 2 describes the design of the international payments system proposed by American and British planners during the Second World War, the actual scheme adopted, and the various modifications which have taken place since that time. The following three chapters take up structural changes in the world economy as they affect the economic relations among countries and, in particular, their ability to pursue independent domestic policies. They imply that change is inevitably taking place; we cannot stop it, but we can influence its direction. Chapter 6 summarizes and analyzes the consequences for national economic policies of this increasing economic interdependence. Chapters 7, 8, and 9 take up in turn the three broad categories of measures for dealing with payments imbalances—internal measures, liberal financing, and external measures—with a view to their past and possible future application. Finally, Chapter 10 seeks the best combination of these measures and offers some brief concluding remarks.

CHAPTER TWO

The Postwar International Payments System

The broad outline of our international payments system was laid down in 1944 at an international conference at Bretton Woods, in New Hampshire. That system has, of course, evolved over the years to meet changing circumstances. Some subsequent developments were not generally anticipated, and some developments which were anticipated failed to materialize. As a result, the features of the payments system today are in some respects very different from those designed by the British and American officials who were charged during the Second World War with the task of drawing up a framework for international trade and payments in the postwar world. It is nonetheless instructive to see how those officials attempted to solve the central problem set forth in the preceding chapter: how nations may enjoy the benefits of international commerce while still leaving themselves free to set and pursue successfully their own national economic objectives.

The payments system in the postwar period has involved all three of the major methods for coping with imbalances in international payments, but the relative emphasis among external measures, internal measures, and provision for financing has varied from country to country and has altered in the course of time. What is striking, however, is the contrast between the postwar system and the heavy reliance on internal measures before 1913 and on external measures in the 1930s.

This contrast is not accidental. The architects of the postwar international monetary system, fearing a major postwar depression, were preoccupied with avoiding the monetary disasters of the 1930s. Between 1931 and 1936, one country after another had depreciated its currency in terms of gold, partly to correct acute balance-of-payments difficulties, partly to generate domestic income and employment by raising exports. At the end of this process, exchange rates were not very different from what they had been in 1930—in effect, the sequence of devaluations merely represented an extremely clumsy method for raising the price of gold. Tariff warfare had started even earlier, with the Australian tariff of 1928 and the Hawley-Smoot Tariff of 1930 (which raised American tariffs to their historic peak). Britain abandoned almost a century of nearly free trade and established its tariff preference area at the Ottawa Conference in 1932; and in 1934 Nazi Germany adopted the Schachtian system of discriminatory trade preferences with Eastern Europe and Latin America. Others, too, induced or coerced their trading partners into discriminatory trading blocs, which were sometimes virtually closed to outside competition through high tariffs, quotas, and exchange controls.

Measures such as these, employed by a single country, can improve its balance of payments and raise its employment, but only at the expense of employment and external balance in other countries. They become self-defeating if they are widespread; they do not represent a viable system.

The British and American officials sought to devise a system which would avoid the disruptive and pointless rise in trade barriers and the competitive depreciations which had occurred during the interwar period. They wanted to permit countries to enjoy the benefits of foreign trade unencumbered by direct government interference and to cushion strictly temporary imbalances in international payments, while at the same time eliminating permanent, "structural" imbalances by mutual agreement. And they wanted to avoid, insofar as it was possible, the uncomfortable policy choice between maintaining "internal" and "external" equilibrium; they wanted to permit policies in pursuit of full employment without creating serious balance-of-payments deficits.

If the disorders of the 1930s were unacceptable, the pre-1914 gold standard mechanism for maintaining external balance, even if it could have been restored, was equally unacceptable. It attached too much importance to the objective of external balance, too little to full employment. The experience of the Great Depression resulted in a reversal of priorities in economic objectives, with maintenence of international balance clearly taking second place to preservation of a high level of domestic employment. This contrasted sharply with the 1920s, when Britain, for example, endured persistent unemployment in excess of 10 per cent of the labor force for the sake of restoring the pound sterling to its 1913 parity and keeping it there. In addition to full employment, the reconstruction of damaged industry, inauguration of certain social programs, and other domestic objectives were given high priority after the Second World War.

The International Payments System of Bretton Woods

The system agreed upon at Bretton Woods therefore set out, in the words of the Articles of Agreement of the International Monetary Fund, "to facilitate the expansion and balanced growth of international trade, and to contribute thereby to the promotion and maintenance of high levels of employment and real income and to the development of the productive resources of all members as primary objectives of economic policy." Negatively, the rules it established were designed to avoid the cumulative disorders of the interwar period, to avoid resort "to measures destructive of national or international prosperity."

As originally conceived, the Bretton Woods system contained five broad features intended to permit the simultaneous long-run achievement of internal and external equilibrium:

1. It permitted the national pursuit of domestic economic objectives, which were assumed to include maintenance of high levels of employment and income.
2. It required the removal of artificial exchange restrictions on trade and other current payments, so that mutually beneficial international specialization could take place.
3. It called for fixed exchange rates, so that trade would not be hampered by the fluctuations of rates and so that governments would not be tempted to use exchange depreciation as an instrument for stimulating domestic demand.
4. With national pursuit of national objectives, fixed exchange rates, and the abolition of exchange controls, countries were bound from time to time to develop balance-of-payments difficulties. Therefore

the system provided medium-term credit facilities for countries which did encounter difficulties.

5. It also provided for occasional changes in the fixed rates of exchange when it became apparent that a country was experiencing fundamental, or "structural" imbalance in its international payments.

The system permitted national governments to pursue national (but not nationalistic) economic policies, within a broad set of objectives and rules governing such policies. Within reason, it also provided financing for any resulting deficits for a period long enough to ascertain whether a change in exchange rates was really needed. In the meantime, countries were barred from introducing artificial barriers to payments for goods and services either for balance-of-payments reasons or to stimulate employment.

This agreement was to be complemented by an elaborate arrangement governing tariffs and trade, designed to lower trade barriers and to permit them to be raised only to provide temporary relief to a country's balance of payments, and then only under well-defined and internationally agreed circumstances.[1] In brief, the Bretton Woods system was heavily market-oriented for trade in goods and services; movement was to be as free and unfettered by controls as possible.

The same favorable treatment was not accorded to capital move ments. Not only was freedom of international capital movement thought to be unnecessary to achieve the objectives of high income and employment and efficient growth in world trade, but also the experience of the interwar period had indicated that such freedom might actually be harmful and disruptive to the pursuit of those objectives. While the Bretton Woods Agreement does not actually encourage or require the regular use of controls over capital movements as a method for maintaining external balance, the technique is certainly not discouraged. An early British version of the proposed system permitted the new international institution to *require* the control of outward movements of capital as a condition for borrowing beyond a certain point, and at American insistence an early interpretation of the Bretton Woods Agreement prohibited the International Monetary

---

[1] The far-reaching agreement covering trade and the establishment of the International Trade Organization was never put into effect, but most of the principles were incorporated in the General Agreement on Tariffs and Trade (GATT), adopted in 1947.

Fund from lending to cover deficits arising from large international capital flows.[2] Moreover, the Agreement instructs all members to aid in enforcing the legitimate capital controls of other members.[3]

The International Monetary Fund.   The Bretton Woods Agreement established a new international institution, the International Monetary Fund (IMF), and charged it with the dual task of policing the rules and of lending to member countries to cover temporary balance-of-payments deficits. The Fund grew from its original membership of 44 in 1947 to 107 twenty years later, and it has played an increasingly important role (after some years in eclipse) as a lending institution, as a source of financial advice to member countries, and as a forum for discussing international monetary problems of general interest.

The mechanics of IMF operations are complex and technical, and it is unnecessary to describe them in detail. Each member's relationship with the Fund revolves around its quota, which serves the threefold function of specifying the member's obligation to lend to the Fund (its subscription, 25 per cent to be paid in gold, with certain exceptions, and the remainder in its own currency), of defining the member's right to borrow from the Fund (its "drawing rights," equal to 125 per cent of its quota, with the possibility of further borrowing in certain cases), and of indicating the member's voting power in IMF decisions.[4]

The IMF has divided each country's drawing rights into five tranches, each equal to 25 per cent of its quota. The first of these is called the "gold tranche" because it corresponds to the member's subscription in gold; the others are called the first through the fourth

[2] "Proposals for An International Clearing Union," United Kingdom, Cmd. 6437, April 1943, Sec. 6(8)(b)(ii); and Resolution No. 6 of the Inaugural Meetings of the Board of Governors, International Monetary Fund, *Summary Proceedings* (Washington: IMF, 1946), p. 106. This interpretation was relaxed in 1961. Article VI of the Articles of Agreement of the International Monetary Fund proscribes a member from using IMF resources to finance large or sustained capital outflows, and authorizes the IMF to request a member to exercise controls to prevent such use.

[3] Articles of Agreement of the International Monetary Fund, Article VIII, Sec. 2(b).

[4] Voting rights do not correspond exactly to quotas, since each member gets 250 votes plus one vote for each $100,000 of its quota.

credit tranches. Under current practice, borrowing in the gold tranche is virtually automatic, while borrowing in the first credit tranche is liberal. Borrowing beyond that involves increasing degrees of scrutiny by the IMF of the drawing country's economic policies, and the Fund often stipulates certain conditions which a drawing country must meet before it is permitted to borrow. A borrowing country must repay the Fund within three to five years, and outstanding drawings (beyond the gold tranche) are subject to payment of interest on a scale which increases with the number of credit tranches used.[5]

The Bretton Woods Agreement called for total quotas of $8.8 billion,[6] compared with total reserves of member countries amounting to about $38 billion in 1947. Quotas have been increased twice since they were originally set, by 50 per cent in 1959 and by 25 per cent in 1966. With the addition of new members, the second increase brought total IMF quotas to nearly $21 billion.

Each member is supposed to declare to the Fund a par value for its currency, and is obliged to keep the actual exchange rate within 1 per cent of its par value. Provision is made for changing par values when a country experiences a "fundamental disequilibrium" in its balance of payments. It can make changes up to 10 per cent of the original par value on its own, but changes beyond that are supposed to be made only after consultation with the IMF.

Early Plans for the Postwar Payments System

The Bretton Woods Agreement was the outgrowth of two plans put forward by British and American officials in 1943. Each plan represented "purer" versions of the alternative methods for coping with imbalances than did the IMF system that emerged. It is of some interest to see what these wartime planners produced, before the inevitable compromises were made, since the two versions will serve as useful reference points.

[5] Technically, a member does not "borrow" from the IMF at all. It "purchases" foreign currencies it needs with its own currency, with the result that the Fund's holding of the foreign currency goes down and its holding of the drawing member's currency goes up. Repaying the fund involves a "repurchase" of the member's currency from the Fund.

[6] Including $1.2 billion from the Soviet Union, which never joined the Fund.

With respect to basic objectives, the British proposal for an International Clearing Union, whose principal author was J. M. Keynes, stated clearly that any plan should involve "the least possible interference with internal national policies, and the plan should not wander from the international terrain," and that "the technique of the plan must be capable of application, irrespective of the type and principle of government and economic policy existing in the prospective member states." [7] The following year, in defending the Bretton Woods proposals in the British House of Lords, Keynes emphasized the importance of an international setting "within which the new domestic policies can occupy a comfortable place. Therefore, it is above all as providing an international framework for the new ideas and the new techniques associated with the policy of full employment that these proposals are not least to be welcomed." [8] It is clear that the British placed heavy emphasis on preserving domestic freedom to pursue policies leading to full employment. The plans for international institutions were being discussed precisely at the time when Sir William Beveridge's *Report on Social Insurance and Allied Services* and the British government's *White Paper on Employment Policy* were in the process of becoming the foundations for British economic policy.

At the same time, however, the British proposal recognized that there might be occasions when poor judgment in framing economic policies could lead a country into balance-of-payments difficulties. It stated that "we need a system possessed of an internal stabilizing mechanism, by which pressure is exercised on any country whose balance of payments with the rest of the world is departing from equilibrium *in either direction,* so as to prevent movements which must create for its neighbors an equal but opposite want of balance." Thus, it permitted the Clearing Union's governing board to recommend to any member state that had borrowed half its quota "any internal measures affecting its domestic economy which may appear to be appropriate to restore the equilibrium of its international balance." [9]

[7] "Proposals for an International Clearing Union," cited, preface.

[8] J. M. Keynes, "The International Monetary Fund," a speech before the House of Lords (1944), reprinted in Seymour E. Harris (ed.), *The New Economics* (New York: Alfred A. Knopf, 1947), p. 377.

[9] "Proposals for an International Clearing Union," cited, para. 1(d) and 6(8)(b).

This ambivalence reflects recognition that payments deficits may arise from a variety of sources, some inside any given country, some outside, some due to inappropriate economic policies, some due to changes in economic structure. An underlying and unresolved difference of opinion in most debates on the international monetary system is whether imbalances arise primarily within each country due to faulty domestic economic policy—especially excessive credit creation—or whether responsibility properly lies with changes in underlying economic factors or with changes in demand emanating from abroad. The British view clearly attached most importance to fluctuations in economic activity abroad: "There is great force in the contention that, if active employment and ample purchasing power can be sustained in the main centers of the world trade, the problem of surpluses and unwanted exports will largely disappear . . ." [10] This of course reflected the widespread view that a major disturbing element in the postwar world would be a depression in the United States. It was incumbent on the United States to avoid such a depression, but other countries must be suitably armed to defend their levels of employment if depression should come.

This was to be accomplished by access to large and readily available resources to finance deficits resulting from full employment at home in the face of depression abroad. The British proposal permitted any member country to draw up to half of its quota over a span of two years—and the quotas were to be large, one suggestion placing them at 75 per cent of the sum of a country's exports and imports, or nearly $33 billion for the world as a whole—at its own initiative and without having to adjust its policies or explain them to other countries. Beyond that point, the governing board of the Clearing Union could demand collateral, could require controls over outward capital movements, or could even require a depreciation of the member's currency.[11] But up to that point drawing rights on the Clearing Union could be used as freely as "owned reserves," to use the modern term, such as gold holdings.

The Clearing Union proposed by the British would have created a new form of international money (called bancor) rather than rely on the use of national currencies or gold for its operations, as the IMF does. Member countries would still be limited by their own

10 Same, para. 18.
11 Same, para. 6(8).

quotas in the amount they could borrow, but the Clearing Union did not have to concern itself with having enough resources to honor members' quotas; it could simply credit its books to the drawing country, just as a central bank credits its books to a commercial bank which borrows from it. What made the system work was the obligation of all member countries to accept (in principle, without limit) claims on the clearing union in payment for net exports of goods and services to other members. Theoretically, a single country might be required to "extend credit" via this machinery by accumulating bancor up to the total value of the quotas of all the other members. Practically, the United States feared that during the postwar recovery of Europe it might be called upon to do just this (to an amount in excess of $30 billion, under the British suggestion for quotas, or $15 billion if allowance were made for the stringent action to be taken by countries borrowing more than 50 per cent of their quotas.) For that reason the United States favored a system like the IMF which limited each member's lending to the Fund as well as its borrowing.[12]

In terms of the categories developed in Chapter 1, the British Clearing Union proposal involved provision of ample liquidity in order to permit unfettered trade in goods and services and simultaneously to insulate domestic economic policies from the "discipline" of the balance of payments. It corresponded to a point like J in Figure 1–1. If a country used too much liquidity too rapidly, however, it might reflect imprudent domestic policies and the international authorities could require the country to take corrective action, involving, if necessary, devaluation of its currency.

The original proposal put forward by the American side, drafted largely by Harry Dexter White, allowed for less national autonomy in domestic policy. While this proposal shared with the British one the broad objectives of freedom for international transactions and maintenance of a high level of domestic economic activity, it permitted an international institution to oversee these objectives. The new institution could supervise domestic economic policy in member countries

[12] In the event, the United States provided Europe with *grants* exceeding $16 billion under the Marshall Plan, in addition to extensive loans. Under Keynes' Clearing Union these would have built up credits which the United States would have welcomed fifteen years after the Bretton Woods Conference.

and it could even alter exchange rates. It takes on the character of an economics ministry in a world government.

By comparison with the British proposal, the American one offered meagre financing resources—only $5 billion in all. This was consistent with the broad powers to be held by the international authority. With rapid adjustment, countries require relatively low reserves. Balance-of-payments adjustment would be assured by the requisite changes in domestic policies or, if appropriate, in exchange rates. This proposal represented a point close to the upper vertex in Figure 1–1 —like the gold standard, but with the difference that national policies would be centrally coordinated to ensure a minimum of disruption to the world economy arising from divergent policies, while at the same time avoiding the kind of destabilizing downward spiral of trade and economic activity that occurred in the 1930s. Exchange rates could be adjusted, but not on national initiative. The system thus restricted severely the scope for individual national action in the realm of economic policy.

The implied loss of national sovereignty not only made Britain recoil but it was unacceptable to most Americans as well. Particularly as negotiations proceeded and as the various proposals were subjected to public discussion, it became clear that the American Congress would not welcome any international institution which could interfere with domestic economic policies. So the American position took on a certain ambivalence. On the one hand, officials recognized that effective operation of an international financial system would require occasional interference in domestic policies so long as external measures, such as direct controls, were ruled out as a method of preserving international balance and so long as the financing liabilities of potential creditor countries were to be kept within modest limits. On the other hand, the suggestion of "foreign" interference in domestic American economic policy offended the sensibilities of the American Congress and, no doubt, the majority of the informed public. The final version of the American proposals was therefore much closer to the British view with respect to preservation of national autonomy, but lacked the provision for ample financing to make that possible without restrictions on trade.[13]

[13] At the Bretton Woods conference the Australian delegation attempted, without success, "to see Governments specifically accept the obligation to main-

The Bretton Woods Agreement which finally emerged was thus something of a compromise between the two proposals. It involved a much smaller provision for financing and (as it has developed) somewhat more direction of national economic policy than envisaged by Keynes in the British plan, but somewhat more generous financing and much less direction of national policy than was envisaged in the earlier versions of the American proposals.[14] This left something of a gap in the logic of the arrangement, since there might be occasions in which the resources available for financing were inadequate to protect the domestic autonomy which was permitted.

A number of academic economists, especially in Britain, criticized the proposals for the postwar monetary system on the grounds that they attached far too much importance to the removal of restrictions on international trade and payments and to the nondiscriminatory application of any restrictions that had been retained. These critics felt that, in the face of a major industrial slump abroad, a commitment to multilateralism and nondiscrimination would force countries to choose between abandoning the benefits of trade altogether and abandoning stabilization policies at home. It would be far better, in their view, to preserve something of both by permitting discrimination against those countries whose imports had fallen sharply.

The Articles of Agreement of the IMF bowed to this view to the

---

tain employment . . ."; i.e., to reduce national autonomy with respect to domestic policy as well as international policy, on the grounds that domestic policy was equally important for the course of world trade. This recognition was expressed explicitly in the Charter for the International Trade Organization in 1947, but since only Liberia ratified the Charter, it failed to go into effect.

[14] While each country's quota was larger under the IMF than it would have been under the White Plan, the total amount of funds *available* was substantially less than would have been true under Keynes' Clearing Union with the same total value of quotas. Of the $8.8 billion originally programmed for the IMF, only $4.3 billion would have been in gold and dollars. Because a country's quota defined (and limited) its lending obligations as well as specifying its drawing rights, there were *two* limits to the ability of any country to use the Fund: the limits imposed by its own drawing rights and the limits possibly imposed by the Fund's lending resources. This dual limitation on the Fund's operations with any country dictated a conservative attitude toward lending in its early years and in addition it became important later, as we shall see, not because the Fund's holdings of dollars were depleted but, on the contrary, because weakness of the dollar in the early 1960s induced the Fund to use other currencies, of which it held only small amounts relative to its needs.

extent of including an escape clause in the form of Article VII, the so-called "scarce currency clause," which could be invoked if the Fund's supply of a particular currency were in danger of being exhausted. This clause released adherents to the Agreement from rules governing restrictions on international payments with a country which ran a large and persistent surplus in its international payments. Members could then restrict payments to the intractable country, but not to other members. This "controlled discrimination" thus provided the system with an ability to withstand particularly difficult circumstances without experiencing total reversion to chaos and mutual recrimination in international payments.[15] British officials, especially, attached much importance to this provision, for one of their principal concerns was the asymmetry inherent in a system in which countries in deficit are sooner or later compelled to take action, while countries in surplus can, if necessary, avoid corrective action simply by accumulating international reserves indefinitely—or until the deficit countries are finally forced to reduce the imbalance.[16]

The IMF system, in terms of the triangle in Figure 1–1, involved a combination of modest financing and main reliance on internal measures to correct imbalances, but with allowance in extreme cases for external measures: devaluation if a single country ran a persistent deficit[17] and systematic trade discrimination against a country which ran a persistent surplus.

[15] The same end could be accomplished, of course, by an appreciation of the currency of the country running the payments surplus, or by a massive devaluation of all other currencies against that currency. Under the rules adopted, however, there was no way to compel a country to appreciate; and large-scale devaluation was probably thought to be impracticable because of the degree of coordination required. In fact such a widespread devaluation came in 1949, led by the devaluation of sterling. It is worth recalling that at the time many experts doubted the effectiveness of devaluation as a technique for eliminating payments deficits.

[16] See R. F. Harrod, *The Life of John Maynard Keynes* (London: Macmillan & Co., 1951), pp. 543–44; and J. M. Keynes, in S. E. Harris, cited, pp. 372–73.

[17] Concern with protecting national autonomy is reflected in Article IV, Sec. 3(f) of the IMF Articles of Agreement, where the IMF is obliged to approve a proposed change in a country's par value if that country is judged to have a "fundamental disequilibrium": in particular, the Fund "shall not object to a proposed change because of the domestic social or political policies of the member proposing the change." It was noted in Chapter 1 that ideolog-

Evolution of the Payments System since Bretton Woods

The IMF did not prove up to the task of coping with the heavy demands of reconstruction and other expenditures in Europe.[18] The period of "normalcy" in which the Bretton Woods system was supposed to function efficiently was not formally acknowledged until 1961, fourteen years after the IMF began operations, and was nearly three times longer than the transition period anticipated. The interim period was filled with a number of expedients such as the Anglo-American loan of 1946, the Marshall Plan aid program, the formation of the OEEC, with its committees for discussion and for coordination of economic and trade policies, and the European Payments Union (EPU), designed to make international payments *within* Europe multilateral. During this period, the IMF was unable to play the central role in the international payments system for which it was designed, and it could not transform the momentum of its formative period into actual practice.

The reasons for this long transition period [19] are many. Recon-

ical differences among the industrial countries of the non-Communist world have narrowed substantially in the last three decades.

The concern with national autonomy is also reflected in GATT, Article XII, Sec. 3(d), drawn up in 1947: "a contracting party . . . shall not be required to withdraw or modify restrictions [on trade] on the ground that a change in policies [directed toward the achievement and maintenance of full and productive employment or towards the development of economic resources] would render unnecessary restrictions which it is applying under this Article."

[18] Heavy reconstruction demands were anticipated, and the IMF was not in fact expected to carry this burden. A "transition period" of five years was allowed before members were expected to accept all of the IMF obligations; and the International Bank for Reconstruction and Development (IBRD) was established as a parallel institution to the IMF, endowed with borrowing powers and nearly $8 billion in subscriptions to finance long-term lending. But the IBRD early adopted the practice of financing only bankable projects, whereas general balance-of-payments support was often needed. The IBRD did lend over $500 million to European countries in its first few years of operation, but it too shifted its activity primarily to other countries during the Marshall Plan.

[19] In legal terms, the "transition period" lasted until IMF members renounced their right under Article XIV of the Articles of Agreement to retain exchange controls and accepted the general obligations set forth in Article VIII, which calls for removing all restrictions on payments for current trans-

struction was difficult and in some countries it was complicated by political turmoil. Cooling relations with the Soviet bloc, the rearmament of Europe, and the outbreak of war in South Korea put further strains on the economies and the payments positions of European countries. Finally, one condition of the Anglo-American Loan of 1946 required Britain to make the pound sterling fully convertible within one year. Britain complied briefly in the summer of 1947, with disastrous effects to British reserves. This premature experience with convertibility no doubt made British and other officials unduly cautious about subsequent approaches to currency convertibility and acceptance of the general obligations of the Bretton Woods Agreement.

The result of these circumstances was an acute "dollar shortage" for most of the Fund's members. The Fund itself experienced no such shortage, for it early curtailed its lending to countries receiving U.S. aid under the Marshall Plan. After a few years characterized by heavy restrictions on trade and payments by most countries outside of North America, the European countries in 1950 formed the EPU, which amounted to a club for systematic discrimination against payments to the "dollar area." This represented a functional substitute for invoking the scarce currency clause of the IMF, a move which was never formally taken.

In the immediate postwar period most industrial countries had only modest means for financing deficits, so they imposed heavy restrictions on international transactions. Selective relaxation of these restrictions during the 1950s and U.S. payments deficits of the 1960s dominated payments developments in the ensuing years.

Postwar Liberalization. The OEEC, formed in 1948 to allocate Marshall Plan aid equitably among the claimants, saw the close two-way connection between rapid recovery and restoration of mutually beneficial international trade. OEEC members therefore agreed to remove quantitative restrictions on at least 50 per cent of *intra-*

---

actions and for the removal of any discriminatory or multiple currency practices. Only seven countries, all in the Western Hemisphere, accepted the obligations of Article VIII within five years after the Fund began operations. Eleven more countries, including the major European countries, formally accepted Article VIII in February 1961, and Japan did so in 1964. At the end of 1967, 31 member countries out of a total of 107 had accepted the obligations set forth in Article VIII. Most European currencies had been convertible *de facto* for nonresidents since the end of 1958.

European trade by the end of 1949. Liberalization was to reach 75 per cent by 1951, with the additional requirement that 60 per cent liberalization apply to each of the three separate categories: foods and fodder, raw materials, and manufactures. In 1955 the required liberalization was extended to 90 per cent, with 75 per cent in each of the three commodity categories. State-traded goods were excluded from the calculations, but state trading for resale was discouraged. A series of rules and interpretations associated with trade liberalization were incorporated in 1950 into a Code of Liberalization, which was subsequently modified and extended until it lapsed in 1961 with the transformation of the OEEC into the Organization for Economic Co-operation and Development (OECD).

Trade with the dollar area was not subject to these liberalization targets, and indeed was not subject to any particular targets at all, beyond the general objective of reducing restrictions on trade as rapidly as the situation permitted.

Trade liberalization within Europe was based on presumptive reciprocity. It was recognized that member countries would be reluctant to liberalize trade unless their trading partners also did so; yet to limit the process of liberalization to the pace of the most reluctant member would unduly impede the restoration of intra-European trade. The rules for liberalization therefore applied in principle to all members; but various exceptions were allowed, usually based on balance-of-payments considerations. Thus the *pace* of trade liberalization became an important feature of the adjustment process. Countries in surplus liberalized their transactions early, while those in deficit delayed until their payments position permitted it.[20] Severe payments difficulties could even justify deliberalization, but the case would have to be put before the OEEC to avoid retaliation by the major countries. Britain and Germany deliberalized in 1951, and France deliberalized in 1952 and again in 1957.

Adjustments in timing of liberalization in intra-European trade helped avoid imbalances in payments, but the principal element of adjustment was not so much the reciprocal reduction of trade controls within Europe as the timing of reduction of controls on imports re-

[20] This variation in timing of trade liberalization differs sharply from the tariff reductions which have taken place under auspices of the GATT. For the industrial countries, these are based on strict reciprocity in tariff reduction. This issue will be taken up in Chapter 9.

quiring payment in dollars. During the period of dollar shortage, discrimination against North American goods was severe, and these restrictions were relaxed only as the over-all payments positions of European countries improved. A rough indication of the discrimination against dollar goods is given by the fact that, in 1953, only 11 per cent of total imports from the "dollar area" into the OEEC countries (all of western Europe) were free from quantitative restrictions, compared with 71 per cent of intra-European trade. By 1961, these figures had risen to 89 per cent and 94 per cent, respectively.[21]

The liberalization of intra-European trade was facilitated by the EPU, which served the twofold purpose of putting all European currencies on a par as far as intra-European settlements were concerned and of providing credit to countries in payments deficit. The first purpose was achieved by channeling all intra-European payments through the EPU, so each country could cease to be concerned about its bilateral payments position with each of the other members and need only be concerned about its over-all position with the EPU (which included the currency areas of several European countries, and most notably the Sterling Area).

In addition, the EPU extended credit to its members. This credit was automatic and unlimited for periods up to 30 days, since settlements between each member and the EPU were made only at the end of each month. Members in deficit also received automatic credits from surplus countries for some portion of the deficit at the monthly settlements—the credit was originally on a sliding scale starting at 80 per cent of the monthly deficit, and was gradually reduced over time to a flat 25 per cent—so long as the over-all debtor position of the deficit country with the EPU fell within its EPU quota. Credits beyond the quota required special negotiations with the creditor countries under the auspices of the EPU. In contrast to the IMF at the time, this system provided, within limits, automaticity and relative absence of publicity, and the EPU under these circumstances provided a genuine addition to international liquidity. Creditor and debtor positions at the EPU were denominated in a unit of account and, like transactions with the IMF, were thus guaranteed against capital losses due to currency devaluations.

In 1958 the EPU was liquidated and supplanted by the European

[21] OEEC, *Twelfth Annual Economic Review* (Paris: OEEC, 1961), p. 186.

Monetary Agreement (EMA), whose credit provisions are much more limited in size and are not automatic. The move to full currency convertibility for nonresidents by most European countries in 1958 [22] reflected the growing strength of European currencies and a passing of the need for an anti-dollar discriminatory bloc, which the EPU represented; the "dollar shortage" was officially ended. The EMA, moreover, provided substantial incentive to make most currency conversions through the exchange markets rather than, as under EPU, through its institutional machinery for multilateral settlement. Private markets took over the function of foreign exchange clearing. Most of the EMA's lending resources have been devoted, in effect, to the economic development of Turkey, and only $37 million in payments have been made through its multilateral system of settlements. [23]

U.S. Payments Deficits and the Role of the Dollar.

Just as the possibilities for selective relaxation of restrictions on trade and payments as a limited device for balancing payments were becoming exhausted, the need felt by most countries to adjust their payments positions diminished sharply. This was due to the emergence, in 1958, of a large deficit in the U.S. balance of payments. While it varied from year to year, the U.S. deficit remained very large for the following decade. [24]

[22] These countries did not, however, give up their right under Article XIV of the Bretton Woods Agreement to apply restrictions on exchange transactions until 1961.

[23] Multilateral settlements through the EMA take place at the maximum buying price or the minimum selling price for each currency. Thus, central banks normally save money by using the exchange markets. The European Fund of the EMA grants credit for two to five years, and it has made credits available to Greece, Iceland, Spain, and Turkey. Turkey has accounted for most of the drawings. See European Monetary Agreement, *Fourth Annual Report to the Board of Management, 1962* (Paris: OECD, 1963); and Bank for International Settlements, *Thirty-Seventh Annual Report* (Basle, 1967), Chap. V.

[24] There is an extensive debate over how the U.S. payments deficit should be measured. In terms of "official settlements"—reserve losses plus increases in U.S. liabilities to foreign central banks—the deficit rose from $3.0 billion in 1958 to $3.4 billion in 1960 and then fell to $1.3 billion in 1965. A small surplus in 1966 was followed by a $3.4 billion deficit in 1967. For a discussion of measuring the U.S. payments deficit, see R. N. Cooper, "The Balance of Payments in Review," *Journal of Political Economy*, LXXIV, August 1966, pp. 379–95.

This is not the place to discuss the various causes of the U.S. deficit; there is a confusing array of explanations.[25] What is important is the consequences for the international payments system. Large U.S. deficits meant that other countries had comfortable payments surpluses. While payments positions varied from country to country and from time to time, balance-of-payments pressure on the rest of the world, taken as a group, was eased very substantially. Indeed, the final relaxation of controls over trade and payments and the acceptance of the obligations of Article VIII by the industrial countries of Europe reflected this easier position. When countries did occasionally run into balance-of-payments difficulties, it was generally because domestic demand had run far ahead of the capacity of the economy to produce, so there was little conflict between domestic and international objectives: both pointed toward some restraint of demand. On the few occasions when this was not the case, large amounts of special balance-of-payments support was amassed, as will be described below.

But what about the United States itself? If other countries felt little balance-of-payments pressure because of large U.S. deficits, did not the United States feel acute balance-of-payments pressure?

Although this pressure was felt, and was reflected in a number of domestic and international policies during the period, it was considerably less acute than might have been expected from the size and duration of the deficits, for several related reasons. First, the United States had very large gold reserves. They had accounted for over 70 per cent of the world's total monetary gold stock in 1947, and even by 1957 the United States held 59 per cent of the world's monetary gold. Some redistribution was thought to be positively desirable. Second, the world economy had lived through more than a decade of "dollar shortage," and large U.S. deficits were welcome for a change, particularly since it was widely, if erroneously, suspected that they would be short-lived. Finally, foreign countries were willing to hold many of the dollars which they acquired through their surpluses, rather than converting them into gold. Since the Second World War the dollar had become a "reserve currency," an asset which central banks and governments held in their international reserves. Foreign official hold-

<hr>

[25] A useful summary of the debate can be found in Chap. 8 of M.O. Clement *et al.*, *Theoretical Issues in International Economics* (New York: Houghton Mifflin Co., 1967).

ings of dollars had been negligible before the Second World War. In 1946 they amounted to about $3 billion, and by 1966 they amounted to over $13 billion. In addition, nearly $14 billion were in the hands of foreign commercial banks and other private holders.

The evolution of the dollar as a reserve currency was an unforeseen but quite natural development. The reasons for this development are given below. The point here is that foreign willingness to hold dollar assets amounted to lending to the United States, and helped to finance the U.S. deficits.[26] The net effect was a weakening of the influence of the U.S. payments deficit on its domestic and/or foreign economic policies, compared with what would have been the case if the full burden of financing the payments deficits had fallen on U.S. gold reserves.[27] In effect, the United States provided ample liquidity to the rest of the world through its deficits, and these deficits in turn were financed by the willingness of surplus countries to lend at short term to the United States by holding liquid dollar assets.

Still, the insulation which this financing provided was not complete. The United States was very much conscious of its weak balance-of-payments position, and this weakness inhibited the use of expansionary monetary and fiscal policies which, on domestic grounds alone, would have been desirable before 1965. It also induced the United States to begin to restrict its external transactions in a number of important respects. Moreover, the surplus countries became increasingly restive about what they felt to be the inflationary impact of their payments surpluses and the limitations that freedom of international capital movements placed on their ability to restrict domestic demand through monetary action.

While dollars will continue to be accumulated by many countries, the voluntary accumulation of dollars on a very large scale is un-

[26] There is of course the possibility, which should not be dismissed lightly at least for some countries and for some periods, that foreign acquisition of dollars was the *cause* and not merely the *consequence* of the deficits.

[27] In addition to its gold reserves, the United States had IMF drawing rights in excess of $5.0 billion. It was reluctant to use these, however, partly because it was felt that a U.S. drawing would weaken confidence in the dollar, partly because of the inadequacy of the Fund's usable resources to meet a large drawing by the United States and at the same time carry on its normal lending operations when the dollar was weak. The United States did begin to draw on the Fund in 1964, in small amounts and for technical reasons having to do with the ability of debtor countries to repay the Fund.

likely to recur. For the first time in many years, no dollars were added to total official reserves in 1965, and large liquidations of official dollar holdings occurred in 1966. The surplus countries began a conscious attempt to introduce greater "discipline" into the U.S. balance of payments by indicating extreme unwillingness to accumulate more dollars and, in the case of France, by converting large dollar holdings into gold.

The payments system after 1950 moved gradually away from reliance on external measures toward greater reliance on financing and on internal measures, as shown in Figure 1–2; but in the 1960s pressure mounted against financing the U.S. deficit, and a reversion toward external measures developed. This is discussed in Chapter 9.

Adaptation of IMF Practices. During this time the IMF shifted toward much greater reliance on internal measures to assure international balance, with less emphasis on financing temporary deficits than had been envisioned by some of the participants at Bretton Woods. In the mid-1960s, however, there seems to have been some shift in the other direction, back toward easier and more abundant financing facilities.

A hardening of the Fund's view on the ease with which member countries could draw was already evident at the beginning of its operations.[28] The Fund feared that its resources might be used for reconstruction purposes without actually ensuring balance-of-payments equilibrium after reconstruction, so it attempted to conserve its resources for those cases in which Fund help offered reasonable prospects for tiding a country over a temporary crisis. In 1948 the Fund decided not to lend to countries receiving Marshall Plan aid. New lending dropped sharply, and in 1950 no lending took place.[29] Marshall Plan aid ended in 1951, and the Fund took a series of decisions which have guided its operations since that time. In an apparent effort to conserve its resources in anticipation of large drawings, the Fund (a) required repayment of drawings in 3 to 5 years, a requirement much stiffer than the "repurchase" provisions of the Articles of Agreement; (b) required consultation on "excess" Fund holdings of

---

[28] See for example the First Annual Meeting of the Board of Governors, *Report of the Executive Directors* and *Summary Proceedings* (Washington: IMF, 1946), p. 24.

[29] Figures on Fund lending are given in Table 8-1, on page 211, below.

any country's currency after three years rather than seven, as previously; (*c*) raised the schedule of charges on outstanding drawings; and (*d*) directed that in its lending operations "the Fund will be guided . . . by its judgment whether a member's *policies* are likely to be adequate to overcome its problems within a temporary period." [30]

The Fund at this time passed major responsibility for maintaining international monetary stability directly to the countries themselves, stating, in an apparent endorsement of restrictions then widely prevalent, "It is important, therefore, that countries follow commercial [sic] policies that will enable them to build up reserves in periods of prosperity which would provide a first cushion to absorb the shock of a recession." [31] Members were, however, given "the overwhelming benefit of any doubt" in requests to draw up to the amount of their gold subscription. And in the following year the Fund restored a certain degree of flexibility to its operations by creating the "stand-by," whereby a member country can open a line of credit at the Fund for a specified period of time, say a year. These stand-bys were established "to remove the doubts that have led some members to the view that in formulating their policies they could not rely on Fund assistance." [32]

Further flexibility in the face of changing circumstances appears in the Fund's attitudes toward changes in exchange rates. Before the devaluations of 1949, Fund pronouncements suggest unmistakably that the initial par values established by some countries were out of line and should be changed. During the 1950s the Fund took a relatively passive position on changes in par values, especially for less developed countries. But in the early 1960s it seems to have acquiesced in the widespread official view that changes in exchange rates among major currencies are undesirable.[33] At the same time, the Fund

[30] IMF, *Annual Report, 1952*, p. 42. Italics added. IMF charges on outstanding drawings in the fourth credit tranche were lowered again in 1963.

[31] Same, p. 46.

[32] IMF, *Annual Report, 1953*, p. 51.

[33] In its 1964 *Annual Report*, p. 28, the Fund discusses the process of balance-of-payments adjustment. It is extraordinary that this discussion mentions changes in par values only once, and then with some apparent reluctance: "Adjustments in exchange rates are of course not precluded by the par value system, and are indeed foreseen by the Articles in the event that a country has fallen into fundamental disequilibrium; but such situations should arise less frequently to the extent that the policies described above are followed."

showed considerable tolerance of members that failed to establish uniform par values. It often agreed to floating rates where a realistic par value seemed difficult to establish, as for Canada in 1950. In other cases, too, it accepted multiple exchange practices as necessary fiscal devices, although with evident reluctance.

Several steps have been taken to increase the lending resources of the Fund. In addition to selective quota increases from time to time, a general quota increase of 50 per cent occurred in 1959 and another general increase of 25 per cent took place in 1966. Moreover, since larger quotas increase drawing rights as well as lending resources, the Fund in early 1962 made provision through the General Arrangements to Borrow (GAB) to replenish its holdings of convertible currencies by as much as $6 billion by borrowing from the major industrial countries.

Need for additional resources under the GAB arose from a basic asymmetry in the original quota structure of the IMF: the preponderant size of the quota of the United States. There were two reasons for establishing such a large quota—36 per cent when the IMF started operations in 1947, although with the accession of new members and special quota increases by others, this had dwindled to 22 per cent by 1965.[34] First, the United States obviously was to be the largest creditor to the Fund in the foreseeable future; the rest of the world needed U.S. dollars, and this postwar fact dominated the Bretton Woods negotiations. It was natural, therefore, that the United States should

---

Much the greater part of its discussion of adjustment focusses on the need to pursue appropriate domestic policies.

[34] With the accession of new members, the U.S. and British share of total votes has fallen sharply, while the voting share of the present members of the EEC has remained roughly constant because of the accession of Germany in 1952. Because of multiple representation on the Executive Board, members of the EEC cast votes amounting to 21 per cent of the total in 1965.

Percentage Share of Total Votes at the IMF

	1947	1965
United States	36	22
United Kingdom	17	11
Members of the EEC	16	16

The rationale for the structure of IMF quotas is given by Oscar L. Altman in "Quotas in the International Monetary Fund," IMF, *Staff Papers*, August 1956, pp. 136–42.

provide a disproportionately large subscription, and that it would want a correspondingly disproportionate influence in the Fund's decisions. The formal symmetry among members preserved in the wording of the Bretton Woods Agreement was quite overshadowed by the asymmetry in quota sizes, hence drawing rights and voting power. The large U.S. quota provided the Fund ample resources for others to draw, but possibly left insufficient resources to honor a large U.S. drawing without depleting the Fund's usable assets. The General Arrangements to Borrow were designed to supply the Fund with the necessary resources for a U.S. drawing, but they did so only by inserting a new decision-making group—the Group of Ten—into the process of Fund lending.[35]

The second reason for the large quota of the United States and the United Kingdom—which gave the two countries together 52 per cent of the original total subscriptions—was the important role that the dollar had begun to play, and that sterling had played for many years, in international transactions. These large quotas represented some tacit recognition of the "key currency" arguments advanced against the global conception of the IMF in the 1940s.[36] Member countries draw dollars from the Fund not only because they are running deficits with the United States; they draw dollars because they use them in international transactions with other countries as well. Until 1960 virtually all drawings from the Fund were made in U.S. dollars, whether or not the United States was in over-all surplus.

So long as countries were willing to add U.S. dollars to their international reserves, use of the dollar by the Fund would not tax U.S. reserves even when the United States was running a payments deficit. Drawings of other currencies, in contrast, typically have to be converted into dollars for exchange market operations and thus will tend,

[35] The ten GAB adherents, with their maximum lending commitments in millions of U.S. dollars, are Belgium (150), Canada (200), France (550), Germany (1000), Italy (550), Japan (250), Netherlands (200), Sweden (100), the United Kingdom (1000), and the United States (2000). In addition, Switzerland, though not a member of the IMF, has agreed to lend up to $200 million when the GAB is invoked. Invocation of the GAB requires a separate decision by the Group of Ten (plus Switzerland), and any country can in effect veto the use of its currency. Thus any Fund operation which requires invoking the GAB involves a separate hurdle for the ultimate borrower.

[36] See John H. Williams, *Postwar Monetary Plans and Other Essays,* 3rd ed. (New York: Alfred A. Knopf, 1947), Chaps. 3, 4.

unless it is in surplus, to reduce directly the gold or foreign exchange reserves of the country whose currency is drawn.[37] At the same time, countries in debt to the Fund frequently find it natural to repay in dollars (or in gold), since that is the form in which they hold their reserves or in which they routinely add to reserves from exchange market operations.

However, if countries are unwilling to add dollars to their foreign exchange reserves, drawings from the Fund in dollars would result in conversions into gold at the U.S. Treasury unless the United States were running a surplus in its balance of payments. In periods in which its balance of payments was itself weak, these gold outflows could aggravate the difficulties of the United States. In 1961, therefore, the Fund adopted some conventions on the choice of currency for its lending operations, linking the choice both to the reserve level and to the balance-of-payments positions of the countries whose currencies are to be used.[38] Since 1961 only one fourth of the new IMF lending has been in dollars and the bulk of it has been in the currencies of continental European countries. The Fund's holdings of dollars rose steadily as repayments continued to be made in them and in 1964 they reached the point (75 per cent of the U.S. quota) at which further repayments in dollars were not technically permissible, so the United States itself drew from the Fund for the first time. It would then sell the currencies it drew, for dollars, to the countries wanting to repay the Fund, and those countries would repay the Fund in the currencies drawn by the United States. This circuitous operation prevented the repaying countries from converting their dollars into gold in order to repay the Fund, but it illustrates the complications arising from heavy reliance on a single national currency in a system formally symmetric among currencies.

[37] Use of a country's currency does increase that country's virtually automatic drawing rights at the Fund—or, if it is in debt to the Fund, such use reduces indebtedness. But by the mid-1960s only one or two countries regarded their IMF drawing rights as an integral part of their international reserves.

[38] Between 1947 and 1959 the U.S. dollar was used for 90 per cent of all drawings, totalling $3.4 billion. The pound sterling was used in 7 per cent of the drawings, and small amounts of Belgian francs, Canadian dollars, Dutch guilder, French francs, and German marks had also been used. The U.S. dollar was used for only half of the drawings in 1960, and for only one-third of the large drawings in 1961.

Developments Outside the Fund. Following the restoration of convertibility for European currencies in the late 1950s, a number of special arrangements for official international credit arose outside the IMF. The Federal Reserve System of the United States established a series of bilateral "swap" arrangements with the central banks of eleven other countries and the Bank for International Settlements. Under these facilities either party can, in effect, acquire a short-term loan of three to twelve months' duration at its own initiative. They are called "swaps" because they take the form of an exchange of currencies, so initially the foreign exchange reserves of both participants rise when a swap is set in motion. By early 1968 these swap facilities totalled $7.1 billion (of which $1.5 billion were with the United Kingdom), exceeding in amount the American quota at the IMF, and available on much shorter notice. Being short term, they are used largely to offset private transactions which are expected to be limited in duration and reversible, such as large movements of interest-sensitive or speculative short-term capital.[39]

Institution of the Federal Reserve swaps was preceded by the so-called Basle Arrangements, an *ad hoc* agreement whereby European central banks accumulated sterling and supported it in other ways to the extent of $910 million during the sterling crisis of 1961.[40] These too represented strictly short-term support, probably for 90 days but extended another 90 days, on the assumption that part of Britain's deficit was due to speculative withdrawals from sterling which would

[39] For a description of these and other international financial operations of the United States, see the excellent summaries published in the March and September issues of the *Federal Reserve Bulletin,* starting in September 1962. See also Robert Z. Aliber, *The Management of the Dollar in International Finance,* Princeton Studies in International Finance No. 13 (Princeton: Princeton University Press, 1964), pp. 47–48.

[40] See Bank of England, *Quarterly Bulletin,* I, December 1961, pp. 9–10. The Basle arrangements were in fact a series of bilateral arrangements between the Bank of England, on the one hand, and the central banks of Belgium, France, West Germany, Italy, the Netherlands, Sweden, and Switzerland, on the other, made in Basle following a joint communiqué of the central bankers in March 1961, pledging mutual support against currency speculation. The various creditors were not informed about the extent to which other central banks were also supporting the pound. See IMF, *International Financial News Survey,* March 8, 1963, p. 66.

soon be reversed. Similar credits were extended to Britain in 1964 and again in 1966. In the first two cases a subsequent drawing on the IMF permitted Britain to repay these short-term credits when they matured. These arrangements, in effect, complement the Federal Reserve swaps, which are bilateral with the United States.

Large-scale balance-of-payments assistance was also extended directly to Canada in June 1962 and to Italy in March 1964. The lines of credit amounted to over a billion dollars in each case, including minority participation by the IMF and a major role for the United States, involving both the use of swaps and of other lines of credit.

In addition to these new sources of international credit, new forums have developed for discussing balance of-payments policies and other economic developments in the industrial countries. Perhaps the most significant of these are the monthly meetings of central bankers at the Bank for International Settlements in Basle, Switzerland, Working Party Three on the Promotion of Better International Payments Equilibrium in the OECD, and the committee of deputies of the Group of Ten. Working Party Three has been charged with the responsibility of "multilateral surveillance," involving discussions of the size of payments deficits and how they are to be financed; and the Group of Ten meetings have been primarily concerned with long-range improvements in the international payments system, especially the generation of international liquidity, a topic discussed further in Chapter 8.

All of these new arrangements, both for credits and for discussion, tend to detract from the role of the IMF. There is perhaps even the implication that the Fund should play a secondary role with respect to the major industrial countries, confining its operations primarily to the less developed countries and to occasional "bail out" operations for industrial countries heavily burdened by short-term credits which cannot quickly be repaid, as was the case with Britain in 1961 and again in 1965. A role as a relatively passive medium-term lender—and as the principal forum for assisting and cajoling the less developed countries into sensible monetary and balance-of-payments policies—is far removed from the central role in international finance that had been envisioned for the Fund by its architects in 1944. The tendency to shift the principal locus of discussion and action away from the Fund, whether or not it was conscious, has not been entirely successful, however, and during 1966 the IMF was re-established as the principal forum for considering the important question of international liquidity.

International Reserves. This survey of developments since Bretton Woods would be incomplete without a brief discussion of the evolution of international reserves. At present, international reserves take three principal forms: holdings of gold, holdings of foreign exchange, and (virtually) automatic drawing rights at the IMF. At the end of 1965 these three forms of reserves amounted respectively to $41 billion, $23 billion, and $5 billion, for a total of $70 billion for all countries together (Table 2–1). In addition, the U.S. "swap agreements" and the IMF stand-by agreements in excess of gold tranches both represent automatic lines of credit, although in both cases the maturities of any resulting borrowings are relatively short. They add to international "liquidity" even though they are not part of international reserves.

New gold production has accounted for modest increases in international reserves during the last two decades. In most countries gold production has actually declined, but these declines have been more than offset by a rise in production in the Union of South Africa, which now accounts for about three-fourths of new non-Communist gold production amounting to some $1.4 billion a year. New supplies of gold have been augmented by net gold sales from the Communist countries. The Soviet Union is believed to be second only to South African gold production, and it is a normal if erratic seller in the London gold market. Communist China, on the other hand, was a net buyer in the mid-1960s. Only a part of new gold supplies—and a declining part in recent years—is added to national monetary reserves, however, because of the demands of private industry and of private hoarding of gold. Official gold holdings actually declined in 1966 and even more heavily in 1967 to less than $40 billion.

IMF gold tranche drawing rights are acquired in two ways. When a country accedes to the Fund, it must deposit a certain fraction of its quota—normally 25 per cent—in gold. Against this gold deposit it has "virtually automatic" drawing rights; the only requirement is that the drawing country "represent" that it has a balance-of-payments deficit. The general quota increases, 50 per cent in 1959 and 25 per cent in 1965, also increased gold tranche drawing rights. This was

TABLE 2-1   International Reserves [a]
($ billion, end of year)

	1945	1955	1965
1. Gold	33.3	35.8	41.4
2. of which: United States	20.1	21.8	14.1
3. Foreign Exchange [b]	14.3	17.0	23.0
4. of which: U.S. dollars	4.2	8.3	15.9
5. Sterling	10.1	7.6	6.7
6. Gold Tranche Position at the IMF [c]		1.9	5.4
7. Total	47.6	54.7	69.8
8. Addendum: World Exports	34.2	84.0	165.4

[a] Official holdings of all countries except the U.S.S.R., Eastern Europe, and Mainland China; includes holdings of the Bank for International Settlements and EPU.

[b] Reported assets (line 3) generally differ from sum of dollar and sterling liabilities to official holders, lines 4 and 5, because of differences in concept and errors in measurement. Sterling liabilities for 1945 represent a rough estimate of official holdings of sterling outside of British colonies (valued at $4.03 per £), reported in *Report of the Committee on the Working of the Monetary System* (Radcliffe Report), (London HMSO, 1959), p. 230. For 1945 and 1955, dollar liabilities are short-term liabilities to official holders as reported by banks in the United States. *Total* dollar liabilities to official holders were perhaps half a billion dollars higher.

[c] Including super gold tranche.

Sources: Federal Reserve Bulletin, Supplements 14 and 15 to *Banking and Monetary Statistics; International Financial Statistics*.

merely a *quid pro quo* for deposits of gold at the Fund, so total reserves were not increased; gold reserves were transformed into automatic drawing rights at the Fund. Indeed, many countries in 1959 purchased gold from the United States for their additional subscriptions, so they really transformed foreign exchange into drawing rights at the Fund and thereby reduced total international reserves.[41]

The second method of acquiring gold tranche drawing rights does increase international liquidity. It arises when the IMF uses a country's currency in its normal lending operations. If the Fund's holdings

[41] This practice was limited in 1965 by special arrangements. See IMF, *Annual Report, 1965,* Chap. 4.

of any country's currency falls below 75 per cent of that country's quota, the country acquires additional drawing rights [42] in corresponding amount. Thus Fund lending to one member will typically increase the international liquidity of some other member. It will also, of course, increase the liquidity of the borrowing member if such borrowings are beyond the gold tranche; but these "borrowed reserves" must be repaid, under present practices, in three to five years.

Most of the increase in international reserves since the Second World War, and especially since 1959, has been in foreign exchange, and most of that increase has been in U.S. dollars. While the pound sterling is still held in official reserves in substantial amounts, these holdings are largely in the Sterling Area, and in aggregate they have shown little change (in sterling value) over the years.

It is the foreign exchange component of reserves that has recently become so troublesome. Growing world trade and payments require growing reserves, and under present arrangements this growth has been satisfied largely by accruals of dollars resulting from deficits in the American balance of payments. If the deficits continue, however, confidence in the dollar—and hence in a major component of world reserves—will be undermined. If the deficit is stopped, world liquidity will not grow rapidly enough and the growth in world trade will be retarded by internal or external measures. [43]

The reserve currencies—dollars, sterling, and in a limited sphere the French franc—serve not one role but several. They are international means of payment, widely used in settling international transactions. In addition, the dollar is a currency of intervention, used by other countries to support the par values of their own currencies in private markets. All three, finally, are reserve currencies in the strictest sense of the word: they are currencies in which the international reserves of at least some nations are denominated and held.

These three roles are conceptually quite distinct and in practice they are separable, although of course it is not entirely coincidental

---

[42] Sometimes called "super gold tranche" drawing rights.

[43] This difficulty was first underscored by Robert Triffin in two articles in the *Banca Nazionale del Lavoro Quarterly Review* in 1959, reprinted as *Gold and the Dollar Crisis* (New Haven: Yale University Press, 1960). This dilemma, though not Triffin's resolution of it, has been widely accepted as a correct characterization of the problem.

that the same currencies perform the same roles. Of the three, the dollar is by far the most important in the second two roles; the "key currency" role of sterling and the French franc is limited to areas, notably former colonies, retaining special political ties with Britain and France.

Both sterling and the dollar play an extremely useful role in international finance. It is highly convenient to have an international currency of exchange to act as intermediary between other monies. About 110 distinct national currencies exist. Without a currency of exchange, there would in principle have to be nearly 6,000 different bilateral currency markets, and the number of transactions going through most of them would inevitably be small and sporadic. Matching buyers and sellers at reasonably firm prices would be difficult and foreign trade would be discouraged. Under these circumstances, the question is not *whether* a currency will emerge as an intermediary between others, but which one(s).

Over one-third of world trade was estimated in the mid-1950s to have been transacted in sterling,[44] and at least another third was undoubtedly denominated in U.S. dollars. Britain and the United States are the world's largest importing countries, together taking 22 per cent of world imports. But much international trade between other countries is also denominated in these currencies. Just as we avoid commodity barter domestically by using money as an intermediary, we avoid bartering money internationally by using just a few currencies as intermediaries between the others.

Similarly, countries in actual practice maintain exchange stability under the Bretton Woods system within narrow margins around par values not by buying and selling gold at fixed prices but by intervening in the foreign exchange markets to buy and sell the domestic currency as required. Under this procedure domestic currency must be exchanged against some other currency, and it is entirely natural to use the principal currency of exchange, which provides an active and well-developed market in other currencies. In fact, most central banks support their currencies by buying and selling U.S. dollars. Private arbitrage keeps exchange rates between other currencies in line.

This vital function of the dollar—a currency of exchange and by virtue of that a currency of intervention—is conceptually quite separable from its function as a *reserve* currency. Reserves are stores of

[44] *Midland Bank Review,* August 1963, p. 3.

value, and they can be held in virtually anything so long as they are readily convertible into international means of payment. Corporations and banks do not hold all of their liquid assets in currency and demand deposits; on the contrary, they typically hold amounts in excess of working balances in Treasury bills or other earning assets, confident that they can convert these assets into cash on short notice and with little or no loss. The importance of efficient financial markets is obvious here. Gold is a useful form in which to hold international reserves because it is readily convertible into external sterling in London or U.S. dollars at the United States Treasury at a known price. By the same token, reserves could be held in other forms—even wholly new and artificial forms—so long as they can be converted quickly into international means of payments when needed.

The separability of different roles for the key currencies is illustrated by sterling, which was an important means of international settlement long before 1913 but which was not held in international reserves except in small amounts. Sterling has remained an important transactions currency in international trade since 1945 even though reserve holdings of sterling have declined since that time, and even when the principal means of stabilizing exchange rates is by dealing in dollars or (before May 1953) by periodic settlements made at par directly between central banks without being routed through private exchange markets. As with all money, domestic as well as international, the value of any international asset arises from widespread acceptability by the relevant groups, in this case other central banks. International reserves can be held in any form whatever so long as they are widely acceptable for settlement of international payments or so long as they can be converted readily and at relatively low cost into forms which are acceptable.

Summary

This chapter has attempted to describe and interpret the various solutions which the postwar payments system produced for the central problem posed in Chapter 1 (how to enjoy the many benefits of international commerce while preserving considerable freedom for nations to set and pursue successfully their own economic objectives); to indicate how those solutions were compromised and modified in the payments system actually devised; and to show how the payments system evolved in the two decades following the Second World War. The original American and British plans both represented more complete and self-contained systems than the institution and its rules that emerged, the first implying full coordination of national economic policies by an international body, the second providing ample liquidity to support moderate divergences in nationally determined economic policies. Adaptations both inside and outside the International Monetary Fund have compensated in part for its original deficiencies, but rapid changes in the world economy are continually placing new demands on the international payments system. It is to these changes that we now turn.

PART II

Structural Changes
in the World Economy

CHAPTER THREE

Increased Sensitivity of Foreign Trade

No fair assessment of an international payments system can be made without reference to the characteristics which govern international trade, capital movements, and labor migration: the ease with which merchandise, funds, and people can cross national boundaries and the readiness with which they do so. Relationships among the industrial countries have changed very markedly in these respects during the past two decades in the direction of greater international economic intercourse. A sketch of these developments is given here and in the next two chapters.

Growing international intercourse both reflects and causes a much higher sensitivity of international transactions to economic developments in the countries of North America and Western Europe. Trade responds more rapidly to changes in incomes and prices, and capital responds more readily to differences in yields. These changes, in turn, have a profound influence on the ability of countries to manage their economic affairs in their own way.

This chapter deals with international trade in goods and services. The following chapter considers international factor movements of capital, labor, and technology, with emphasis on direct investment in foreign countries. Chapter 5 takes up international movements of relatively liquid funds and financial intermediation among nations. Finally, Chapter 6 indicates the implications of these changes for economic policy in the countries most affected.

Trends in Foreign Trade

The outstanding feature of international trade since the Second World War, especially trade among industrial countries, is its ex-

ceedingly rapid growth. In the two decades following the Second World War, world trade grew by over $120 billion to a total of $165 billion in 1965. Even in the ten years 1955–65, after European reconstruction permitted its re-entry into established markets, world exports doubled. Trade among the non-Communist industrialized countries more than doubled—growing by an astounding 7.6 per cent per annum—to a total of $85 billion.

Traditionally trade was thought to be based on an exchange of "land-using" goods for "labor-using" goods. David Ricardo's classic statement of the doctrine of comparative advantage involved trading Portugal's wine for England's cloth. The illustration was not chosen at random. Classical economists believed that trade was founded on the exchange of manufactures, which required labor skills, for foodstuffs and materials; as population grew, land must become scarcer everywhere and the basis for trade would decline.

This argument assumes that a country's comparative cost structure is determined primarily by natural advantages—by fertile and well-watered plains; by a felicitous climate; or by extensive deposits of high-quality ore or fuel. Strong differences in comparative costs would give countries a powerful incentive to trade, and those luckless areas with few or no natural advantages could concentrate their economic activity on labor-using products. Standards of living in such places would necessarily be low, but trade would still be beneficial.

Much international trade today is still of this character: an exchange of foodstuffs and raw material for manufactures. Indeed, a large number of primary producing (and usually less developed) countries, both in the free world and in the Soviet bloc, have become increasingly restive at the perpetuation of this "classical" type of trade and wish to graduate from the status of providers of foodstuffs and raw materials to the industrial countries.[1]

But the most rapidly growing type of world trade is not at all of this traditional type; it involves the exchange of manufactures for manufactures. As can be seen in Table 3–1, exports of manufactures

---

[1] See John Pincus, *Trade, Aid, and Development* (New York: McGraw-Hill, for the Council on Foreign Relations, 1967). For the strains created over this issue within the Soviet bloc, see John Michael Montias, "Background and Origins of the Rumanian Dispute with Comecon," *Soviet Studies,* October 1964, pp. 125–51.

have grown from less than 40 per cent of world trade in 1928 to nearly 60 per cent in 1966. During the period 1953–64, world exports of manufactures rose 228 per cent, compared with a growth of 84 per cent in other products. Trade in manufactures accounted for two-thirds of the total *growth* in world trade during this period.

Trends in the direction of trade also suggest a growing exchange of manufactures for manufactures. Trade between industrial countries accounted for a much larger share of total world trade in 1965 than

TABLE 3–1 World Trade by Commodity Class [a]

	($ billion)			Manufactures as a Per Cent of Total
	Total	Manufactures [b]	Primary Products [c]	
1928	31.7	12.4	19.3	39
1937–38	22.9	9.1	13.8	40
1953	71.4	32.3	39.1	45
1966 [d]	177.7	105.8	71.9	60

[a] Excluding trade among the present members of the Communist bloc and, for 1953 and 1966, U.S. special category exports.
[b] Defined as Groups 5–8 in the Standard International Trade Classification.
[c] Including residual.
[d] Partially estimated.

Sources: GATT, *Trends in International Trade* (Geneva, 1958), and *International Trade 1966* (Geneva, 1967); League of Nations, *Industrialization and Foreign Trade* (Geneva, 1945), Appendix B.

a decade earlier (Table 3–2), while exports of the nonindustrial areas declined as a proportion of world trade. Greater time perspective shows that the change in the geographical pattern of world trade between 1953 and 1965 to some extent represented a return to the pattern which prevailed in 1928. But in 1928 a large part of the trade among industrial countries represented an exchange of foodstuffs and raw materials for manufactures, particularly exports from the United States and Canada to Europe; and trade between the Communist bloc nations was much smaller than in the postwar period. Moreover, a number of "nonindustrial" countries today are in fact substantial exporters of manufactured products, particularly textiles. If allowance is made for these three developments, the growth in exchange of manufactures for manufactures has been even sharper than the figures in Table 3–2 suggest.

The rapid growth in trade is due in large measure, of course, to the

TABLE 3–2   The Network of World Trade
(Per cent of total world trade)

Exports from	Year	Exports to			
		Industrial Areas	Nonindustrial Areas	Eastern Trading Area	Total, World
Industrial Areas					
	1928	42.2	18.8	5.0	66.0
	1953	37.1	20.4	1.1	58.6
	1965	46.5	16.4	2.5	65.4
Nonindustrial Areas					
	1928	18.7	5.8	1.1	25.6
	1953	22.8	8.0	0.5	31.3
	1965	16.1	5.2	1.5	22.8
Eastern Trading Area					
	1928	5.3	1.2	2.0 [a]	8.5
	1953	1.5	0.6	8.0	10.1
	1965	2.5	1.6	7.6	11.8
Total, World					
	1928	66.2	25.8	8.1	100.0
	1953	61.4	29.0	9.6	100.0
	1965	65.1	23.2	11.6	100.0

[a] The figure of 2.0 per cent for intra-Eastern trade in 1928 was assumed on the basis of fragmentary evidence in the United Nations, *Statistical Yearbook,* 1956, Table 150.

Sources: 1953 and 1965: GATT, *International Trade 1965* (Geneva, 1966); 1928: GATT, *Trends in International Trade* (Geneva, 1958).

rapid growth in output and incomes which the industrial countries have experienced in the postwar period. But the growth in trade outpaced the growth in output, and this was still more true for the growth in trade in manufactures. The tremendous growth in trade in manufactures within and between Western Europe, North America, and Japan is all the more striking because the economic basis for manufacturing is far less specific than is the basis for exports of foodstuffs and raw materials. Modern manufacturing is less dependent on the qualities of the soil or climate than are mining and agriculture; thus, more countries should be able economically to satisfy their own needs. As we shall see later, there are some grounds for believing that the cost structure in manufacturing has become much more similar among industrial countries, and that this trend will continue. Thus, the basis for trade might seem to be diminishing rather than expanding.

Forces for Expansion in Foreign Trade

Three important forces have been working in the opposite direction, however. And all three bear on the sensitivity of trade flows to national economic developments. Changes in commercial policy, reductions in transportation costs, and broadening of business horizons have all acted to enlarge the volume of trade, especially among the industrial countries.

Commercial Policy. The most obvious reason, apart from the rise in incomes, for rapid postwar growth in trade among industrial countries is the lowering of artificial barriers to trade. World trade was hampered by the high tariffs of the 1930s; it was further depressed immediately following the Second World War because productive capacity was inadequate to produce for export and to rebuild war-damaged economics at the same time. Reconstruction of industrial capacity, combined with improvements in arrangements for international payments—notably the re-establishment of multilateral clearing through the EPU, described in Chapter 2—permitted a gradual elimination of the extensive direct controls on trade and payments which most European countries had mounted to keep payments to foreigners in line with receipts and to allocate scarce foreign exchange to their most appropriate uses.

Success in trade liberalization under the OEEC, already alluded to in the previous chapter, is indicated by the fact that the percentage of private intra-European trade freed from quantitative restrictions rose from 56 per cent in 1950 to 84 per cent in 1955 and to 94 per cent in

1961.[2] State trading for resale to the public, important right after the war, was sharply reduced. And as the payments positions of the European countries improved, they also liberalized their trade with North American and other countries. In early 1953 only 11 per cent of total imports from the "dollar area" into the OEEC countries were free from quantitative restrictions, but this percentage rose steadily to 89 per cent in 1961.

While the OEEC was removing quantitative restrictions on trade within Europe, the contracting parties to the GATT were attempting to do so on a global level, and tried to go even farther and reduce tariffs as well. From the first round of multilateral tariff reduction in 1947, when the GATT was drawn up, to the Kennedy Round of tariff negotiations begun in 1963, there were six major multilateral tariff-reducing sessions. The extent of these tariff reductions is not easily summarized, but the first round in 1947 resulted in substantial tariff cuts, and the Dillon Round of 1961–62 resulted in tariff cuts of 20 per cent on a modest range of industrial commodities. Tariff reduction thus contributed in some measure toward the great growth in trade, and again especially among the major industrial countries who were participants in the tariff negotiations. Many less developed countries did not participate in these negotiations to the extent of lowering their own tariffs, but in most cases tariff reductions by industrial countries were extended to them under most-favored-nation treatment.[3]

Finally, commercial policy changes have given a fillip to trade in recent years through the formation of the EEC and the EFTA, both of which are pledged to eliminate tariffs and other barriers to trade within each region. Tariff reductions within the EEC began on Janu-

[2] OEEC, *Twelfth Annual Economic Review* (Paris, 1961), p. 185. It has sometimes been claimed that use of 1948 trade patterns as a base for calculating the degree of trade liberalization imparts an upward bias to it. An OEEC computation using 1957 trade as a base shows, however, that the difference was very slight for total imports, raw materials, and manufactures. For foodstuffs the difference was more substantial, reaching 30 percentage points in the case of one country. Reported in Irving B. Kravis, *Domestic Interests and International Obligations* (Philadelphia: University of Pennsylvania Press, 1963), p. 141n.

[3] It should be noted, moreover, that the steady rise in prices had some effect in lowering the protective value of tariffs, since many of the tariffs inherited from the interwar period were based on quantity rather than value.

ary 1, 1959, and by mid-1966 tariffs had been reduced to only 20 per cent of their 1957 levels. EFTA tariff reductions on industrial products began a year and a half later but were completely eliminated at the end of 1966. Trade within both areas grew at a rate of around 10 per cent a year in the 1960s, while imports from non-members grew at a slower rate.

Commercial policy will probably continue to move in the direction of liberalization. The Kennedy Round holds out the promise of substantial across-the-board tariff reductions by 1972. In its Trade Expansion Act of 1962, the United States expressed the hope that virtually all tariffs of industrial countries could be halved. Although the Kennedy Round fell substantially short of this objective, further reductions in barriers to trade seem likely over the next few decades—unless trade policies are used deliberately for balance-of-payments purposes, a possibility discussed further in Chapter 9.

Transportation Costs. A second explanation for the rapid growth in international trade since the Second World War is the reduction in ocean transportation costs per dollar of traded goods. For many products, transportation costs exceed tariffs as a barrier to trade.[4] Like tariffs, transportation costs have fallen over the years relative to the value of goods shipped. There are two reasons for this: freight rates have not risen so much as have wholesale prices generally; and the composition of world trade has shifted, as we have seen, away from low-value primary products to high-value manufactured products, without a corresponding increase in transportation costs.[5]

---

[4] Mordechai Kreinen, "Freedom of Trade and Capital Movement—Some Empirical Evidence," *Economic Journal*, LXXV, December 1965, pp. 748–49.

[5] Between 1950 and 1966 tramp freighter rates on general cargo rose only 6 per cent, compared with a rise of 22 per cent in U.S. wholesale prices and a rise of 14 per cent in unit value of world exports. Ocean freight rates did not even participate fully in the inflation during the Second World War, rising only 57 per cent between 1938 and 1950 compared with a rise of 102 per cent in U.S. wholesale prices and generally higher increases in other countries. See C.P. Kindleberger, *The Terms of Trade* (Cambridge, Mass.: The M.I.T. Press, 1956), pp. 19, 336–40, for these data and for some of the difficulties associated with data on freight rates.

Ocean freight rates are among the most volatile prices of the contemporary world; abstracting from the wide swings upward and downward, however,

New methods of bulk and containerized shipping promise to lower even further transportation costs relative to the value of goods shipped. Hauling and handling are operations in which standardization and economies of scale are important, and both new ships and port facilities are capable of much larger loads than in the past. For high-value commodities, air freight will become a cheaper and increasingly important mode of shipment, although it will carry only a small proportion of world trade for a long time to come.[6]

Broadening of Horizons. The rapid growth in international trade has been partly in response to relatively lower transportation costs, and partly in response to much lower government barriers to trade in the form of tariffs and direct controls. But a part of this rapid growth in trade may also be attributable to a "broadening of the horizons" of businessmen or, in the terms of the following chapter, to an enlargement of their decision-making domains across national boundaries. It is difficult to adduce evidence on the importance of this point. One might expect three observable consequences from such a broadening of business horizons: an increase in the number of firms which export, an increase in the share of output exported by such firms, and

---

ocean transportation costs reveal a modest downward trend since 1950, as indicated in the following tabulation:

Freight and Insurance Costs as Percentage of
the Landed Value of Imports

	1949–51	1962–63
Germany, Federal Republic of	9.0	7.5
Italy	11.4	10.4
Japan	22.6	15.8
United Kingdom	10.7	10.6
United States	8.4	7.4

Source: Computed from data given in the notes to the IMF *Balance of Payments Yearbook;* for the United States, from the IMF estimate of U.S. imports, c.i.f., compared with U.S. imports, f.o.b., found in *International Financial Statistics.*

[6] International air shipments from and to the United States have trebled over the last decade, while international air shipping rates fell from an average of $.34 per ton-mile in 1955 to $.27 in 1963. Computed from data in the Federal Aviation Agency's *FAA Handbook of Aviation,* 1964.

changes in the structure of corporate leadership to give a more important role to foreign sales.

Direct information of sufficient scope to confirm these developments is unfortunately not available. Much anecdotal evidence suggests that the management of a number of corporations has given foreign operations greater importance in its thinking, and that many firms, both American and European, have entered export markets for the first time. But it is not clear how general this phenomenon is. Even the United States, with more complete information on the foreign operations of its firms than other countries, lacks the information required for comparisons over time. The best we can do is observe that the sharp rise in foreign trade relative to total output of goods and services in the industrial countries—and the even sharper rise in merchandise trade relative to the production of goods alone [7]—is perhaps explained in part by factors other than falling tariffs and transportation costs, and that "broader business horizons" were probably important.

The effects of a broadening of horizons on the growth of trade cannot be operationally distinguished from other influences. Indeed, new opportunities for profitable foreign trade opened up by reductions in trade barriers and transportation costs may themselves have induced some broadening of horizons, if we use that term loosely. But the effect of which we are speaking is irreversible, leaving a higher level of trade even if tariffs were raised again. Two developments support the view that some enlargement of the business decision-making domain has occurred. First, as we will see in the next chapter, direct investment in other industrial countries, both by American and by European firms, accelerated very sharply in the late 1950s and early 1960s. Second, international travel for business purposes has grown at an astounding rate. In 1965, 112,000 Europeans came to the United States on business, compared with only 43,000 eight years earlier. And in 1964, 115,000 Americans went to Europe on business, and another 95,000 combined business and pleasure, nearly 90 per cent more than in 1957. Furthermore, it is difficult to believe that the general explosion in international travel (Table 3–3) has not resulted in wide discovery of new opportunities for sales and of new

---

[7] The share of total U.S. production of goods which went into exports rose from 6.2 per cent in 1950 to 7.9 per cent in 1965. But this, of course, is the phenomenon we are trying to explain.

products to buy. Management techniques or products successful in one country but untried in another will be noticed more readily if there is extensive opportunity to observe, which even vacation travel can provide. Moreover, nearly one million American troops and their dependents are stationed in Europe under NATO. This group is constantly rotating and thus exposing an even larger number of Americans to European life, and Europeans to American ways of living.

TABLE 3–3   International Travel

	1955	1960	1965
Americans to Europe	482,000	832,000	1,405,000
Europeans to the United States	131,000	274,000	584,000

Source: U.S. Department of Commerce, *Survey of Current Business.*

All these factors lower natural, political, and psychological barriers to trade, and help explain the rapid growth in postwar trade. But they do more than that; they should make trade flows much more sensitive to economic developments within national economies. Smaller incentives than in the past should be required to induce a firm to enter a foreign market as the barriers of ignorance, tariffs, and transport costs fall away. But before turning to the implications of this increase in sensitivity, it is well to consider a more subtle and perhaps more powerful, if slower, process which also points in the direction of greater sensitivity of trade flows to national economic developments: the gradual convergence of cost structures among the industrial countries—an evolution which results in narrowing the economic basis on which foreign trade rests.

Changes in Comparative Costs and the Structure of Production

Trade has traditionally been rooted in different natural endowments and in the different relative sizes of national labor forces. In some cases it was also based on specialized knowledge and skills, such as British supremacy in producing cotton textiles early in the industrial revolution or Switzerland's primacy in watch-making today. When a country was well endowed with resources or special skills, wages would be high; when the labor force was large relative to resources, they would be low. The reverse would be true for land rents and other factor rewards. The pattern of trade would be heavily influenced by these relative differences in wage and other factor costs.

Three broad developments have tended to diminish both relative factor cost differences (wage to rent ratios, etc.) and absolute cost differences among countries (wages in one country as compared with wages in another, under fixed exchange rates). They are the accumulation of capital, the higher rate of investment in low wage countries, and the movement of capital and managerial knowledge across national frontiers.[8]

Capital accumulation plays a key role in narrowing the relative rewards to different factors of production. It is fruitful to regard capital as a highly flexible factor which can be used to improve the "natural" factors of production, labor and resources.[9] In the form of irrigation ditches or fertilizer, capital improves the land and farming "climate"; in the form of technical or college education, it improves labor. Alternatively, capital can be regarded as a close substitute for either land or labor, depending on how we mold it. As skyscrapers, for example, capital multiplies many times the usable space of Manhattan Island by substituting for land; as tractors and machinery, it substitutes for labor.

Either way we view it, the accumulation of capital reduces greatly the *natural* differences among nations on which traditional trade was based. Some resources are highly specific to the production of certain goods and can be used in the production of other goods only with greatly increasing cost. A rise in the capital stock relative to other factors reduces this specificity in production. But if the basis for profitable trade is the difference in factor endowment, a given amount of trade becomes less profitable over time as these relative factor en-

[8] These developments are at work throughout the world, but they are much more pronounced within the industrialized world. Indeed there is much concern that capital accumulation and skill formation in the less developed countries—the second process above—will fall behind capital accumulation and skill formation in the developed countries, and much attention is directed to preventing this from happening. See Pincus, cited.

[9] This idea is suggested by Peter B. Kenen, "Nature, Capital, and Trade," *Journal of Political Economy*, LXXIII, October 1965, pp. 437–60. See also R. N. Cooper, "Growth and Trade: Some Hypotheses About Long-term Trends," *Journal of Economic History*, XXIV, December 1964, pp. 609–28.

dowments give way to an enlarged capital stock capable of widespread substitution for any of the more specific factors. In a relatively labor-short economy capital is likely to be substituted for labor; in a relatively resource-short economy, it is more likely to be substituted for land and other natural resources.[10] This kind of substitution will tend to narrow factor price differences among countries.

In addition, capital has been accumulating at different rates in industrial countries, and there is apparently an inverse relationship between the rate of capital accumulation and the wage rate. The net investment rate is highest in low-wage Japan and among the lowest in high-wage Canada and the United States, with Western European countries arrayed in between.

Finally, these two developments have been augmented, especially in the last decade, by the increasing freedom with which capital, technology, and even labor move across national boundaries. (This development will be discussed in the next chapter.) If technology and special skills are rapidly transmitted from one nation to another, trade based on these factors also becomes less insulated from other economic developments.

To the extent that this is a correct description of the economic forces at work, cost differences among industrial countries should have narrowed substantially, and the *potential* structure of production—the array of goods which each country could produce profitably at given alternative patterns of prices—should have become much more similar over the course of time. Any historical advantages in resources or location would gradually diminish as capital accumulation compensated for the disadvantages of other countries.

Finding direct evidence for this process is very difficult. It is clear, however, that wage levels among industrial nations, while still varying greatly from country to country, have narrowed substantially over the course of the last decade. Wages have risen much more rapidly in the low-wage countries than in the high-wage ones, and the inverse correlation between wage levels and rate of wage increases over the

[10] This view regards capital as a highly flexible substance, like nutty putty, which can be easily molded throughout its life. It is more realistic to conceive of capital as being initially flexible but hardening like clay once a real investment is made. Thus, fixed capital also becomes highly specific to the production of certain goods. In this case, the magnitude indicating the flexibility of production is gross investment, not the total capital stock.

period 1956–65 was very high (Table 3–4). Only Germany experienced wage increases far out of line with those of its "wage neighbors," and Japan experienced rather lower increases than might have been expected on the basis of its low-wage levels. But the general trend toward convergence of wages is unmistakable.

As we will see in the next two chapters, international differences in the cost of borrowing investment funds also narrowed among industrial countries in this period largely because of the growing international mobility of funds.

Unfortunately, it is not possible to observe directly the production potentials of the industrialized economies—what they *could* produce under different circumstances—with a view to discovering whether they have become more similar. This is especially true when we take a somewhat long-term view and permit depreciation allowances on the existing capital stock to be reinvested in totally different lines of activity. But the hypothesis that production possibilities have converged over time does find some confirmation in data on the actual structure of output. This is true both among regions within the United

TABLE 3–4   Wage Movements in America, Europe, and Japan

	Hourly Earnings In Manufacturing in 1959 [a]	Percentage Increase in Hourly Earnings in Manufacturing, 1956–65
United States	2.68	34
Canada	1.89	39
Sweden	1.05	70
Germany, F.R.	.78	117
United Kingdom	.77	72
Belgium	.74	67
France	.71	97
Italy	.61	102
Netherlands	.57	103
Japan	.29	97

[a] Converted at official exchange rates of 1959. Except for Sweden, data include fringe benefits.

Sources: United Nations, *Monthly Bulletin of Statistics;* and French National Institute of Statistics and Economic Studies.

States and, for a more limited period of time, among industrial countries.

There is nothing peculiarly international about the foregoing arguments. The different regions of the United States are variously endowed with soil, climate, and resources; much capital has accumulated over the last century and it has been free to move from region to region. Looking at the United States to see the operation of these processes has the advantage of permitting a much longer-term view. Thanks to a long series of decennial censuses, information on the regional and industrial structure of employment goes well back into the nineteenth century. The hypothesis sketched above points to a convergence in the structure of comparative advantage among the regions of the United States over the last century; economically, each region should look more like the other regions than it did one hundred years ago. It is clearly not feasible to construct a complete profile of the production possibilities for each major region within the United States, but a look at the actual structure of output or employment can give a rough idea of the production possibilities.

Table 3–5 indicates the regional variation in employment by ma-

TABLE 3–5   Regional Specialization
in Economic Activity in the United States [a]
(Distribution of number of persons engaged)

Industry Group	1840	1920	1960
Agriculture	.13	.54	.57
Mining	.88	.68	.89
Commerce	.66	.18	.08
Manufacturing	.58	.42	.23
Transportation	1.02	.17	.11
Professional services	.30	.23	.08
Public services	n.a.	.27	.22

n.a., not available.

[a] Coefficient of variation in labor force shares for seven regions in 1840 and for nine regions in 1920 and 1960. The regions follow the definition of the U.S. Census Bureau. A declining coefficient means less regional specialization and greater similarity among regions.

Source: Richard N. Cooper, "Growth and Trade: Some Hypotheses About Long-Term Trends," *Journal of Economic History,* XXIV, December 1964, p. 617.

jor industry for 1840, 1920, and 1960.[11] Except for agriculture and mining, the figures indicate much less regional variation in the structure of employment in 1960 than in 1840. As might be expected, commerce and professional services are most widely dispersed today, although that was less true in the frontier days of 1840. Manufacturing as a whole is substantially more scattered now than 40 and 120 years ago. In agriculture, however, there is a clear movement away from subsistence to regional specialization and trade. Mining retained its high regional concentration and, except for transportation in 1840, shows the greatest regional variation in all periods, as is to be expected.[12]

Again except for mining and agriculture, the convergence of regions toward the national average seems to have been persistent, with the observations for 1920 lying between those for 1840 and 1960. Most of the regional specialization in agriculture had already taken place by 1920, with little further change since then.

Additional evidence for the period since 1899 shows diminishing variation from region to region even for the various branches of manufacturing, enough so to lead one scholar to conclude that, as a result of changes in the location of manufacturing, "the comparative industrial structures of the various states became more nearly equal." [13]

[11] Each entry is the ratio of the standard deviation of employment shares in the various regions to the average for all regions. In 1840, for example, the share of the labor force in each region in manufacturing varied from 28 per cent in New England to 6 per cent in East South Central—enough variation to result in a standard deviation of 58 per cent of the average employment share of 14.7 per cent in manufacturing in all regions. A declining coefficient indicates greater dispersion of the industry throughout the United States. For the construction of these coefficients, see R. N. Cooper, cited.

[12] The high variation for transportation in 1840 results from the concentration of shipping in New England and may well reflect some under-reporting for other regions.

[13] Victor R. Fuchs, *Changes in the Location of Manufacturing in the United States Since 1929* (New Haven: Yale University Press, 1962), especially pp. 282–83, 290. Using a "coefficient of scatter," Fuchs shows that of 221 branches of manufacturing considered, 127 showed greater geographical dispersion in 1954 than in 1929, 54 remained the same, and only 40 showed a decrease in scatter. The "coefficient of scatter" is the smallest number of states needed to account for 75 per cent of the industry's total value added. An earlier study finds a lower "index of concentration" for a score of major manufacturing industries in 1929 as compared with 1899. F. B. Garver, F. M. Boddy, and A. J. Nixon, *The Location of Manufactures in the United States,*

This evidence points to the reduction of regional differences in economic activity within the United States. Industries seem to have become somewhat more "footloose" or market-oriented, less dependent on highly specific locational advantages, supplies of materials, or labor skills. As a result, the various regions have come to deviate less from the national average in their structure of manufacturing output and employment.

The same tendency may be occurring between nations, although it is not so readily observable. Comparable data exist only for a much shorter period of time, and international specialization is much more heavily influenced by variations in commercial policy than is regional specialization within the tariff-free United States. But fragmentary evidence over two decades tends to support the view that similar developments are taking place. Table 3–6 suggests that within manufacturing, inter-country specialization declined during the period 1938–61. Ten out of thirteen manufacturing sectors show declines in variation among countries and no sector shows a sharp increase in specialization. Not surprisingly, international specialization declined even more sharply between 1938 and the autarkic year of 1950, when war-stimulated industries were still thriving under the protection of extensive trade controls. In the period 1950–61, inter-country specialization increased in six of the sectors, but specialization continued to decline in six others despite widespread trade liberalization during the period.[14]

The data in Table 3–6 cover too short a period to be decisive, especially since the period spans a major world war which spawned new national industries in response to non-economic forces. Still, the data for Europe conform with observations for regions within the United States covering a much longer period of time, and they too suggest an increasing similarity in the structure of production. And the greater similarity in actual production in turn suggests—without showing conclusively—that the structure of costs has become much more similar among these countries.

1899–1929 (Minneapolis: University of Minnesota Press, 1933), especially pp. 17, 33, 87.

[14] Data for West Germany and the Netherlands are not available for 1938, so they have been excluded to permit comparisons over time. Addition of these countries to the calculations results in an even sharper decline in specialization between 1950 and 1961 than that indicated in Table 3–6.

The convergence of cost structures among industrial countries, which is likely to continue as capital accumulates and as technical knowledge flows ever more easily across national boundaries, has important implications for the operation of the international monetary system and for economic relations among industrial countries. One implication, which will not much concern us here, is that interna-

TABLE 3–6   Specialization in Manufacturing
Activity in Industrial Countries [a]
(Distribution of number of persons engaged)

Manufacturing Group	1938 [b]	1950 [c]	1961 [d]
Food, beverages, and tobacco	.35	.26	.26
Textiles	.37	.40	.34
Clothing, footwear, made-up textiles	.32	.28	.31
Wood products, furniture	.40	.28	.31
Paper and paper products	.60	.47	.51
Printing and publishing	.34	.23	.25
Leather and leather products excepting apparel	.44	.48	.46
Rubber products [e]	.30	.19	.14
Chemicals, petroleum, and coal products	.26	.34	.37
Non-metallic mineral products	.28	.23	.26
Basic metals [f]	.27	.20	.17
Metal products [f]	.15	.18	.17
Others [g]	.80	.75	.58

[a] Coefficient of variation in manufacturing-group share of employment in total manufacturing activity for eight industrial countries: Canada, France, Italy, Japan, Sweden, Switzerland, United Kingdom, United States.
[b] Number of employees in 1937 for Switzerland; only firms with 5 or more operatives for Japan; only firms engaging more than 10 persons in 1935 for United Kingdom; 1939 data for United States; 1937–39 census for Italy.
[c] 1951 for Japan.
[d] 1960 for Sweden.
[e] Excludes Switzerland, France.
[f] Excludes Switzerland.
[g] Excludes Italy.

Source: Raw data from United Nations, *The Growth of World Industry, 1938–1961* (New York, 1964).

tional trade becomes less valuable from the viewpoint of increasing economic welfare. The basic economic rationale for relatively free trade is that it permits each country to concentrate its production on those goods which it can produce relatively efficiently, and to exchange its surplus production for goods which it produces relatively inefficiently. But if the cost structure is very much the same from country to country, the gains from this kind of specialization will be correspondingly small. The United States can produce bananas or coffee only at great cost, but it can provide grain cheaply; trade between temperate and tropical countries may result in large mutual gains in national income. But an exchange of manufactures between Germany and the United Kingdom, while perhaps mutually profitable, would not seem to offer the same increase in real national income per dollar of trade, since, if it were necessary, each of these countries could produce the goods it imports from the other, or close substitutes, at costs little if any higher than the goods it exports for them.[15]

Greater Sensitivity of Foreign Trade

Another implication of the convergence of production cost structures among industrial countries is that international trade flows become much more sensitive to relatively small changes in incomes, costs, prices, and exchange rates. Reductions in trade barriers and transportation costs reinforce this sensitivity. A slight reduction in costs abroad, due, say, to a technological improvement, or a slight increase in prices at home will invite a greater worsening of the trade balance than would be the case if there continued to be "natural"

[15] This observation must be qualified if economies of scale in production are important. Then, even two trading countries with identical potential production structures can gain greatly by each concentrating on the production of only a limited range of goods, exporting the excess of production over domestic consumption to enjoy the reduction in costs permitted by large scale production. Too little is known about economies of scale, but several of the countries under consideration have sufficiently large domestic markets to reap most benefits likely to flow from large scale production even without trade. The importance of economies of scale, and hence the gain from trade, obviously increases as the economic size of a country diminishes. For this reason relatively small countries have a larger national stake than do large countries in a smoothly operating payments system free of barriers to trade. It is no accident that among industrial countries small nations such as the Netherlands and Sweden have relatively low tariffs and strongly favor further lowering of tariffs.

protection afforded by geographical distance or by special cost advantages due to natural resources, or than would be the case if import quotas or high tariffs restricted trade.

This greater sensitivity of international trade flows to changes in costs and prices means that potential imbalances in trade will tend to be larger as well as more frequent, unless economic "disturbances" in the future are smaller than they have been in the past. Yet the prospect for smaller disturbances to trade flows arising from technological changes or from changes in the pattern of demand—as distinguished from the level of demand—seems distinctly dim. On the contrary, such disturbances are a hallmark of economic progress. A vigorously growing world economy will inevitably experience important technical innovations which affect patterns of trade, and it is likely to be subjected from time to time to divergences in national rates of growth which also will affect international trade both directly and through changes in relative prices.

On the other hand, international trade flows, even while they are becoming more sensitive to changes in the level of business activity, may be subjected to fewer such changes as national control over economic fluctuations improves. The experience of Europe since the Second World War has been very encouraging in this respect. National control over fluctuations in economic activity, including the appropriate degree of monetary expansion, is a subject which must be treated at greater length in Chapter 7. A number of economists and officials, especially in Europe, hold that national divergences in the rate of monetary expansion are the principal if not the exclusive cause of imbalances in international payments. The foregoing arguments regarding increased sensitivity of foreign trade flows to small changes in prices and money incomes suggest that this factor, however great or little its significance in the past, will be increasingly significant in the future.

Just as increased sensitivity of trade flows to small changes in relative prices or to small divergences in the movement of national price levels increases potential imbalances in international payments, the same factors should also make correction of imbalances easier. Small changes in exchange rates, slight differences in the rate at which national price levels rise or fall, or the application of uniform tariffs and subsidies of modest size should have a prompt effect on the value of imports and exports. Applied in the right way, these measures could be used to help restore international balance.

Three   Qualifications

These generalizations about increased sensitivity must be qualified in three respects. Product differentiation, economies of scale, and increased protection of agriculture all limit price and cost sensitivity. As manufactured goods account for an ever larger portion of trade, and as the sophistication of manufactured goods increases, the possibilities for product differentiation and the resulting establishment of firm purchaser-supplier relationships also increase. Domestic production may not be able to displace imports or enlarge exports in response to small price changes because of inflexibilities in consumer preferences or because purchasers are "locked in" to particular types of machinery, say, by the need for servicing and spare parts from the manufacturer or by the obvious economies in inventory and maintenance from dealing with a limited number of different brands of equipment. As is well known, product differentiation raises barriers to entry, and this is no less true of foreign markets than of domestic ones.

At the same time that product differentiation introduces a certain rigidity into consumer habits and supplier relationships, it has probably contributed to the rapid growth of trade. It is noteworthy, for example, that the great growth of trade within the EEC since its formation has tended to take place within product groups rather than between groups. That is, the reduction of trade barriers has not yet resulted in greater national specialization *among* industries, as the traditional theories of trade might have led one to predict, but rather in greater specialization *within* industries. Despite a sharp reduction of internal tariffs since 1959, only rarely has a member country of the EEC experienced a *decline* in exports to other member countries in any major industry group of products.[16] Instead, France and Ger-

---

[16] This analysis depends very much, of course, on the system of commodity classification used. We assume that production substitutability is much higher within product classes than between product classes.

Balassa has carried out a more sophisticated analysis of intra-EEC trade which confirms this generalization. He finds that the rank order of national export industries in intra-EEC trade is not only positively correlated but has become more similar between 1958 and 1963 in every case, taking EEC members in pairs. See his "Tariff Reductions and Trade in Manufactures Among the Industrial Countries," *American Economic Review,* LVI, June 1966, p. 470.

many have both increased their exports of automobiles, chemicals, electrical machinery, etc., to each other. This result is entirely consistent with a convergence of production capabilities combined with product differentiation resulting in *intra*-industry specialization rather than *inter*-industry specialization.

It is, of course, too early to tell whether inter-industry specialization will take place in the long run. Capital, while highly flexible before investment takes place, becomes highly specialized in the form of plants and equipment after investment takes place, and European firms have not had time to readjust much of their capital stock to the formation of a large common market. Furthermore, the impact of product differentiation on the total value of trade may offset the rigidities it introduces into consumption patterns.[17]

A second qualification involves economies of scale in production or marketing. If these are important, price sensitivity will be correspondingly lower. However, seven of the major industrial countries have total output in excess of $50 billion and it is likely that internal markets of this size have long since overtaken economies of scale in all but a few industries. Thus, foreign trade is not necessary for reaping the benefits of scale, and price sensitivity should play an important role among countries producing at optimum scale.

Finally, it should be mentioned that some of the arguments advanced above do not apply to agriculture. Commercial policy remains highly restrictive in many countries, and indeed new ways are being introduced to reduce the price sensitivity of trade flows in agricultural goods.

[17] The growing sensitivity of trade to changes in prices can be summarized concisely with the following formulation: $\Delta M = M (1 - E) (\Delta p/p)$, where M is the *value* of imports (as it enters the balance of payments), p is the price of the imports, E is the price elasticity of demand for imports (defined to be positive, following convention), and Δ indicates the change in the variable it precedes. It can be seen that the impact of a given percentage change in price on the value of imports will depend on the sizes of M and E. In effect, this chapter has argued that M has grown because of reductions in tariffs and transport costs, and because of a broadening of business horizons. The removal of quantitative restrictions on trade, the reduction of specific tariffs and *ad valorem* tariffs containing "excess" protection, and the convergence of cost structures have all tended to raise E. Increasing product differentiation has raised M, but it has probably tended to lower E, at least in the short run. On balance, ΔM will be larger for a given $\Delta p/p$, assuming other prices unchanged.

A similar analysis applies to export goods.

Recent Experience. Despite these qualifications, recent experience, while hardly conclusive, does tend to support a view that price sensitivity is reasonably high—certainly higher than the estimates of price sensitivity drawn from the 1930s and the early postwar period. In recent years there have been a number of cases where relative prices of imports and domestic products have been influenced as a matter of policy. In practice it is difficult to sort out the effects of price changes from the effects of growing demand and output. But the Canadian devaluation of about 8 per cent in 1962, the German and Dutch revaluations of 5 per cent in 1961, and the gradual lowering of tariffs within the EEC over the period 1959–65, all tend to confirm high sensitivity to relative price changes. The imposition of 15 per cent import surcharges by Britain in 1964 gives somewhat less conclusive support.

Summary

The main thesis of this chapter is that many factors have conspired during the last two decades to increase the sensitivity of foreign trade to changes in economic conditions. Transportation costs have fallen somewhat, tariffs and other barriers to trade have fallen much more, "horizons" have broadened to provide greater receptivity to foreign goods. Moreover, the accumulation of capital and the international transmission of technical knowledge have caused a convergence in the potential structure of production in industrial countries so that national advantages arising from climate, resources, or unique technological skills are less successful in insulating a country from foreign competition than they once were.

These general characterizations of international trade do not dominate the modern world economy. Comparative advantage in the traditional forms still plays a significant role in determining the pattern of trade, even among industrial countries, as annual American exports of nearly $4 billion in raw materials and agricultural products to Europe testify. But they indicate the direction in which the world economy is moving. The implications of this greater sensitivity for the functioning of the international payments system are explored in Chapter 6. But first we turn to other changes in the character of international transactions.

CHAPTER FOUR

International Movements
of Capital, Technology,
and Labor

Significant changes in the volume and character of foreign trade over the past two decades have been accompanied by equally important changes in the movement of factors of production—capital, technical and managerial skills, and labor. Foreign trade directly influences the pattern of consumption and production in a trading country; international factor movements influence its capabilities for production as well as its actual pattern of production. By adding to domestic savings, inflows of capital from abroad increase the amount of investment which a country can undertake. Transmission of technical knowledge across national boundaries can improve the efficiency with which capital, labor, and land are used. And immigration from other countries raises the labor force and hence both enlarges potential output and influences the optimum combination of labor with other factors of production.

This chapter considers all of these factor movements—capital, knowledge, and labor—but with heavy emphasis on international movements of capital, for these have been most prominent in recent years and therefore influence most decisively the effectiveness of national economic policies. Moreover, the following discussion is further limited principally to foreign direct investments—that is, investment which carries with it decision-making control by the foreign investor. Portfolio investment—international investment which involves the purchase of foreign securities or other financial claims on foreigners, without management control—is considered separately in the following chapter because much "international investment" of this type between industrial countries has not, strictly speaking, involved international factor movements at all, but has merely represented an exchange of financial claims. Some portfolio investment does of course result in a transfer of real saving among countries, and not all direct investment does so. The distinction between portfolio and direct investment drawn here thus exaggerates the real differences between them.

The main conclusions of this chapter can be anticipated. As with increased trade flows, the increasing international mobility of factors of production increases the sensitivity of each national economy to developments outside. International movements of capital, technical knowledge, and even labor contribute to the convergence of cost structures among industrial countries noted in the preceding chapter. And the quicker and larger these movements are, and the more responsive they are to national economic developments, the more quickly they transmit developments in one country to another. This is most notably true of international capital movements, and of their sensitivity to differences in monetary conditions from country to country. But the increasing international mobility of business enterprise carries with it implications for national economic autonomy beyond its possible effects on the balance of payments; it also greatly weakens the ability of national governments to regulate effectively the activities of business. As we shall see, it creates pressures for greater international coordination of national policies.

International Capital Movements, 1950–65

There is no doubt about the vast increase in the international flow of capital, including direct investment, among the industrial countries since 1950. This is true not only of the amounts involved, but also of the number of establishments which have participated in international capital movements. While outstanding U.S. direct investment in the world increased roughly threefold from the early 1950s to the early 1960s, direct investment in Europe increased more than tenfold. Net private long-term U.S. portfolio investment in Europe also increased very markedly during the same period, although here the contrast with increases in investment in the "rest of the world" (mainly, in this case, Canada) is less striking. Tables 4–1 and 4–2 show the net

TABLE 4–1 New U.S. Direct Investment Abroad
($ million per year)

	Total		Europe		EEC		United Kingdom		Canada		Japan	
	Net Outflows	Retained Earnings	Net Outflows	Retained Earnings	Net Outflows	Retained Earnings	Net Outflows	Retained Earnings	Net Outflows	Retained Earnings	Net Outflows	Retained Earnings
1950–52	660	716	60	69	32	68	15	86	317	189	19	2
1953–55	742	830	74	197	43	64	15	112	388	306	13	6
1956–58	1,858	1,158	322	261	116	113	172	130	567	359	2	8
1959–61	1,555	1,132	724	308	246	129	325	128	397	349	20	17
1962–64	2,015	1,373	1,056	404	627	109	167	156	305	467	66	26
1965	3,418	1,542	1,479	388	857	–3	317	242	912	540	19	49
1966	3,543	1,716	1,805	434	1,140	105	384	190	1,087	539	31	49

Source: U.S. Department of Commerce, Survey of Current Business.

TABLE 4–2   Private U.S. Capital Movements
Other Than Direct Investment [a]
($ million)

	Total			To Europe	
Year	Long Term	Short Term	Errors and Omissions [b]	Long Term	Short Term
1953	185	167	366	180	−24
1954	−159	−635	191	38	−240
1955	−241	−191	515	−47	−25
1956	−603	−517	568	−114	−158
1957	−859	−276	1,184	−63	−97
1958	−1,444	−311	511	−176	−62
1959	−926	−77	423	−147	154
1960	−863	−1,348	−941	−141	−421
1961	−1,025	−1,556	−1,006	−375	−47
1962	−1,227	−544	−1,159	−262	−177
1963	−1,695	−785	−352	−750	−87
1964	−1,961	−2,147	−1,011	−480	−437
1965	−1,080	761	−429	281	25
1966	−664	−6	−383	477	−544

[a] Negative sign signifies net outflow from the United States.
[b] Residuals in the balance-of-payments accounts. Changes in errors and omissions are usually assumed to represent unrecorded capital movements. The large change between 1959 and 1960 is noteworthy.

Source: U.S. Department of Commerce, *Survey of Current Business.*

outflows of private U.S. capital for direct and portfolio investments abroad, respectively.[1]

American investment in Europe and Canada takes a wide variety of forms—direct investment, purchases of stocks and bonds, European and Canadian bond issues in the United States, short- and long-term bank lending. This is in sharp contrast to the flow of capital to the less developed countries, which has been predominantly in the form of direct investment (largely in the extractive industries) and

[1] "Net" here means net of repatriations by U.S. residents, not net of inflows of foreign capital into the United States. As will be made clear in the following chapter, *gross* international flows of U.S. portfolio capital were substantially larger than these net outflows suggest.

short-term trade credit. Investor interest in claims on Europe and Canada is evidently much broader than in claims on other countries, although interest in Japan and several Latin American countries takes an intermediate position.

Information on the *number* of American firms operating in Europe is more difficult to obtain than information on the flow of funds.[2] One survey shows that there were over 3,700 "new operations" —acquisitions, expansion of existing plant, or new establishments— by American firms in Europe in the eight years 1958–65, of which over 2,800 were in the countries of the EEC and most of the remainder in the United Kingdom and Switzerland. More than 60 per cent of these operations represented new establishments, 20–30 per cent were acquisitions, and the remainder were expansions of existing direct investments.[3] Several new operations, of course, can be undertaken by a single American parent firm; but the large number of new operations undertaken every year, with acquisitions and new establishments accounting for 80 per cent or more of the total, suggests that many American firms began operations in the European market for the first time.[4] At the same time, the large firms which already had

[2] The latest census of American investments abroad, taken for the end of 1957, showed 2,696 respondents with operations in Europe at that time, and only 1,225 respondents with operations in the member countries of the EEC. More recently, an extensive compilation of published information on new business activity by American firms abroad in 1960–64 shows that 2,042 American companies undertook 5,244 "new operations" (2,954 new establishments, 983 expansions, and 1,307 licensing agreements), of which 2,633 were in Europe. Over 30 per cent of the new operations (1,155 in all) were undertaken by companies with only one new operation, suggesting that they were operating abroad for the first time. Ninety per cent of the 2,042 American companies had five or fewer new operations abroad. Booz, Allen, and Hamilton, "New Foreign Business Activity of U.S. Firms, 54 months—1960–1964" (1965), pp. 19, 26.

[3] The Chase Manhattan Bank, "Report on Western Europe," No. 40, February–March, 1966, and earlier issues. The survey suggests that *acquisitions* of existing European firms by American firms took place at a rate of 150–200 per year in the early 1960s.

[4] American investments in Europe are not financed entirely from the United States. A large sample of American firms operating in Europe in 1963, for instance, drew only 18 per cent of their funds from the United States, the remainder having been raised locally—partly from depreciation allowances (24 per cent) and retained earnings (24 per cent), partly from local borrowing (34 per cent). Moreover, while the share of new investment in Europe by

TABLE 4–3   Foreign Direct Investment
Flows of Britain and Germany
($ million)

	1958	1964
New British direct investment ª in:		
EEC	22	104
Other Europe	17	25
North America	106	120
New direct investment ª in Britain by:		
EEC	3	53
Other Europe	14	31
North America	202	364
New German direct investment in:		
EEC	21	92
Other Europe	26	90
North America	13	15
New direct investment in Germany by:		
EEC	29	78
Other Europe	3	47
North America	2	150

ª Including reinvested earnings.

Source: U.K. Central Statistical Office, *United Kingdom Balance of Payments, 1966;* Deutsche Bundesbank, *Monthly Report,* December 1965.

some foreign operations have apparently extended them in several dimensions.

Although American investment has attracted the most attention and has accounted for the largest flows, businesses in other countries have stepped up their foreign investments too.[5] Table 4–3 shows direct investment flows in 1958 and 1964 between Britain and

American firms financed from the United States rose sharply to 26 per cent in 1960, it fell steadily thereafter.

[5] Data on direct investment by other countries are very scanty, although increasing rapidly. There is very little information on European direct investment before 1960. A notable exception is the excellent article—the first of its kind—on German direct investment in the Deutsche Bundesbank, *Monthly Report,* December 1965. It is noteworthy that EEC staff studies of direct investment have relied primarily on U.S. data.

TABLE 4–4   Direct Investment Flows, 1964
($ million)

From: ↓ *To:* →	*United States*	*Canada*	*United Kingdom*	*EEC*	*Other OECD*
United States	—	253	214	807	355
Canada	35	—	3	18	
United Kingdom	120		—	104	25
EEC	165	15	21	386	175
Other OECD	28	12	31	289	n.a.

n.a., not available.

General Note: National data on direct investment flows are still incomplete and highly imperfect. This table gives the order of magnitude of flows but involves, apart from basic inaccuracies in the data, the following imperfections: Belgian flows to Canada have been recorded with EEC flows to the United States; Dutch and Italian flows to Canada are included with other OECD; Belgian data include some long-term capital movements other than direct investment; and Belgian flows to and from the United Kingdom are included with other OECD. British figures include reinvested earnings as well as new capital outflows.

For the United States, the United Kingdom, Canada and the EEC, data have been taken as recorded by the capital-exporting countries; for other OECD countries, as recorded by the capital-importing countries. This involves some error, for different sources do not always agree on the same flow. In 1964, for example, Canada recorded a $174 million inflow of direct investments from the United States, but the United States recorded an outflow of $253 million to Canada.

Sources: U.S. Department of Commerce, *Survey of Current Business;* Dominion Bureau of Statistics, *The Canadian Balance of International Payments, 1964;* EEC, *General Statistical Bulletin,* 1965, N. 12; U.K. Central Statistical Office, *The United Kingdom Balance of Payments, 1966.*

Germany, on the one hand, and the EEC, the rest of Europe and North America on the other. New British investment in the EEC, for example, increased fivefold between 1958 and 1964; and new EEC investment in Britain showed an even sharper rise. The pattern of direct-investment flows among industrial countries is shown in Table 4–4, where it can be seen that while American outflows are larger than those from other countries, foreign direct-investment flows between other countries were by no means inconsequential.

Motives and Causes for Direct Investment Flows

Why has this vast increase in investment abroad—not only from the United States to Europe but also in the opposite direction and within Europe itself—taken place?

Capital is said to move from where it is abundant to where it is scarce, from where rates of return are low to where they are high. This undoubtedly goes a long way toward explaining why the United States is a major exporter of capital. But it does not explain why there are substantial two-way flows of capital, especially direct investment capital. Some of these two-way flows reflect a desire for "portfolio balance," an attempt by investors to spread their risks and reduce the variability in their returns. But a major motivation for direct investment is undoubtedly the desire by an investing firm to exploit some quasi-monopoly it holds, whether special skills, patent rights, or "good will." [6] Thus, European firms with patentable products may set up subsidiaries in the United States to produce and market them—either because production costs are lower or because tariffs and transport costs make importation from Europe costly—while American firms with patentable products do the same in Europe, and for the same reasons. This explanation of direct investment in foreign countries would lead one to expect the controlling corporation to hold a very high proportion of equity in its foreign subsidiaries, since firms with unique advantages will be reluctant to share with foreign owners the quasi-rents resulting from them. Debt capital, on the other hand, would be borrowed wherever it is cheapest or most convenient. Joint ventures will occur only when the foreign partners also have something to contribute to the enterprise, as, for example, when the U.S. manufacturer of a new product forms a subsidiary with a foreign company to exploit the latter's distribution facilities.[7]

[6] Stephen Hymer has emphasized this factor in his "Direct Foreign Investment and International Oligopoly," June 1965, mimeo.

[7] This is very much the pattern which is actually observed, as indicated in the following figures for financing foreign investment. In 1957, 84 per cent of the equity of European firms in which Americans held a controlling interest was owned by Americans, leaving only 16 per cent for foreigners. Foreigners, in turn, owned 86 per cent of the equity of foreign-controlled firms in the United States in 1959. This contrasts sharply with the sources of debt capital: U.S.-controlled firms in Europe raised 89 per cent of their debt capital abroad,

This explanation probably accounts for much of the investment in foreign manufacturing operations. But it can explain a rapid growth in foreign investment only to the extent that the special advantages of the investing firms are increasing. Some industries—pharmaceuticals and electronics come to mind—no doubt are subject to such rapid change as a result of technological developments that firms in the forefront have perhaps increased their special advantages through patentable research and development. However, a substantial fraction of new U.S. operations in Europe—46 per cent in 1964, a rise from previous years according to the survey cited earlier—do involve European partners, indicating that special advantages are not the sole explanation, or at a minimum that the European partners have complementary advantages.

The explanation for the rapid *growth* in investment after 1955 undoubtedly lies in the recovery of Europe, viewed in its most general sense, rather than in long-standing differences in capital-labor ratios or in special advantages of the investing firms. A number of factors converged simultaneously in the late 1950s, although all reflected tendencies which were evident earlier: full currency convertibility for nonresidents was established for most European currencies at the end of 1958; the Rome Treaty establishing the European Economic Community was signed in 1957 and went into effect in January 1958; the Soviet Union launched its sputnik and ushered in the era of intercontinental ballistic missiles in 1957; and de Gaulle eliminated political instability in France and ended the Algerian war in the years after 1958.

All of these events undoubtedly played some role in inducing

---

and only 11 per cent in the United States; foreign firms in the United States raised 81 per cent of their debt capital in the United States, and brought only 19 per cent from abroad. The same pattern can be observed for American investments elsewhere in the world. It appears from these figures that debt financing is done predominantly in the host country, suggesting that the principal motivation for investment is not the "shortage of capital" but the opportunity to exploit some special factor. Data are from the U.S. Department of Commerce, *U.S. Business Investments in Foreign Countries* (Washington: GPO, 1960), p. 108; and *Foreign Business Investments in the United States* (Washington: GPO, 1962), pp. 42–46.

The United States Department of Commerce, which is responsible for collecting information on U.S. investment abroad and foreign investment in the United States, defines "controlling interest" to involve ownership of at least 25 per cent of the equity.

American firms to locate in Europe. Currency convertibility not only assured unrestricted repatriation of earnings and capital from investments in Europe, but it also signaled the steady improvement which had taken place in Europe's economic condition over the preceding decade. Incomes were growing rapidly and currencies had become strong.[8] It is a perverse characteristic of international capital that it fails to move when it is most needed; it shunned Europe in the early fifties during the period of dollar shortage, but moved in great volume after the dollar shortage had ended and European recovery was complete.

In addition, the political and military position of Europe had gradually improved. The prospect for direct invasion of Europe became more remote after Stalin died and the cold war settled into a peaceful if uneasy coexistence with strategic deterrence. At the same time, Soviet missiles could threaten direct and large-scale physical damage to the United States, a new and unaccustomed possibility for Americans. Thus, both the reduction in physical security in the United States and, far more, the improbability of physical destruction in Europe served to reduce one of the psychological barriers to investment by Americans in Europe.[9]

Finally, the formation of the European Common Market promised a large tariff-free market comparable to the United States in population if not yet in standard of living, a market in which incomes were growing rapidly and consumers were beginning to buy automobiles and other durables in substantial quantity. Production could supply the entire Common Market from a single location if economics of scale so dictated. Moreover, this same attractive market was to be

---

[8] International capital movements were also encouraged by the removal of government impediments. In 1959 the OEEC adopted a Code of Liberalization of Capital Movements which reflected the willingness of most member countries to eliminate or reduce national controls on a wide range of capital movements, notably direct investment and capital movements associated with the movement of persons. This code "bound" its adherents to allow certain types of capital movements to take place freely except under exceptional circumstances. The code was revised and extended under the OECD in 1963.

[9] American investors apparently did not accept the Gallois and official French theory that strategic deterrence via intercontinental ballistic missiles increases, rather than decreases, the vulnerability of Europe to land invasion.

protected against imports from outside by quite a stiff common external tariff, typically the arithmetical average of high French and Italian tariffs and low Benelux and German tariffs preceding the formation of the EEC, but excluding certain tariff reductions in force in Italy and Germany. Thus both the positive attractions of the market and the formidable tariff barrier induced Americans and others to invest heavily in Europe.

At the same time, Article 67 of the Rome Treaty establishing the EEC calls on its members to abolish restrictions on movements within the Community of capital belonging to residents "to the extent necessary for the proper functioning of the Common Market," and Article 71 urges members to liberalize capital movements even further to the extent that their balance-of-payments positions permit it. In 1960 the Council of the EEC approved a directive which freed direct investment and short- and medium-term commercial credit transactions within the Community. Moreover, a number of steps have been taken under Articles 52–58 of the Rome Treaty to extend the right of establishment in each country to residents of other member countries and to harmonize the national requirements for establishing a business.

These changes no doubt stimulated the movement of some European capital across frontiers. It seems, however, that the firms most willing to cross boundaries within the EEC have been American firms—those which were already international in orientation and locational-decision-making. The "broadening of business horizons" mentioned in the previous chapter is reflected in increased American investment and at the same time is fostered by foreign investment.

Decision Domains and Government Jurisdictions

Before examining the implications of this greater mobility of business enterprise for national economic policy, it is useful to introduce the notion of a business "domain" of decision-making and the parallel notion of a government's "jurisdiction."

The *domain* of a business enterprise is the geographical area over which its activities range. This might better be designated the firm's horizon, but the term "domain" carries a geographical connotation and "horizon" is often used to indicate the distance into the future for which a firm plans or projects—its time horizon. Obviously the domain of a firm will vary according to activity, and it is useful to distinguish a firm's domain with respect to (*a*) sales, (*b*) sources of capital, (*c*) sources of management personnel, and (*d*) location of production facilities. For the typical firm we might expect these various domains to decline in size from the first to the fourth, although there are important exceptions. Large international firms may have larger domains for location than they do for top personnel; and there may even be cases where investment in production precedes sales from the parent.

A firm's sales domain, for example, is the geographical area over which the firm actively attempts to sell its products—the area involved in its marketing plans. For a very small firm, this might be a single buyer who traditionally takes all its output. The firm merely decides how much to offer the buyer on each occasion. For a larger firm the marketing strategy will be more complicated than this and may range over many buyers in many locations. Similarly, in the other areas of the firm's decision-making there will be a region, a domain, which it regularly encompasses in framing its plans.

A similar concept is applicable to labor: a worker's domain is the geographic area over which he is willing to work. And again it is useful to distinguish the domain for temporary work from that for permanent settlement, and the domain over which he is willing to work (at some employer's initiative) from the domain which he automatically considers when job-hunting. Labor organizations also have decision domains over which they seek membership and leadership.

A *jurisdiction* is the geographical area over which a given governmental unit governs or could govern, in the various dimensions of economic policy. Jurisdictions often coincide with nations, and hence with many other functions of national government. But this coincidence is not necessary. It is possible to imagine jurisdictions in certain regulatory matters, in government services, in monetary matters, and even in taxation which either transcend or fall short of national governments. The taxing and regulatory powers of the High Authority of the European Coal and Steel Community illustrate a jurisdiction which transcends national governments, while any federal system such as those found in Australia, Canada, Germany, and the United States abounds in illustrations of jurisdictions which fall short of national governments. As with a decision domain, the size of a jurisdiction will vary with the particular power of government in question, and it is usually governed by constitutional or conventional relationships among the different levels of government.

Various jurisdictions can, of course, cooperate in pursuit of their objectives, and extensive cooperation may lead to *coordination* of policies and measures to regulate business and labor, to stabilize employment and prices, and to assure a satisfactory rate of economic growth. As concerted action among jurisdictions increases, their behavior approximates more closely that of a single enlarged jurisdiction.

Identifying business and labor domains is obviously fraught with imprecision and arbitrariness. Human behavior moves continuously through a spectrum, usually without defining sharp lines. In discussions of international economic problems it is customary to dichotomize the world of economic activity into "national" and "international." Many business firms are national in their activities, but if they produce abroad they are considered "international." This practice obscures a process which is usually much more gradual than "going international" implies. The domain of most businesses is not national at all, but strictly local. Only gradually do successful firms become "national" in their various dimensions, and many have domains which extend beyond local activity but stop far short of nationwide activity.

The same is true internationally. A firm may broaden its domain in one dimension or another to include territory outside the nation in which its head office is located, but still remain far short of being global in scope. For many American firms "going international" means having operations in Canada, nothing more. Thus, enlarging the domain of a firm is seen to be a continuous process, not a discrete one.

A need to draw lines, however, arises from the legal requirements of governmental jurisdictions. There must be geographical and (usually) functional limits to the powers of government. Considerable interest attaches to the size of business and labor domains compared with governmental jurisdictions. If the former are substantially larger than the latter, this can set severe limits to the effectiveness of economic policy.

The evidence on trade adduced in the preceding chapter and that on direct investment here, although fragmentary, does suggest that the decision domains of a number of business enterprises have increased. This is apparently true with respect to sales, location of production, and sources of capital. Many American corporations are firmly planted in Europe as well as North America, and top management devotes an increasing amount of time to overseas investments. In the future these foreign operations will become a routine part of managing the business, just as national firms routinely scan the entire United States when attempting to expand sales or considering new domestic investment.

The growth of business decision domains, increasingly spanning national boundaries, has a number of implications. One, noted in the previous chapter, is that trade flows tend to become much more sensitive to small changes in prices and incomes—with a broader base of operations, firms will be quicker to discover new opportunities and to take advantage of them.[10] These international firms also become conveyors of technical knowledge between countries, reducing any national advantage from technological advances.

Second, international firms will have both the knowledge and the credit rating to borrow in a variety of national capital markets; they can shop around for capital in an international market. This will contribute to making international capital movements more sensitive to differences in national monetary conditions than they have been. This development is taken up in the next chapter, where movements in financial capital are discussed.

Both of these developments are reflected through a country's balance of international payments, and the main problems which they pose for national economic policy arise through the balance of payments. These problems are considered in detail in Chapter 6. In addition, however, as business decision domains grow more rapidly than government jurisdictions (as they have during the past decade), they complicate the pursuit of national economic policies in a number of ways which do not involve the balance of payments as such. It is these which are taken up here.

[10] This tendency may be weakened by the reluctance of subsidiaries to buy from suppliers other than their parents. Thus, in some industries, supplier-purchaser relations across national boundaries may become more rigid than they are today, even though the area of ignorance about alternative sources of supply is reduced.

International Business and National Control

Problems created for national control by the international mobility of business can be considered under three headings: problems created, or allegedly created, by the foreign-owned enterprise for the countries in which investment takes place; problems created for the country of the parent firm; and problems created for host countries by the government of the home country.

Problems Created for the Host Country. The periodic debate over the merits and dangers of direct foreign investment usually hinge on the costs entailed by the host country in having a substantial part of its economic activity controlled by foreigners. It is important here to note again the feature which distinguishes direct investment from other forms of international capital movement: direct investment involves *management control,* and the control is by foreigners. Foreign control has from time to time become a sore point in those nations which are hosts to major foreign investment. In Canada, where 59 per cent of total capital in manufacturing is controlled by foreigners (over 40 per cent by Americans), serious efforts have occasionally been made to discriminate against foreign investment.[11] France has also attempted to check the intrusion of foreign control into its economy, and its concern has struck a sympathetic chord in some other countries.

The charges against foreign control are varied: that foreign firms do not export enough, that they give preference to suppliers in the home country and hence enlarge imports, that they ignore local employment practices, that they do not contribute to local charities, that they rob the country of research, that they interfere with national planning.

While concern over foreign control of domestic industry is perhaps

11 In 1963, for example, a new tax measure provided that Canadian companies without Canadian equity holdings of at least 25 per cent and corresponding Canadian representation of the board of directors, be taxed at a rate somewhat higher than Canadian corporations which meet this requirement. See A. E. Safarian, "Foreign Ownership and Control of Canadian Industry," in Abraham Rotstein, ed., *The Prospect of Change: Proposals for Canada's Future* (New York: McGraw-Hill Book Co., 1965), for a description and criticism of this and other Canadian proposals.

understandable in psychological terms, solid grounds for fearing foreign control are far from evident. In writing for the Royal Commission on Canada's Economic Prospects, two Canadian economists noted that a profit-maximizing firm will behave in precisely the same way no matter what the nationality of its management.[12] An American-owned Canadian firm will buy supplies in the United States if it is cheaper to do so, and in Canada if that is the lowest cost source of supply. A profit-maximizing, Canadian-owned Canadian firm should behave in the same way. This view, of course, assumes that the firms in question already have "broad horizons," that they scan the whole array of possible markets, sources of supply, and points of location. If a firm's domain is more limited, there could be some merit in the charge. American firms abroad might buy from American sources simply because they are familiar with them, thus unknowingly perhaps overlooking cheaper local sources.

Nonetheless, some of the charges that have been levied against foreign-owned firms—for example that they prefer to export from the home country and hence are not so aggressive in exporting from the host country as domestically owned firms would be—seem to be empirically unfounded.[13]

It is also claimed that foreign ownership may stifle scientific research and development work in the host country. Because of important economies of scale, many firms prefer to concentrate their research and development work, and they tend to concentrate it in the home country.[14] Subsidiaries abroad may benefit fully from any commercial developments. But it is widely believed that research and

[12] Irving Brecher and S. S. Reisman, *Canada–United States Economic Relations,* Royal Commission on Canada's Economic Prospects (Ottawa: Queen's Printer, 1957).

[13] American-owned firms in Canada accounted for 50 per cent of Canadian exports of manufactures in 1957, for example, while controlling 43 per cent of capital invested in manufacturing. A. E. Safarian, cited, especially pp. 229–35.

[14] To cite one rough illustration: in 1960, 68 per cent of all patents issued in Canada were issued to American nationals (i.e., excluding American-owned Canadian firms), while 0.7 per cent of patents issued in the United States were to Canadians. Cited in Howe Martyn, *International Business* (New York: The Free Press of Glencoe, 1964), p. 74. See also John R. Shipman, "International Patent Planning," *Harvard Business Review,* March–April 1967. This pattern of relative dominance is not necessarily related to direct investment, however.

development expenditures have important and valuable external effects quite apart from the particular products which are developed, in the form of training scientists and technicians, providing encouragement and the incentive of prospective employment to university students willing to study scientific and engineering subjects, stimulating related research outside of the firm, etc. These benefits accrue largely to the country in which the research is located. Indeed, concentration of research in a few places may even induce scientists and technicians to leave their home country for the country in which the research is going on. Thus, the United States is said to have induced a "brain drain" from Europe and Canada, while Britain and France, in turn, have induced a drain of technical talent from their respective former colonial areas. This tendency for research to concentrate in a few centers may result in substantial though somewhat intangible loss to those countries wishing to pursue scientific research independently, a loss which is mitigated only in part by the tendency, discussed below, for technical knowledge to be transmitted with ever greater speed across national boundaries. Lessening of national capability to carry on independent research, as distinguished from the capability of manufacturing the products of recent research, weakens both national power and national prestige.

Finally, international corporations may be less subject to moral suasion or other pressures exerted by national governments to achieve national objectives. France has relied for some years on a system of "indicative planning" to guide investment decisions in the French economy. The object of such planning is to achieve a rapid rate of growth without at the same time risking temporary overcapacity and unemployment which results from over-exuberant investment booms. The principal function of each plan is to lay out a national investment program based on *mutually consistent* projections of final demand. It is often in the self-interest of business firms to conform with the investment guidelines set forth in the plan, but on those occasions when firms have interpreted their own interests differently, the French government has applied moral suasion and, when necessary, has withheld financial resources to enforce compliance. Foreign and especially American firms disturb the French planners because of their access to sources of funds outside the country; they do not rely, as most French firms do, on government approval to raise funds necessary for new investment. (For the same reason, foreign firms will perhaps be less subject to the effects of restrictive national monetary policy.)

It should be noted that this source of difficulty posed by foreign direct investment will gradually diminish with further integration of the international economy. Foreign firms will continue to be able to thwart restrictive monetary measures, but so, increasingly, will purely domestic firms, as banks and other financial investors expand their lending domains, and as domestic firms learn to seek funds abroad. As we will see in the next chapter, large and reputable firms of any nationality can increasingly find short- and even medium-term funds in the Eurodollar market, national regulations permitting.[15] Moreover, the basic assumptions of indicative planning on a national level, as it is practiced in France, are gradually eroded as national barriers to imports from the other Common Market countries are eliminated. Concern with the consistency of output and investment plans involves "closed economy" thinking; the more open the economy, the more easily domestic shortfalls in production can be met from abroad and, more important, the more likely it is that well-laid plans can be disrupted by incursions of foreign goods, the product of new investment outside the country.[16] It is noteworthy that the EEC has begun to undertake indicative planning, not at the national level, but for the community as a whole.

Problems Created for the Home Country. Far less attention has been paid to the potential problems that high mobility of business establishment creates for the home country. These problems involve both national regulation and national taxation. In both cases it is the possibility of escape that creates difficulties for the regulators.

An obvious example of business escape is provided by regulation of water use in the United States. Industrial use of a stream of water often results in its pollution. The effluent must be cooled or decon-

---

[15] In August 1963, France imposed strict limitations on resident borrowing from foreigners; these restrictions were relaxed in early 1967, as France's balance-of-payments position worsened.

[16] See Bela Balassa, "Whither French Planning?" *Quarterly Journal of Economics,* LXXIX, November 1965, pp. 537–54, for a discussion of the implications of the Common Market for French planning. Also Malcolm C. Mac-Lennan, "The Common Market and French Planning," *Journal of Common Market Studies,* III, October 1964, pp. 23–46.

taminated before it can be re-used. This is true cost to society resulting from the industrial activity, but it is not reflected in the costs borne by the upstream users of the water. A strong case can be made for government action in the form of legal requirements governing disposal of waste, cooling of used water, and so on. However, few communities acting alone can make stringent rules effective, for such rules will simply induce firms to locate elsewhere—upstream or downstream from the jurisdiction in question, or on a different river, where they can escape the cost-increasing regulation. Firms already located within the jurisdiction may not actually move because of the costs of doing so, but their expansion plans may be influenced by the regulations. The mere prospect of relocation and slackening of new investment in turn may act as a powerful deterrent to establishing or enforcing regulations which, to be effective, are usually costly.[17]

Illustrations of escape from regulation can also be found at the international level. The United States attempts to protect its investing citizens by requiring public corporations, including mutual funds, to disclose their financial condition. For political reasons, it proscribes American firms from selling to Communist China and Cuba. And to preserve competition, it has anti-trust regulations governing acquisitions and collusion.

In all these cases, American regulations might be circumvented by operation out of some other country. The larger the "domain" of American investors, the more exposure they have to "foreign" brokers, and the readier they are to purchase "foreign" securities, the easier it is to circumvent disclosure regulations. Thus, mutual funds holding largely American securities can advertise and sell to American purchasers from some foreign base of operations; and fraudulent stock operations can exploit American investors from Canada, similarly evading the investor protection afforded by the Securities and Exchange Commission (SEC).[18]

[17] For examples of the erosion of state regulation and taxation of corporations in the United States, see R. N. Cooper, "National Economic Policy in an Interdependent World Economy," *The Yale Law Journal*, LXXVI, June 1967, pp. 1293–96.

[18] A flamboyant example of the attempt to escape national regulations while enjoying the benefits of national markets came a few years ago when two radio stations were established off the shores of Holland and of Britain, outside territorial waters, and beamed at these countries in competition with the national radio services.

To trade with certain proscribed countries, an American firm with some unique advantage in patents or skills may find it profitable to establish itself in a country which does not prohibit such trade, or to license a firm in a foreign country which will export to China and Cuba. In either case the intent of the proscription is violated.

The mere presence of a business firm in several countries offers some opportunities to escape national regulation or taxation. Since the Second World War, most European countries have adopted some form of regulation of restrictive business practices. Nowhere is it as stringent as the anti-trust laws in the United States, but it marks a sharp change in attitude from the inter-war period, when official opinion in many countries encouraged cartelization, market-sharing agreements, and price-fixing. Most of this new regulation, however, explicitly or tacitly exempts exports and foreign operations of domestic firms from regulation, apparently on the dubious ground that exemption is necessary to permit effective competition with foreign firms which enjoy similar exemptions.[19]

With the increasing internationalization of firms, national measures limiting restrictive business practices are greatly weakened, since firms may gather in Country *B* to decide market-sharing and pricing arrangements for Country *A,* and the same firms may work out their market strategy for Country *B* in Country *A.* Enforcement of national regulations under these circumstances is difficult, partly because it is difficult to gather legally acceptable information on firms operating legally in another country, partly because appropriate jurisdiction may be unclear if, for example, export sales are involved. The authorities in the country where the collusion is taking place have no power to act if collusion affects operations elsewhere, and, indeed, they often have no incentive to act.[20]

[19] The United States, for instance, explicitly exempts exports from anti-trust regulations under the Webb-Pomerene Act of 1918. Foreign investment operations are also exempt so long as their collusive activities do not affect sales in the United States. Since Judge Learned Hand's 1945 decision in the Alcoa case, U.S. courts have found several violations of the Sherman Act by American subsidiaries abroad, and fear of such accusation has apparently been one factor inducing American firms to set up wholly-owned subsidiaries abroad rather than joint ventures with competing foreign firms. See Howe Martyn, *International Business,* cited, pp. 32–36.

[20] For a discussion of regulation of restrictive business practices in Europe and some of the difficulties of enforcement, see Corwin D. Edwards, *Trade Regulation Overseas* (Dobbs Ferry, N. Y.: Oceana Publications, 1965).

Mergers across national boundaries may also inhibit competition by bringing into the corporate fold a potential competitor and thereby preventing imports from threatening a domestic market position.[21]

In addition to weakening the effectiveness of national regulation, business firms located in several countries can sometimes escape national taxation by placing some operations in low-tax countries and through intra-corporate sales and pricing techniques. These possibilities can pose problems both for the home country and for some of the host countries.

Switzerland's central location and low taxation made it both convenient and profitable to route sales from all over the world through sales offices there. Products were apparently priced so as to attribute most of the profits to the sales subsidiaries rather than to producing subsidiaries. As such, the profits on sales would be taxable at the lower rates prevailing in Switzerland. The various Swiss cantons compete vigorously with one another in offering attractive terms to new businesses, and tax rates themselves are sometimes negotiated between the prospective firm and the cantonal authorities. Moreover, Switzerland has negotiated a number of tax treaties with other countries which waive or substantially reduce taxes in those countries on dividends paid to nominally Swiss stockholders. In combination with low taxes in Switzerland, these treaties offer a powerful inducement to locate sales offices or holding companies in Switzerland even when manufacturing facilities are located elsewhere.

It is noteworthy that the rate of return on book value of U.S. investments in trading operations in Switzerland in the late 1950s was over 40 per cent, compared with only 20 per cent for the same type of investment in the EEC and still less on U.S. manufacturing investments in all Europe (Table 4–5).

The strong inducement such arrangements give to investment in Switzerland is indicated by the response of American investors to a change in the U.S. tax law governing foreign operations. Before 1962, U.S. taxes on the earnings of American subsidiaries abroad were deferred until the earnings were repatriated to the United States. Legislation in 1962 changed this provision in the case of holding companies and other so-called tax haven operations to make earnings

---

[21] Would the large-scale entry of foreign cars into the U.S. market, and the introduction of the compact car as a competitive response, have occurred if Volkswagen had been under U.S. corporate control, for example?

TABLE 4–5   Earnings on U.S.
Direct Investments Abroad [a]
(Percentage of Book Value at the Beginning of Year)

	1958	1962	1966
Manufacturing			
Europe	16	12	11
EEC	17	14	11
Switzerland	36	11	15
Trade and Other [b]			
EEC	20	18	6
Switzerland	42	40	16
Petroleum			
Europe	5	3	−2
Middle East	60	71	60
Venezuela	21	18	19

[a] After foreign taxes.
[b] All direct investments other than mining and smelting, manufacturing and petroleum.
Source: U.S. Department of Commerce, *Survey of Current Business.*

taxable when earned; thus, the advantage of low tax rates in Switzerland and several other countries was greatly reduced by applying U.S. taxes concurrently to American earnings in those countries.[22] The response was dramatic. In 1961 and 1962, about 40 per cent of new headquarters, sales, and service offices of American firms in Europe were located in Switzerland; in 1963, the proportion going to Switzerland dropped sharply to just over 10 per cent of the total.[23] Switzerland remains an attractive place to locate, but the tax attractions have been reduced. However, a change in U.S. tax laws was required to counteract some broadening of the locational domain of American firms. Moreover, a number of other countries, such as Luxembourg, still offer tax and other attractions which were not offset by the change in tax legislation, indicating the difficulty of correcting such

[22] See Lawrence B. Krause and Kenneth W. Dam, *Federal Tax Treatment of Foreign Income* (Washington: The Brookings Institution, 1964), for a description of U.S. taxation of earnings on foreign investment.
[23] Chase Manhattan Bank, cited, No. 28.

anomalies through national action alone without harming legitimate foreign investment.

Another illustration of intra-corporate pricing to minimize local taxes is provided by the international oil companies. Because depletion allowances offered by U.S. tax laws apply equally to foreign operations, and because these allowances are calculated on the basis of the value of crude oil production, American oil firms operating overseas have a strong tax incentive to enlarge the value of their crude oil production at the expense of their other operations. Thus, reported earnings on refining and distributing operations of American oil firms in Europe provide a rate of return on the book value of assets of less than 5 per cent—hardly enough to make investment there worthwhile, it would seem, but new investment continues—while the rate of return on American oil operations in the Middle East ranged from 60 to over 70 per cent a year (Table 4–5). Because of a particular feature of American tax law, and because of pressures from the oil-producing countries to raise crude oil prices, some of the corporate tax base of oil-consuming European nations is apparently shifted to the Middle East through intra-corporate pricing practices.[24]

All of these cases illustrate the problems which are created for national economic policy when business domains exceed governmental jurisdictions. Some problems are created for the host countries, some are created for the home country, and some are created for both. Although these difficulties exist whenever business is internationally mobile, they are aggravated when the barriers to trade and financial capital movements are low. Thus, there is an important interaction between the increased mobility of goods and the impact of the international mobility of firms on national policies.[25]

Problems Created for the Host Country by the Home Country. As this process proceeds, governmental jurisdictions must expand their scope of operations if they are merely to *retain* effective regulatory control. Sometimes they can alter their own laws in ways which limit the escape from national regulations or taxation, as when the United

[24] Under-pricing of intra-corporate sales, on the other hand, can be used to evade tariff duties unless customs officials are on their toes.

[25] The absence of tariffs is a key feature in the ability of corporations to thwart State regulation within the United States. See R. N. Cooper, *Yale Law Journal,* cited.

States tightened the law governing taxation of foreign income in 1962. In order to make its regulations effective in the face of international mobility, however, a country may be tempted to reach out to its firms operating abroad. This involves the unilateral extension of jurisdiction into areas of potential conflict with other jurisdictions.

The so-called extra-territorial application of national laws has arisen on several occasions when the United States sought to bar American-owned firms in Canada and France from selling their products to Cuba or Communist China, in both cases clashing with the foreign policies of those countries. The SEC has also, under Congressional instruction, attempted to extend its disclosure requirements to foreign firms whose securities are traded in the U.S. over-the-counter market, even when the foreign firm does not encourage such trading. Extra-territoriality can even accompany a nation's exports. The lack of a significant domestic electronics industry was brought home to France recently when it was compelled by U.S. export control regulations to cancel a sale of commercial jet airplanes to Communist China because they contained American electronic equipment which the United States does not permit to be shipped to Communist countries. The process can also work the other way. American anti-trust authorities have on occasion attempted to impose their rules on parent corporations in Britain by putting pressure on their subsidiaries in the United States.[26]

There are, then, a number of complications created by extensive overseas investment so long as the largest governmental unit for making economic policy is the nation-state. The classical advantages of overseas investment, namely, that it raises world output by shifting capital and managerial skill from regions of low return to regions of high return, must be set against these possible disadvantages.

It is not surprising, under these circumstances, to see indications of the expansion of governmental jurisdictions. In the United States, water pollution has become a subject of *national* concern and is being increasingly subjected to national control. Indicative planning in Europe is moving from the national level of France, where its effectiveness has been eroded, to the supra-national level of the EEC. It is no accident that the national anti-trust laws of the United States are considerably stronger than those of the various states, and that the in-

[26] Howe Martyn, cited, p. 36.

cipient anti-trust regulations of the EEC are stronger, at least in intent, than are the national laws of its members. In each case the larger jurisdiction is better able to enforce tighter regulations without concern for jurisdictional slippage.

International Transfers of Technology

National differences in technological skills and knowledge, like national differences in the capital stock available per worker, can provide the basis for profitable specialization and trade. But as in the case of capital, technical knowledge is traversing national boundaries with increasing speed and in increasing volume. The movement of technology is often associated with direct investment abroad; indeed, the rationale for the investment may be special technical knowledge embodied in a patented process or product. But increasingly technology moves by itself, disembodied from capital movements. In 1965, for example, residents of the United States earned over $1 billion in royalties and licensing fees (excluding movie royalties), largely earning on technical know-how; [27] and over $300 million of this was not associated with American direct investment operations abroad. These latter figures were nearly three times the corresponding earnings in 1956. Royalties and fees from the "export of knowledge" rose much more sharply either than U.S. commodity exports or than earnings on U.S. direct investments abroad during the same period of time (Table 4–6).[28]

The number of licensing agreements between American and European firms continues to increase rapidly at a rate of 100–150 per

[27] John Dunning reports that "more than a quarter of U.S. research and development was made available to the U.K. economy through the media of American subsidiaries." "Capital Movements in the 20th Century," *Lloyds Bank Review,* April 1964, p. 38.

[28] Germany, one of the few countries for which such data are available, shows a similarly rapid increase in both foreign payments and receipts from patents and copyrights (in millions of dollars):

	1952	1956	1960	1964
Receipts	8	19	37	66
Payments	21	63	121	174

year; they amount to nearly 20 per cent of new business operations in Europe according to one survey.[29] At the same time, members of the EEC are moving toward a common patent convention and registration. As a prelude to that, 31,000 patents and trademarks have been deposited with the EEC Commission. The ease with which new knowledge can move across national boundaries, and the speed with which it does so, marks a sharp contrast with the ancient practice of prohibiting even the migration of skilled workers and the export of machinery for fear that competitors would learn the technology they embodied.[30]

The extensive trade in technology has two implications: first, as noted earlier, differences in production possibilities based on technology will gradually disappear over time; second, countries such as the United States, which have relied extensively on new products for a strong export position, will find it increasingly difficult to do so, since the new techniques of production may move in international trade as easily as the new products themselves.[31]

International Migration of Labor

In addition to being the consumers for whom all production takes place, people also provide labor for the productive process. As factors of production, they must decide where they will work and at what tasks. As with capital, we can define the "domain" within which given individuals normally consider employment prospects when looking for jobs or when offered jobs. But the locational domain for labor is undoubtedly far narrower than it is for firms. Most individuals, especially in Europe, seek employment within quite a small radius of their birthplace. Labor markets are highly localized. Under

---

[29] Booz, Allen, and Hamilton, cited, pp. 20–21.

[30] Great Britain finally removed its prohibition on the export of textile machinery in 1843; but a legacy of these restrictions can be found in U.S. controls over exports of advanced equipment to the Soviet bloc.

[31] On the importance of "research oriented" goods in American exports, see Erik Hoffmeyer, *Dollar Shortage* (Amsterdam: North-Holland Publishing Co., 1958); also W. Gruber, D. Mehta, and R. Vernon, "The R & D Factor in International Trade and International Investment of United States Industries"; and D. B. Keesing, "The Impact of Research and Development on United States Trade," both in *Journal of Political Economy*, LXXV, February 1967, pp. 20–48.

some external stimulus which exposes individuals to a broader geographical area, such as national service or active recruitment by non-local firms, some may enlarge the area in which they are willing to work.[32] But in general, labor mobility is low even within countries. In Britain, for example, certain areas typically have unemployment rates twice and three times the national average, even through vigorous

TABLE 4–6   U.S. Earnings from Merchandise Exports,
Direct Investment and Technology
($ million)

	1956	*1960*	*1965*
Merchandise exports	17,379	19,459	26,276
Earnings on direct investments	2,171	2,355	3,961
Royalties and fees—direct investments	299	344	909
Royalties and fees—other	133	249	324

Source: U.S. Department of Commerce, *Balance of Payments Statistical Supplement,* 1963; and *Survey of Current Business.*

economic booms. Labor shortages elsewhere apparently do not absorb the regional unemployed fast enough.[33]

Mobility of labor is even lower between countries. The Rome Treaty (Article 48) requires the establishment of complete legal labor mobility within the Common Market, so that nationals of each country will be able to work in any other country on equal terms with

[32] A survey of European opinion in early 1963 revealed that one-fourth of the residents of the EEC would willingly emigrate (the range was from 18 per cent in Luxembourg to 29 per cent in Italy), and nearly one-third of Britain's residents said they would willingly emigrate. These numbers are substantial, and certainly would provide the basis for an international labor market if actual mobility corresponded to them. It is noteworthy, however, that the country chosen most often by the respondents as a destination if they were *forced* to migrate was the United States, not some other country in Europe. (For the French, however, Switzerland was the favorite choice; and for the British it was Australia by a wide margin.) See Reader's Digest Association, *The European Common Market and Britain* (1963), Tables 44 and 45.

[33] See United Kingdom, *Economic Trends,* June 1967. The United States also has regional variations in unemployment, of course, but the disparities are not nearly so sharp, and they narrow in booms. In 1965 the national unemployment rate was 4.6 per cent, while West Virginia, highest among the continental states, had 7.8 per cent unemployed.

nationals of the host country. Many of the legal obstacles to geographical mobility within the EEC have already been removed. Yet, except for Italians, very little actual movement has taken place.

Belgium and Holland have had no barriers to labor migration between them since 1957, yet the number of Belgians who work in Holland plus the Dutch who work in Belgium is small compared with the number of Spaniards who work in both. Significant migration did not take place despite substantially higher wages in Belgium and despite the fact that the Flemish and Dutch languages are very similar.[34] Psychological barriers to movement—traditional animosities, religious differences, and the like—apparently overshadowed legal obstacles as barriers to migration. The locational domain of most Dutch labor does not include Belgium, and vice versa.

The contrast of continental Europe with the United States is sharp. In 1960, 9 per cent of the total U.S. population lived in different states from the ones in which they had lived in 1955, and for several states the figure was above 25 per cent. This marks very high geographical mobility. Moreover, mobility within North America is apparently higher than it is within the EEC; over one million Canadians, equal to roughly 6 per cent of the Canadian population, live in the United States. The locational domain of many Canadians apparently includes the United States as well as Canada (though for many English-speaking Canadians it may include the United States but not French Canada).

Labor mobility in Europe is growing. During the 1950s there was a vast movement of labor out of European agriculture, as farmers' sons went to the cities in preference to staying on the land. This, however,

[34] Belgian census figures show the following number of Dutch and other foreigners living in Belgium (in thousands):

	1947	1954	1961
Dutch	63.7	49.7	49.9
Other foreigners	367.6	379.6	453.5

Net migration of Dutch into Belgium actually declined from around 1,000 a year in the early and mid-1950s to half that in the early 1960s, despite a sharp decline in unemployment in the Flemish regions of Belgium during this time.

On the recent history of labor regulations in Benelux, see J. E. Meade, H. H. Liesner, and S. J. Wells, *Case Studies in European Economic Union* (London: Oxford University Press, 1962), pp. 177–81.

is largely a one-way movement; it is not likely to be reversed even if economic conditions in the cities became less buoyant.

The sharp increase in international labor mobility since the late 1950s has been largely from the less developed countries of Europe —southern Italy, Spain, Greece, Turkey, and Portugal—to the prosperous industrial areas rather than among the industrial countries. In 1965, for example, 81 per cent of the 436,000 immigrants into the six members of the EEC came from these five countries, with the largest number going to Germany.[35] Much of this population is transient—men who come to work for a year or two to earn enough to marry or to buy some land—but increasing numbers of southern Europeans have settled in the northern countries. Foreign workers in 1965 accounted for 5 per cent of the German labor force—2 per cent were from other members of the EEC—and for no less than one-fourth of the Swiss labor force, a fact that has brought cries of alarm from many Swiss.

In addition, selected groups of individuals, usually highly skilled or educated, are developing international mobility. This phenomenon has been dubbed the "brain drain." It is estimated, for example, that about half the annual output of new doctors in Britain emigrates—a sharp rise from the early 1960s. The search for scientists and skilled engineers transcends national boundaries, and often such offers of employment are favored. As this development increases, it will put a severe strain on national wage patterns, for the highly mobile will command a "world" price, while those less mobile—and less actively sought—will command only the local wage. The gap between the highly mobile and the relatively immobile will thus grow in all but the highest income countries. It will also create pressures for aligning income taxes in the relevant income brackets.

Recent concern about the brain drain notwithstanding, labor within Europe does not yet do the international "shopping around" done increasingly by capital.[36] Labor immobility impedes the process of international adjustment. Where the mere offer of jobs or of slightly higher wages will not induce labor to move, where movement

---

35 United Nations Economic Commission for Europe, *Economic Survey of Europe in 1960,* Part I (New York: United Nations, 1966), p. 28.

36 It has been observed, though, that some Italian workers have become close students of the social security laws in European countries and plan to maximize their retirement earnings by meeting minimum social security eligi-

takes place only after prolonged delay and painful adjustment, it is easy for a region or a country to become a "depressed area" in the face of *ex ante* balance-of-payments deficits which it cannot correct through changes in exchange rates or commercial policy and which it has inadequate reserves or credit lines to finance. If enough people leave a depressed area, there will be employment for those remaining, provided that potential output falls more than total demand for products of the area. It is mobility at the "margin" which counts. Not everyone has to move, or even be willing to move. The margin of mobile persons in Europe seems to be growing, but it is still not large enough to provide an effective mechanism of adjustment.[37] Karl Deutsch and his associates have rightly emphasized that labor mobility is a crucial prerequisite to successful political integration.[38] This is a topic to which we return in Chapter 7.

Summary

Like goods, factors of production have greatly increased their movement across national frontiers in the past decade. This is especially true of American business establishments and of technology. Europeans have been much slower to take advantage of the reduction in barriers to direct investment, perhaps because the decline in tariff rates within the EEC and EFTA reduce the incentive to locate in other member countries. But a number of American firms and some European firms show signs of "thinking internationally" when laying

---

bility requirements in a number of countries. This is the beginning of a need for close coordination among national systems. See C. P. Kindleberger, "Mass Migration, Then and Now," *Foreign Affairs,* 43, July 1965, p. 656.

[37] In the German slump of 1966–67, for instance, the decline in the number of foreign workers amounted to about one-third of the deficiency in jobs; a rise in unemployment accounted for the rest. There was, however a sharp decline in foreign workers' remittances from Germany, a further illustration of the impact of growing interdependence on a nation's balance of payments.

[38] They say, "Full-scale mobility of persons has followed every successful amalgamated security-community in modern times immediately upon its establishment," and very often high mobility preceded political integration. As a requisite to political integration, they attach a higher importance to mobility of persons than to mobility either of goods or of money. Deutsch *et al., Political Community and the North Atlantic Area* (Princeton: Princeton University Press, 1957), pp. 53–54.

their plans for expansion. The domains of their decision-making have enlarged. The same is less true of labor, which, except for the substantial flows from southern Europe to the industrial north, shows little tendency toward greater international mobility in search of employment. When the decision-making domains of labor and capital exceed the jurisdictions of governments, the tasks of regulation and taxation are greatly complicated and a strong incentive is provided for inter-governmental cooperation in these matters. But as Chapter 7 shows, a discrepancy in decision-making domains between labor and capital can create difficulties in economic adjustment. Before we return to these problems, the following chapter takes up the international flow of financial capital, as distinguished from business establishment.

CHAPTER FIVE

International Financial Markets

Like direct investment, international portfolio investment increased sharply over the period 1950–65.[1] Net private portfolio capital outflows from the United States rose from $0.3 billion a year in 1950–53 to $1.1 billion in 1957, to $4.1 billion in 1964. With few exceptions, other countries continue to restrict the ability of residents to export portfolio capital. Nonetheless, private exports of portfolio capital from many other countries rose substantially too. And the export of official capital has also assumed major proportions. Except for emergency balance-of-payments support operations, this capital—$5.8 billion in 1965, net of repayments [2]—goes largely to the

[1] It is customary to divide international capital movements into two categories, direct and portfolio. The latter, in turn, is often subdivided into long-term and short-term. Portfolio investment differs from direct investment in that it does not involve direct management control over the decisions of the borrower, although, of course, some scrutiny of the borrower's plans may be made before any loan is completed. The term "capital movement" in fact gives rise to considerable ambiguity, for the movement of funds is confused with a movement of capital goods. The latter adds directly to the importing nation's capital stock, while the former does not. Similarly, the term "international investment" involves the layman's rather than the economist's definition of investment, applying to any purchase of assets (including securities) rather than to purchases of only those assets (e.g. machinery) which raise future output. This terminology has become so well established that it would only confuse matters to attempt to change. In this chapter, then, "international investment" will refer to flows of funds across national boundaries, primarily for portfolio investment. These flows do *not* automatically lead to transfers of real resources from the lending to the borrowing countries, nor do they automatically add to the capital stock of the borrowing nation. Paper assets may be exchanged for paper assets (or gold), and borrowing may take place for public or private consumption as well as for investment.

[2] OECD, *Development Assistance Efforts and Policies* (Paris, 1966), p. 33.

less developed countries and will not concern us here, although it represents yet another manifestation of the inter-linking of national economies and will serve, like capital movements among developed countries, to reduce the specificity in production capabilities which are the legacy of geography and climate.

Motivation for International Flows of Funds

The standard economic rationale for international capital movements is that they shift productive resources from regions of lower to regions of higher return, thus raising total output. As we have seen in Chapter 4, however, direct investment abroad takes place not only because of differences in national rates of return on real capital; special management or marketing skills, technical knowledge and patent rights, trademark "good will," differential taxation, and a host of other factors all may induce foreign direct investment, and there are substantial two-way flows between countries. Similarly, international portfolio investment may take place for many reasons other than national differences in the rate of return on real capital.[3] The yields on securities such as bonds and short-term paper may not correspond closely to this real rate of return. And even if they did, investors might place their funds abroad for reasons other than yield.

Divergences between the yield on securities and the return to investment arise because some borrowing takes place for purposes other than productive investment, because some investments are taxed or subsidized, and because the size of the capital stock cannot be altered radically in the short run. Monetary and debt management policies influence the yield on securities. Net government borrowing will tend to raise interest rates on bills and bonds; net lending, to lower them. Central bank operations also affect security yields by altering the proportions of money, securities, and real assets available for the portfolios of private wealth-holders. In addition, taxes and subsidies to certain forms of activity may substantially alter the demand for funds and, thus, yields on securities. The United States permits states and municipalities to float tax-free issues on the capital market; many countries subsidize housing; some countries tax new bond issues; and so on.

---

[3] I.e., the amount by which an additional dollar's worth of real investment will raise the annual output of goods and services, net of depreciation.

Two further points may be noted. First, time preference may vary from country to country, so that there are differences in the extent of borrowing for consumption purposes. Second, the possibility that rates of exchange between different currencies may change introduces the possibility of speculative gains in moving funds from one country to another.

Even where yields on securities correspond reasonably well with the rates of return on real assets, as they should over the long run, differences in transactions costs, in the breadth of markets, and in the variability of returns may still redirect international capital movements.

Transactions costs may differ substantially between various financial markets. When free to do so, borrowers will be attracted to the market where *borrowing* rates are lowest, while lenders want to invest their funds where *lending* rates are highest. If there is a large gap between these two rates, both borrowers and lenders may leave their domestic financial market for foreign markets where transactions costs and other factors affecting margins are lower. As we see below, the attraction of New York as an international financial center hinges in part on the low costs of transactions, especially for long-term securities.

Second, the liquidity of securities as well as their yield influences their attractiveness to investors. A security is highly liquid if it can be sold on short notice without incurring loss. The larger the loss which may have to be incurred, the less liquid the security. Liquidity depends in part on the characteristics of the financial market, and not merely, as is sometimes assumed, on the maturity of the security. The larger the market, the larger the number of the participants and the greater their activity, the more liquid a security is likely to be. Potential buyers are always ready to snap up any offering. If the market is "thin," in contrast, an investor who needs cash may have to trim his prices considerably in order to sell on short notice. International investors thus may be attracted to a large financial market for the liquidity it offers, even if, as a consequence, they must sacrifice some yield.

Third, high uncertainty about future prices may either attract or repel investors. Many investors are averse to risk, and they will therefore be willing to give up some yield for the sake of lower uncertainty. Other investors may be attracted by the possibility of really high capital gains, even if they also risk losses. Thus the variability of security prices may be an important feature influencing the movement of funds. As in the case of liquidity, variability is influenced by the size of the financial market and the number of participants in it. A market with few participants will demonstrate higher variability in prices than one with many, provided the investment decisions of the many participants are to some extent independent of one another and investors are not easily subject to bearish or bullish fads.[4]

All three of these factors—reversibility, liquidity, and predictability, to use Tobin's terms [5]—are closely related to the absolute size of the financial market in which securities transactions take place. Transactions costs are more likely to be lower, liquidity higher, and predictability greater, the larger the volume of transactions and the larger the number of participants. Size is no guarantee of comparative advantage in these respects; national regulations governing securities sales, collusive agreements among securities brokers, and taxes on purchases of securities can all influence these dimensions of financial transactions. But other things being equal, large size is likely to give a financial market an advantage. The economies of scale implicit in financial transactions are not unlike those involved in using the telephone—the more people who have phones, the more useful it is for everyone to have a phone. And under these circumstances growth is cumulative. Once a dominant market emerges, its advantages over others are likely to increase. Thus, in the United States, the numerous regional markets which thrived in the 1920s have given way almost completely to a national market centered in New York. Unless some substantial shock disrupts the process—as World War II and its aftermath weakened greatly the London market as a center for international finance—agglomeration begets agglomeration.

The foregoing considerations would apply even if there were only a single type of security, traded in different national markets. In reality there is a wide range of securities, varying by maturity, by degree of equity participation, by currency of denomination, by credit worthiness of borrower. The presence of many types of security gives rise to two additional sources of international movement of funds: there are substantial differences in tastes among investors with respect to their

[4] The variability mentioned here is variability around any long-term trend, which is presumably influenced by the more basic characteristics of the economy in which the financial market is located.

[5] James Tobin, *Money*, Chap. 2 (mimeo).

portfolios and they often wish to diversify portfolios to reduce the variability of return. The influence of taste is illustrated by the recent suggestion that transatlantic portfolio capital movements have been governed primarily by systematic differences in liquidity preference between Americans and continental Europeans, with Europeans having very strong preference for highly liquid assets.[6] Such a difference in taste would result in heavy purchases of relatively liquid American securities by Europeans and simultaneous heavy purchases of less liquid European assets by Americans. Second, and quite apart from differences in taste, the desire to reduce the variability in rates of return—whether from changes in monetary policy, economic activity, or exchange rates—may induce some international movement of funds even to centers with relatively low rates of return in the interests of diversification.[7]

Like direct investment, then, portfolio capital may move from country to country for a variety of reasons. Raising real output directly through international capital movements requires a corresponding transfer of real resources to capital-short regions. The effects on output of funds moving from one country to another for the variety of reasons just discussed are much less direct, and they do not require a corresponding transfer of real resources. International movements of portfolio capital can raise output indirectly by fostering greater competition in financial markets, for instance, or by encouraging savings through the higher liquidity of assets available in foreign financial centers. These indirect effects make an accurate assessment of the benefits of freedom of international capital movement much more difficult than would be true if everything moved on the basis of simple comparisons between rates of return.

Development of International Financial Markets Since 1958

The sharp growth in portfolio capital movements after 1958 was due largely to American investors and to the development of the so-

[6] Charles P. Kindleberger, "Balance-of-Payments Deficits and the International Market for Liquidity," Princeton Essay in International Finance, No. 46, Princeton University, 1965.

[7] See Harry Markowitz, *Portfolio Selection,* Cowles Foundation Monograph (New York: Wiley & Co., 1959), or James Tobin, "Liquidity Preference as Behavior Toward Risk," *Review of Economic Studies,* XXV, February 1958, pp. 65–86, for a discussion of the interaction between risk and return in selecting an investment portfolio.

called "Eurodollar market." Although growing, portfolio capital flows between the other industrial countries—apart from their transactions through the Eurodollar market—have been relatively modest in size. International capital movements of the traditional "textbook" type, whereby the citizens of one country buy bonds or short-term securities in another country in response to differences in interest rates (possibly covered by forward sales of the foreign currency to avoid exchange risk) have been relatively small except where the U.S. dollar was involved. The orders of magnitude involved can be seen by comparing the $21.8 billion in short-term foreign assets denominated in U.S. dollars held in 1966 by European commercial banks with $4.3 billion denominated in other currencies.[8] Thus the great bulk—over 80 per cent—of international short-term claims in currencies other than that of asset-holder were in dollars.

Eurodollars. Of the $21.8 billion in dollar claims held by European banks, only $9.3 billion were claims on residents of the United States. The remaining $12.5 billion were part of the Eurodollar market. This is simply a name for the practice, increasing steadily after 1957, of accepting deposits and lending in U.S. dollars by banks outside the United States. According to one estimate, roughly 400 banks participate in the Eurodollar market and the volume of funds moving in this market is estimated at nearly $13 billion if inter-bank deposits are excluded.[9] Most of the transactions in the Eurodollar market are unsecured, so that the "name" of the borrower is important in determining the volume of credit which is made available and the price paid for it. Eurodollar loans are often made to facilitate foreign trade, much of which is denominated in U.S. dollars, although Eurodollars are also "swapped" into local currencies for lending in domestic markets. International banking operations take place in other currencies too, but the magnitude of these transactions in currencies foreign to both borrower and lender is much smaller, with bank claims of this type amounting to well under $2 billion in early 1966.

Various reasons have been given for the existence and the rapid

[8] Bank for International Settlements, *Thirty-Seventh Annual Report* (Basle, 1967), p. 149. Data apply to the end of 1966.

[9] See Oscar L. Altman, "Euro-Dollars: Some Further Comments," IMF, *Staff Papers,* March 1965, p. 1; and BIS, *Thirty-Seventh Annual Report,* cited, p. 141. This estimate excludes foreign currency claims of Canadian and Japanese banks.

growth of the Eurodollar market. It apparently began in 1957, when, as a consequence of extreme pressure on sterling at that time, British banks were prohibited from financing trade between third countries in sterling. In order to preserve a lucrative business, the British banks offered the same financing facilities in dollars instead, attracting the dollars by offering interest on short-term deposits.[10] The advent of convertibility at the end of 1958 and the associated relaxation of exchange controls over banking transactions in a number of European countries gave further impetus to the market since the ability to arbitrage funds between dollars and European currencies is an integral part of Eurodollar activities. European banks would not have been successful in these operations, however, if they had not been able to compete effectively with American banks. That they were able to do so can be explained by the large gap between deposit rates and lending rates in the United States. Until May 1963, a ceiling of 2.5 per cent was imposed by Regulation Q of the Federal Reserve Board on the rates which American banks could offer on 90-day time deposits (1.0 per cent on shorter term), and extensive relaxation of the ceiling did not take place until 1964 (Figure 5–1).[11] In contrast, the prime lending rate in New York—the rate at which large and well-established businesses can borrow—was 4.5 per cent or above after the spring of 1959. Thus, European banks could pay more to depositors than New York banks did and still charge less to borrowers, provided they were willing to operate on small margins. The Eurodollar market is a highly competitive one where conventions and tacit agreements on pricing have apparently not yet been formed among the participants; moreover, the volume of the typical transaction is relatively large. As a result, profit margins are very small. The impor-

[10] Bank of England, "U.K. Banks' External Liabilities and Claims in Foreign Currencies," *Quarterly Bulletin,* IV, June 1964, p. 102.

[11] In October 1962, American banks were permitted to pay higher rates on time deposits by foreign official institutions. In July 1963, the ceiling on 3–6 month deposits was raised to 4.0 per cent for all depositors, and, in November 1964, it was raised again to 4.5 per cent. Interest rates are not permitted on demand deposits in the United States; very short-term (7 day) deposits do, however, command interest rates in the Eurodollar market. In November 1964, time deposits of less than 90 days were permitted to pay 4 per cent; before that time the maximum permissible rate was 1 per cent. In December 1965, both ceilings were raised to 5.5 per cent, and they were lowered to 5.0 per cent in September 1966.

tance of Regulation Q is illustrated by the fact that a number of branches of American banks in Europe have lent Eurodollars to their home offices for use in the United States.[12]

The Eurodollar market has been supplied from a number of sources. Several European central banks, notably the German Bundesbank and the Italian Exchange Office, have from time to time induced their domestic commercial banks to hold dollars by offering attractive forward repurchase terms for domestic currency. The Bundesbank, for example, made short-term dollar investments more attractive than short-term domestic investment in Germany during the period 1960–63 by offering to buy back after 90 days dollars held by German commercial banks at a price which more than offset the difference in interest rates between domestic securities and dollar securities. The German banks naturally preferred to hold their dollars in the Eurodollar market rather than in New York if interest rates were higher in the former market.[13]

In addition, a number of Eastern European banks which normally hold working balances in dollars for their trade with the West apparently had qualms about holding these funds in New York where they were exposed to possible confiscation by the American authorities, and they prefer the anonymity and distance of the Eurodollar market. Such funds amounted to about $360 million in late 1966, when Eastern Europe was in fact a net borrower in the Eurodollar market.[14]

Finally, it is often claimed that the large deficit in the international payments of the United States after 1957 contributed to the growth of the Eurodollar market by providing a plentiful supply of funds to European banks, which they then chose to re-lend abroad rather than convert into local currencies at their central banks.

This surfeit of dollars undoubtedly did contribute to the growth of the Eurodollar market; but it is also true that the existence of the Eurodollar market contributed to the surfeit of dollars. Americans learned that they could earn more for their liquid funds in Europe or Canada than they could in the United States, and sent these funds to

---

[12] BIS, *Thirty-Fourth Annual Report* (Basle, 1964), pp. 136–37.

[13] The Bundesbank's offer in 1964 was confined to dollars held in the form of U.S. Treasury bills, partly because German firms were borrowing Eurodollars to finance domestic expenditure, thus defeating the monetary objectives of the Bundesbank. The offer was withdrawn in early 1966.

[14] BIS, *Thirty-Seventh Annual Report,* cited, p. 140.

FIG. 5-1.
U.S. and Eurodollar Interest Rates
1959-1967

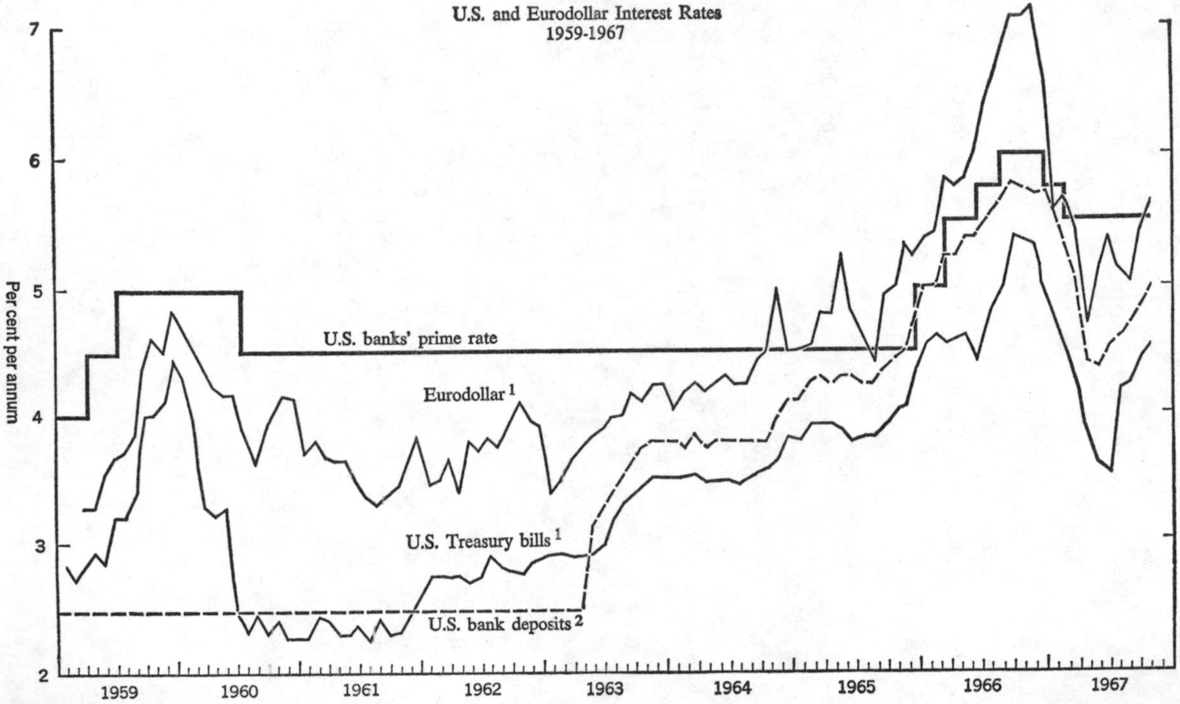

U.S. banks' prime rate

Eurodollar [1]

U.S. Treasury bills [1]

U.S. bank deposits [2]

Per cent per annum

1959 1960 1961 1962 1963 1964 1965 1966 1967

Sources: Bank of England, Quarterly Bulletin.
Federal Reserve Bulletin.
B.I.S.

1. Three-months.
2. The U.S. Bank Deposit Rate 1959-May 1963 is the maximum interest rate payable on time deposits of 90 days to 6 months, as established by the Federal Reserve Board. After June 1963, the rate shown here is for three-month Certificates of Deposit.

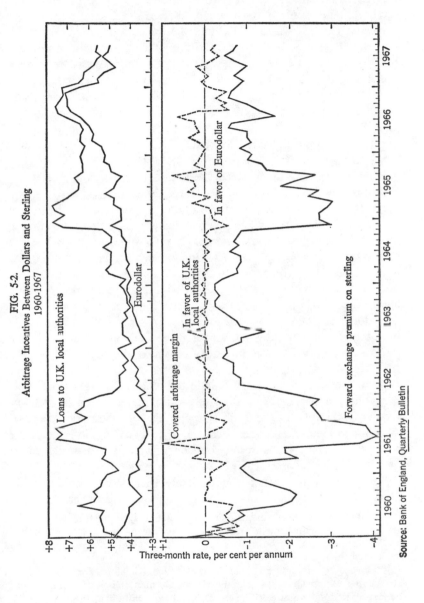

FIG. 5-2.
Arbitrage Incentives Between Dollars and Sterling
1960-1967

Loans to U.K. local authorities

Eurodollar

Covered arbitrage margin

In favor of U.K.
local authorities

In favor of Eurodollar

Forward exchange premium on sterling

Three-month rate, per cent per annum

+8 +7 +6 +5 +4 +3 +1 0 −1 −2 −3 −4

1960 1961 1962 1963 1964 1965 1966 1967

Source: Bank of England, _Quarterly Bulletin_

121

foreign banks for deposit. From 1960 to the end of 1964 the total recorded outflow of short-term capital from the United States to Europe and Canada was $2.3 billion, the great bulk of which was denominated in U.S. dollars. In addition, the "errors and omissions" item in the U.S. balance of payments turned sharply negative in 1960, no doubt reflecting some unrecorded capital movements to Europe and Canada over and above the recorded movements. Moreover, a number of American corporations operating in Europe are known to have held funds in the Eurodollar market, involving either retained earnings not repatriated to the United States or funds sent temporarily from parent firms in the United States.[15]

This movement of American funds into the Eurodollar market illustrates the links which are being forged among domestic money markets in the major countries. As interest rates are raised in any one country, they attract funds from other countries, sometimes directly, more often via the Eurodollar market.[16] The process at work can be seen most clearly for the United Kingdom which, as a deficit country in the early 1960s, generally welcomed capital inflow from abroad. Figure 5–2 shows the very close correspondence between British local authority borrowing rates, covered for exchange risk, and the Eurodollar rates. The forward exchange rate plays the major role in bringing Eurodollar rates and covered local authority rates into correspondence, but the large flows of funds also influence the two interest rates to some extent.

Similar observations can be made for other countries—Eurodollar rates show a parallelism with short-term interest rates in Belgium, Germany, Switzerland, and the Netherlands over the period 1961–64 —although the correspondence is usually less striking, in large part as a result of policy measures to impede unwanted short-term capital movements. These are further discussed below.

The Eurodollar market is not merely an entrepôt through which liquid funds flow from one national market to another. Like any

[15] In the balance-of-payments figures the latter type of transaction might appear as "direct investment" rather than short-term capital and the former would be reflected in a shortfall of repatriated earnings on investment abroad from what they otherwise would be.

[16] Thus, a rise in interest rates in the United Kingdom, for instance, will attract funds from Germany, but the rise in German claims on foreigners will be largely in *dollars*, not sterling; the British banks will change the dollars they receive from Germany into sterling for local lending.

banking operation, the Eurodollar market actually creates credit in the process of transferring funds from ultimate lenders to ultimate borrowers. Only a portion of each dollar deposit is retained in liquid form by the bank of deposit, the remainder being lent at somewhat longer term. If the borrower in turn keeps some of his funds in dollar deposits outside the United States, or if the recipient of the borrower's expenditure does so, the basis is laid for multiple credit expansion. This process is fundamentally the same as that which takes place in any domestic banking system, except that the credit creation is in a currency outside of its homeland.[17] Thus the dollars held outside the United States may exceed by a substantial margin the dollars received by foreigners through deficits in the U.S. balance of payments. A crude guess suggests that every dollar arriving in the Euro-dollar market either directly or indirectly from the United States—i.e. being placed in a European commercial bank—gives rise to credit expansion in the Eurodollar market by a factor of three.[18]

In assessing the potential impact of the Eurodollar market on credit conditions, it is worth noting that total Eurodollar claims of over $21 billion already exceed the money supply in a number of countries; and the total is large with respect to all countries except the United States (Table 5–1). Even the United States is not left un-influenced by the Eurodollar market, however; the pull of only a small fraction of U.S. liquid assets into the Eurodollar market is sufficient to bring U.S. and Eurodollar interest rates into rough conformity. In fact, as Figure 5–1 shows, Treasury bill rates in the United States have risen along with Eurodollar deposit rates. There is, of course, an important question of which is cause and which is effect; credit-tightening in the United States, by reducing the flow of dollars into the Eurodollar market, might be the cause rather than the consequence of a rise in Eurodollar rates. But in at least one case, in November 1964, after Britain had just raised the bank rate to 7 per cent,

[17] To the extent that Eurodollars are swapped for local currencies, the process of dollar credit creation outside the United States is broken.

[18] This crude estimate is arrived at by assuming that foreign banks with dollar liabilities will want to hold some liquid assets in the United States as "reserves" against these liabilities. Total dollar liabilities of foreign commercial banks were about 2.5 times their dollar claims on the United States in the period 1963–65; if Japan is excluded on the grounds of its special banking ties with the United States, the ratio was in the range 3.0–3.3. (Computed from data in BIS, *Annual Report,* cited).

it is clear that the U.S. monetary authorities moved to tighten money (and raised the discount rate) with the Eurodollar market and the pull of Eurodollars into the United Kingdom very much in mind. Moreover, the record of discussion in the Federal Open Market Committee, which determines U.S. monetary policy, indicates clearly that primarily external considerations, and especially the large outflows of short-term funds, influenced the gradual tightening of U.S. monetary policy after 1962.[19]

TABLE 5–1   Money Supply: An International Comparison
(December 1965)

	In Billions of U.S. Dollars	Per Cent of 1965 GNP
Belgium-Luxembourg	6.4	38.2
Canada	8.9	18.5
France	36.2	38.4
Germany, F. R.	18.1	16.2
Italy	22.9	40.3
Japan	29.0	34.6
Netherlands	4.8	25.0
Sweden	3.5	18.0
Switzerland	6.8	48.9
United Kingdom	35.6	36.1
United States	171.9	25.2

Source: IMF, *International Financial Statistics.*

Despite the strong link which the Eurodollar market has forged between national markets, substantial insulation remains, for two reasons. First, the credit-worthiness of any one borrower or group of borrowers is limited. There is as yet no systematic collection of information on total borrowing by individual firms and banks in the Eurodollar market as there is within some national markets, but lending institutions do attempt to ascertain roughly how much has been borrowed—not only by firm, but also by country.[20] Thus Japanese

[19] See, for example, Board of Governors of the Federal Reserve System, *Fiftieth Annual Report*, 1963, pp. 59, 63, *et passim*, and *Fifty-First Annual Report*, 1964, especially pp. 63, 67.
[20] Altman, cited, p. 6.

firms and banks are known to have borrowed heavily in the Eurodollar market on various occasions, and they were able to borrow further only at sharply rising rates. The same thing happened to Italy in 1963. What factors determine, in the lending banks' collective judgment, the maximum safe limits to borrowing is not known; presumably they are influenced not only by the asset position of particular borrowers but also by the over-all foreign exchange position of the borrowing country. Borrowing in the Eurodollar market thus may fall substantially short of what is required to bring a country's domestic interest rates into line with those prevailing elsewhere.

Second, bank borrowing in the Eurodollar market for the purpose of re-lending to domestic banks or businesses in domestic currency requires "swapping" dollars for the domestic currency, an arrangement whereby the bank holding dollars simultaneously sells dollars for local currency and repurchases dollars in the forward market for delivery, say, in three months' time. The attractiveness of this operation depends not only on the local lending rates but also on the forward rate of exchange relative to the spot exchange rate. Lending in local currency purchased with Eurodollars is made more attractive if dollars are relatively cheap in the forward market, i.e., if they sell at a discount relative to the spot exchange rate, and it is less attractive if the forward dollar sells at a premium. Variations in the forward exchange rate relative to the spot rate therefore permit continued divergences between national interest rates. Since the market in forward exchange is usually relatively "thin" compared with national markets in short-term claims, forward rates tend to adjust more rapidly to international flows of funds than do interest rates. When the British bank rate was raised sharply to 7 per cent in 1961 and again in late 1964, local authority deposit rates rose correspondingly at the outset and the forward discount on the pound sterling (vis-à-vis the dollar) increased by almost the same amount. But it takes some movement of funds to induce this change in forward rate. In the first quarter of 1965, $450 million in Eurodollars were swapped into sterling, tending to raise the Eurodollar rate and lower the British local authority rate. The influence of the Eurodollar market on British interest rates was much damped by the movement in the forward rate, but some influence remained.

Movements in forward rates have also insulated other countries from the full equalizing tendencies of an international money market.

There are, however, distinct limits on the ability of forward exchange rates to provide this insulation of national money markets from foreign influence. The forward rate reflects, among other things, a market judgment about what exchange rates will be at the time the forward contracts mature. If the collective judgment of those in the market is that exchange rates will differ markedly from the forward exchange rate, speculators will step in and purchase forward contracts, expecting to liquidate them at a profit by buying the necessary currency in the spot market when they come due. Thus, forward exchange rates cannot long remain outside the bounds within which spot rates are expected to move. Spot rates for most currencies, in turn, are limited in their variation by an obligation imposed by the Bretton Woods Agreement (and, where relevant, by the EMA) on national monetary authorities to hold exchange rates within 1 per cent (three-quarters of 1 per cent for most adherents to EMA) of their par values. They typically do this by buying or selling dollars against their own currencies. So long as par values are expected to remain unchanged, therefore, forward rates will not lie outside the range permitted to spot rates. When they do so for any length of time, it is an indication that a change in the par value is expected.

Two developments should contribute toward limiting movements in forward rates. First, as noted in Chapter 2, official sentiment seems to have hardened against changes in exchange rates—downward or upward—among major currencies. Second, monetary authorities often intervene in the exchange market long before the currency reaches the lowest permissible rate. A decline to the floor is taken as a sign of weakness and is thought to invite speculation. Early in 1965, therefore, following the sterling crisis of November 1964, the spot rate of the pound was not permitted to fall below $2.79, only half the distance between par and the floor of $2.78. And when Italy faced an exchange crisis in early 1964, the Bank of Italy did not even permit the exchange rate of the lira to fall below par. If market sentiment absorbs these two developments—the increasing reluctance to change par values (backed by an apparent willingness by surplus countries to provide very substantial short-term financial support to currencies in difficulty) and the efforts to reduce speculation by official market intervention well above the lowest permissible exchange rate—then in the future forward rates should fluctuate even less in response to differential interest rates than they have in the past.

To sum up, despite the remaining impediments to full integration of national money markets, pressures toward an equalization of interest rates in different centers have been quite strong. As we shall see below and again in Chapter 9, most countries have adopted a number of measures to inhibit these integrative tendencies. Governments want to retain some measure of national autonomy in determining short-term interest rates and national liquidity.

Long-term portfolio capital. Closer links between national capital markets developed far more slowly than they did between national money markets, using the latter term to encompass short-term, liquid funds and the former to apply to long-term securities. It is true that between 1958 and 1965 American long-term portfolio capital moved to Europe in increasing volume, and that following the liberalization of capital movements under several directives of the EEC there was some modest increase in long-term portfolio capital flows within Europe. But these flows have been small relative to those of short-term capital.[21]

For many years most European countries as a matter of policy severely limited the ability of their residents to export capital. In the late 1940s and early 1950s these prohibitions could be justified on grounds of defending the currency. But even after currency restrictions were greatly relaxed for current account transactions, restrictions on capital movements were retained, especially on purchases of securities and long-term loans. In the early 1960s, when the external position of most European countries showed great strength, there was some relaxation of restrictions on long-term capital movements; but there was evident reluctance to go very far in this direction.

[21] There is a difficult problem of measurement involved in comparing capital movements and assessing their "integrative" tendencies. *Net* flows of capital may not reflect the true importance of capital movements if they conceal much larger gross flows in both directions. For example, in 1962, after the French authorities relaxed controls on the purchase of listed foreign securities by French residents, gross sales nearly quadrupled to $340 million and gross purchases increased tenfold to $300 million. These gross flows involved a shift in the composition of the French portfolio of foreign securities, largely from the rest of the world to the EEC. The impact of this shift on national securities markets was far greater than implied by the modest *net* inflow of $40 million. See *A Description and Analysis of Certain European Capital Markets,* prepared by the U.S. Treasury Department for the Joint Economic Committee, U.S. Congress, 1964, pp. 123–25.

One reason often advanced for this resistance to freeing capital movements, and in particular for allowing foreign issues in domestic capital markets, is that Europe is basically a capital-short area and must preserve its limited national saving for domestic needs—first the needs of reconstruction, then the needs of equipping a rapidly growing labor force with modern machinery and eliminating an acute housing shortage. Britain shares many of the same needs as the continental countries, but for political and sentimental reasons kept its capital market open to members of the Sterling Area; France and Belgium also provided special treatment for their respective currency areas.

The argument that the European countries cannot open their capital markets to foreign borrowers because of a "capital shortage" at home sounds odd in view of the extraordinary increase in gold and foreign exchange reserves and other short-term claims on foreigners which the continental European countries accumulated over the period 1950–65. The official reserves of Continental Europe as a whole rose by $26.9 billion between 1950 and 1965 (two-thirds of this increase was in the second half of the period), while private European banks added another $8.6 billion to their foreign exchange holdings. This represents an extraordinary amount of European lending to foreigners.[22] To this extent, therefore, the European countries have put their scarce domestic saving into short-term claims on foreigners rather than into fixed capital formation at home or into long-term claims on foreigners through foreign issues of bonds or stocks in their domestic capital markets.

Viewing national saving in this aggregative way, while exposing an apparent misdirection of "scarce" European capital, does not deny that permitting a greater outflow of long-term capital might have reduced the funds available for housing and other long-term domestic investment. When financial assets are not readily substitutable for one another, that is, when capital markets in the broadest sense are imperfect, then "savings" lodged in one form of asset cannot automatically or even readily be transferred to other uses.

---

[22] From the viewpoint of the disposition of national savings, there is no difference between buying gold from the U.S. Treasury and "lending" to the United States by buying U.S. Treasury bills. So long as gold is willingly purchased by the U.S. Treasury at a fixed price, both represent short-term claims on foreigners—in this case, on the United States.

Much attention has been drawn to the "imperfections" of European capital markets.[23] There are indeed a number of respects in which European capital markets, and especially those of the large countries on the continent of Europe, are imperfect. Issue costs are high (Table 5–2); transactions costs are high; share prices are highly volatile; and the markets are not capable of "absorbing" large issues

TABLE 5–2   Initial Costs of Public Issues, 1962
(Per cent of amount raised)

| | Domestic Companies | | Foreign |
	Bonds	Stocks	Governments
Belgium	3.5–5	5.2–6.3	n.a.
France	6	7.5–8	n.a.
Germany, F. R.	7–8	8–8.5	7–8
Italy	5.5–8.5	n.a.	n.a.
Netherlands	3.25	5.1–5.6	4–5
Switzerland	3–3.5	4.5 [a]	3.5–5
United Kingdom	3	3.25	4.2–4.5
United States	1–2	4–4.5	1.2–4.8

n.a., not available.
[a] This can vary widely.
Source: Bank of England, *Quarterly Bulletin*, June 1963.

with any regularity. But it should not be assumed, therefore, that European capital markets are totally undeveloped. On the contrary, they provide a substantial portion of the financial wherewithal for European investment. As can be seen in Table 5–3, flotation of stocks and bonds accounted for a higher proportion of fixed capital formation in most European countries in 1962 than it did in the United States, which by widespread agreement has the most highly developed capital market. Very few new equities were issued publicly in the

[23] See for example the well-publicized speech by Lord Cobbold (Governor of the Bank of England), reproduced in the Bank of England's *Quarterly Bulletin*, II, December 1963, pp. 263–66; *Rapport par le Comité Chargé d'étudier le financement des investissements* (Lorain Report) (Paris, 1963); and EEC, *The Development of a European Capital Market* (Segré Report) (Brussels, 1966).

United States compared with Europe, even after allowing for the fact that 1962 was a bad year for stocks in the United States; bond issues compared more favorably with those in other countries.

The ability to "digest" new issues depends, however, not on the

TABLE 5-3   Market Financing for New Investment, 1962

	Gross Fixed Capital Formation as a Per Cent of GNP	Net New Issues [a] as a Per Cent of Gross Fixed Capital Formation	
		Total	of Which: Bonds
Belgium	18.8	18.6	12.7
France	19.6	11.8	6.1
Germany, F.R.	25.4	12.6	10.2
Italy	24.6	26.0	15.6
Netherlands	24.3	10.7	6.7
Sweden	22.6	28.6	21.8
Switzerland	27.7	15.5	10.3
United Kingdom	16.5	20.1	16.3
United States	16.1	13.0	12.3

[a] Excluding central government and foreign issues.

Sources: BIS, *Thirty-Fourth Annual Report*, 1964, p. 33; U.S. Treasury, *A Description and Analysis of Certain European Capital Markets*, 1964, pp. 14-21; and OECD, *General Statistics*, January 1965.

size of the market in relation to the economy in which it resides, or even to total investment demand, but on the absolute size of the market, the number of participants, the frequency with which the participants buy and sell, and the extent to which dealers or jobbers speculate in securities for their own account. In terms of the qualities of securities mentioned earlier—reversibility, liquidity, predictability—the absolute size of the market makes a great deal of difference. In these respects the American securities market centered in New York stands far ahead of the markets in Europe, which in turn vary considerably among themselves (Table 5-4). New issues of $50-100 million are absorbed routinely in New York, while $30-45 million can be accommodated easily in London. Issues of these sizes are occasionally found in the continental markets, but they are unusual and require special arrangements. Typical flotations are much smaller, in the $5–15 million range. It is not surprising, therefore, that New York became a major international capital market even apart from exchange restrictions in some European markets. Canadian borrow-

TABLE 5–4   Major Security Markets, 1962

	Market-Value of Securities ($ billion)		Net New Issues [b] ($ billion)	Number of Securities Quoted [c]	Average Turnover [c] ($ million per year per issue)
	Central Government [a]	Other			
Belgium	6.0	10.5	0.9	1,132	0.4
France	3.2	30.7	1.5	2,800	1.5
Germany, F.R.	1.2	23.8	3.0	1,825	n.a.
Italy	4.1	31.6	2.3	351	6.2
Netherlands	4.2	12.7	0.4	2,366	0.2
Sweden	3.0	4.5 [d]	0.9	n.a.	n.a.
Switzerland	n.a.	n.a.	0.5	750	6.5
United Kingdom	46.4	71.2	4.7	9,134	5.8 [e]
United States					
Stocks	—	484.1	2.5 [f]	1,559	30.4
Bonds	110.5	192.6	15.2	1,202	1.2
Total	110.5	676.7	17.7	2,761	17.7

n.a., not available.
[a] Excluding short-term securities.
[b] Including government issues (other than short-term) and foreign issues.
[c] Principle stock exchange only. As a measure of relative activity per issue, average turnover may be biased insofar as it reflects differences in the average prices of securities rather than the number traded.
[d] Excluding stocks.
[e] Last four months of 1964.
[f] Exceptionally low because of the stock market slump of spring 1962. New stock issues were $4.3 billion in 1961. Data include stocks issued by investment companies, amounting to $1.9 billion in 1962.
N.B. Data involve some elements of noncomparability and should be taken only to indicate orders of magnitude.
Sources: U.S. Treasury, *A Description and Analysis of Certain European Capital Markets,* prepared for the Joint Economic Committee of the U.S. Congress, 1964, pp. 14–21; Bank of England, *Quarterly Bulletin,* June 1964, pp. 110–11; New York Stock Exchange, *Fact Book,* 1965, pp. 36, 44; *Statistics Relating to Securities Quoted on the London Stock Exchange,* 1966.

ers regularly come to New York for large sums; but many European borrowers have also gone to New York for funds. Up to 1965, the European Coal and Steel Community (ECSC) had raised about two-thirds ($95 million) of its funds in the New York market and only one-third in various European markets.[24] The governments of Norway, Denmark, Belgium, and Austria all borrowed in New York after 1960, as did municipalities or corporations in these countries and in France, Germany, Italy, the Netherlands, and other European countries.[25]

It is important to note, however, that foreigners have been heavy buyers of foreign securities as well as heavy borrowers in New York. In 1960 over half of the new European issues in the United States was taken up by foreigners. Because of the more rapid growth in private placements compared with public issues, the figure had dwindled to 22 per cent by 1963, but out of a much larger total.[26] Thus, in the case of capital markets, we apparently find the opposite phenomenon from that in the Eurodollar market. A market for short-term dollars developed in Europe at least in part because of a large difference between borrowing and lending rates in New York. In the case of new long-term bond issues, the low transactions costs of New York attracted both borrowers and lenders to that center.[27] In both cases, however, it is significant that the claims are denominated in dollars. The convention of using a common currency broadens the market for all users, both borrowers and lenders. The relative economic importance of the United States makes the U.S. dollar the most natural candidate, but the important fact is the widespread use of a single currency, not so much *which* currency it is.[28]

It has been suggested that the large flows of both short- and long-

[24] BIS, *Thirty-Fifth Annual Report,* cited, p. 159; these calculations exclude a loan of $100 million from the U.S. government in 1954.

[25] U.S. Dept. of Commerce, "New Foreign Securities offered in the United States, 1952–1964," Mimeo, 1965.

[26] In 1964, foreign purchases accounted for 55 per cent of European issues in New York, but the total had been drastically reduced to a mere $51 million by the interest equalization tax, compared with $350 million the year before.

[27] The possibilities for tax evasion may also have provided an incentive for European lenders to buy European securities in New York.

[28] Further testimony to the value of a common currency is given by the rapid growth of *dollar* bond issues in Europe in 1964–66, when the interest equalization tax limited access to the U.S. market.

term capital across the Atlantic reflect a basic difference in liquidity preferences between North America and Europe.[29] Continental European households, it is argued, have a strong desire to hold their savings in highly liquid form. They have had in this century too much experience with long-term debt either defaulted or eroded through inflation to hold long-term securities willingly; they desire assets which they can liquidate quickly when necessary. The personal rate of saving is high in such countries as Germany and France, but long-term interest rates also remain high because of this strong liquidity preference. At the same time, European financial institutions apparently do not provide an adequate bridge between this demand for liquid assets and the desire of borrowers to incur long-term debt rather than liquid liabilities.

In contrast, Americans are much more willing to hold long-term securities, either directly, or indirectly through life insurance companies and pension funds. (More generous, government-sponsored provisions for social security in continental Europe deprive the European countries of the latter source of demand for private securities.) And American financial institutions, such as savings and loan associations, more readily accept short-term liabilities and make long-term investments. On both counts, American savings flow into long-term investments and reduce long-term rates, so the gap between short- and long-term interest rates is much smaller than in Europe.

Under these circumstances, long-term capital will tend to flow from North America to high-interest-rate Europe, while countering flows of short-term capital will move westward across the Atlantic. As Table 5–5 indicates, these counter-flows have in fact taken place. Long-term private capital flows from the United States to Europe were more than offset by reverse flows to the United States in the form of short-term lending, special compensatory official lending,[30] and purchase of gold. It is noteworthy, on this hypothesis, that the distinction between private and official capital—or even the distinction between private capital and gold movements—is blurred. Europeans desire to hold liquid assets. Perhaps private claimants will choose to hold their liquid assets in dollars, but maybe they will convert the dollars received from long-term capital inflow into local liquid assets. The central banks ultimately receiving the dollars, in turn,

[29] Charles P. Kindleberger, cited.
[30] Including prepayment of long-term debt to the United States.

may hold the dollars in the form of short-term assets or they may convert the dollars into gold. In either case, however—and so long as the U.S. Treasury supports the price of gold through its standing offer to buy it at $35 an ounce—the Europeans can use the United States to mediate between their need for long-term investment and their de-

TABLE 5–5   Transatlantic Financial Exchange, 1962–64
($ million, annual average)

	Net U.S. Purchases of European Assets	Net European Purchases of U.S. Assets
Direct investment	1,044	11
Long-term private portfolio investment	511	86
Long-term government	166	705 [a]
Short-term capital, private	213	452 [b]
Short-term capital, official	105	
Gold [c]	—	533
Total	2,076	1,787

[a] Largely special transactions involving prepayment of debt, prepayment of military expenditures, and purchases of foreign-currency bonds ("Roosa bonds").
[b] Breakdown into private and official not available before 1964. European official purchases of short-term claims on the United States, other than gold, amounted to $0.4 billion in 1964, while private purchases were $1.1 billion.
[c] Gold sales by the United States involve a flow of funds from Europe to the United States.

Source: Computed from U.S. Department of Commerce, *Survey of Current Business,* June 1965.

sire for liquid assets. The real savings of Europe were not increased by the long-term capital inflow; Europe instead was borrowing long and lending short, while the United States was doing the reverse.

Regrettably, this view of what has happened in the early 1960s is not easily distinguishable empirically from the European claim that their economies were surfeited with unwanted (long-term) dollars, including direct investment, and that they were unwilling to countenance the domestic monetary expansion which would be required to translate this inflow of funds into real external savings, i.e., an import surplus. Therefore some countries induced their private banks to hold short-term dollar claims in order to reduce the expansionary effect of the capital inflow on the domestic money supply, while others chose to demand gold in the hope that this would force the United States to take action to reduce its capital outflow.

Some indirect evidence, however, suggests that liquidity preference does not differ substantially between Americans and Europeans. The United States at 85 per cent leads all in the ratio of liquid assets to gross national product. This might merely be one reflection of the proportionally larger capital stock in the United States. In terms of new acquisition of financial assets by households, Americans in the period 1959–61 took only 48 per cent in liquid form (currency, demand and savings deposits), compared with 67 per cent in Germany and 73 per cent in France.[31] Large relative amounts (38 per cent) put into life insurance and pension funds in the United States account for the high percentage of long-term assets taken there. But if the increase in long-term *liabilities* of households in the form of home mortgages is taken into account, the household sector in the United States is much more liquid in its net position than the above figures would suggest. Mortgage debt is much less common in France and Germany, so the offset of liabilities would not be nearly so great. Moreover, as already noted, the efficiency of U.S. financial markets makes many long-term assets relatively liquid; and policy-holders can typically borrow against their life insurance policies quickly and on fairly favorable terms.

High long-term interest rates in several European countries, notably France, Germany, and Italy, might, in combination with low short-term rates, be taken as an indication of high liquidity preference. But these high rates often reflect a heavily subsidized demand for long-term capital, especially for housing. Thus, high long-term rates greatly overstate the cost of credit to those borrowers who are compensated in the form of subsidies or tax breaks.[32]

[31] U.S. Treasury, *A Description and Analysis of Certain European Capital Markets,* cited, p. 26.

[32] An outstanding example of domestic savings being diverted into particular channels is offered by the German effort to induce home construction. Through a variety of tax privileges, accelerated amortization, and subsidies, the German government encourages new housing, which accounted throughout the 1950s for more than one-fourth of total investment in Germany. The devices used included large premiums paid on savings and loan accounts which

Eliminating the "imperfections" in European capital markets can contribute to lowering long-term rates there and also to reducing the two-way flow of funds across the Atlantic. If more intermediation took place between savers who want liquid assets and borrowers who want long-term funds, and if the costs of issue were greatly reduced, Europeans would be better able to place long-term issues in their domestic markets. But the basic advantages of the American market —its large size and number of participants—would remain. It has even been argued that New York is more likely to provide integration of European capital markets than is any European market.[33] Because of economies of scale in transactions costs and the effects of large scale on increasing liquidity and predictability, the financial market gaining an initial lead will tend to grow at the expense of others.

More integration of international capital markets has probably already taken place than is superficially evident. The large volume of European borrowers *and* lenders in New York has already been noted. Large portfolios of foreign securities are held in Switzerland and Britain, principally by investment trusts, and their activity can best be indicated by the *gross* transactions by foreigners in outstanding securities in the United States. Gross purchases of American stocks by Europeans amounted to nearly $2.0 billion in 1963, for example, compared with net purchases of only $166 million. Britain and Switzerland accounted for roughly three-fourths of the gross purchases; but the Swiss purchases were largely for the accounts of

---

were devoted to housing construction. An estimate for 1955 by Karl Roskamp places the yield to a saver with an annual income of $9,500, taking into account tax privileges and the savings premium, at 8.1 per cent. Interest rates on the mortgages for which such savings were used were substantially lower. Under the circumstances, it is hardly surprising that the typical German saver was not enthusiastic about buying bonds on the market. The tax- and subsidy-induced diversion of savings into mortgages naturally raised long-term interest rates on unsubsidized assets in Germany and made long-term investment abroad correspondingly unattractive. It also impeded the growth of a broad market in bonds, which is required to give long-term securities high liquidity. For a description of the methods used and the sums involved, see Frederick G. Reuss, *Fiscal Policy for Growth Without Inflation, The German Experiment* (Baltimore: The John Hopkins Press, 1963), pp. 113, 196–200, 252.

[33] Charles P. Kindleberger, "European Economic Integration and the Development of a Single Financial Center for Long-Term Capital," *Weltwirtschaftliches Archiv*, Band 90, Heft 2, 1961, pp. 189–210.

others. Gross sales by Europeans of foreign bonds, at nearly $500 million, exceeded net sales by a factor of ten, and again Switzerland and Britain were heavy dealers.[34] The investment trusts balance risk and yield on a wide range of securities from many countries, and their activities should serve not only to keep prices of comparable securities in line in different markets, but also—unless their managers are more prey to market fears than ordinary investors—to keep stock prices in some rough correspondence with the real performance of national economies.[35]

Also, as discussed in the previous chapter, many business firms are becoming more international in their operations, investing and borrowing as well as selling abroad. These firms themselves provide a force for greater integration of national capital markets, since they are typically alert to the possibilities for inexpensive debt financing and are of sufficiently high credit-standing to be able to borrow wherever funds are available.

Finally, the introduction of the interest equalization tax in the United States illustrates the speed with which international flows of funds can adjust to a new disturbance, and this flexibility is itself one measure of the degree to which capital has become more international in outlook. The interest equalization tax was proposed in July 1963 as a measure to deter long-term portfolio capital outflow from the United States, particularly new issues by foreigners, which in 1962 and early 1963 had reached a volume alarming to the American authorities. The tax did not prohibit such outflows, but it made them more costly to the borrowers.[36]

The response to the tax was rapid. Taxable capital outflows dropped very quickly to negligible amounts in 1964, but nontaxable outflows rose to fill the gap. The most substantial increase took the

---

[34] Data on gross transactions by foreigners in foreign and domestic securities can be found in the U.S. *Treasury Bulletin,* monthly.

[35] Except where these international transactions are distorted by differences in tax laws and by the possibilities for tax evasion.

[36] Legally, the American lender was liable for the tax, but in practice the borrower would have to absorb most or all of it, since the after-tax yield would have to be competitive with comparable domestic securities in the United States. For a description and analysis of the interest equalization tax and its effects on the U.S. balance of payments, see Richard N. Cooper, "The Interest Equalization Tax: An Experiment in the Separation of Capital Markets," *Finanzarchiv,* Vol. 24, Fasc. 3, 1965, pp. 447–71.

form of term bank loans to European business firms, with the term usually running from one to three years. Such loans had amounted to less than $100 million a year in 1961 and 1962, but rose to nearly $600 million in 1964. A part of this increase was apparently independent of the tax, but the rapid development of this type of lending was no doubt accelerated by the tax. American banks thus broadened the "domain" of their lending operations in a short period to include normal business loans to European firms of sufficient standing.

A second response was the great expansion of foreign issues in European capital markets. New foreign bond issues in Europe [37] rose from less than $200 million in 1962 to nearly $1.5 billion in 1966 (Table 5–6). This development too was partly independent of the interest equalization tax, but was accelerated by it. Nearly one-fifth of the new foreign issues in Europe in 1964, for instance, were made by Japanese borrowers, normally heavily reliant on the American market. Many other borrowers, including borrowers in Norway, Denmark, and Belgium, were well known in the New York market and very likely would have borrowed there in the absence of the tax.

A significant feature of this sharp rise in foreign bond issues in Europe was the leading role played by issues denominated in U.S. dollars, which in 1966 exceeded $1.2 billion. These issues were typically arranged by some banks and underwriters acting together, usually centered in London but often including continental participation.

The tremendous growth in bond issues in 1965 and 1966 was stimulated by the U.S. voluntary credit restraint program, under which U.S. firms were requested to finance their overseas direct investments as much as possible from foreign sources. As a result, U.S. firms borrowed over $300 million in the European foreign currency bond market in 1965 and about $700 million in 1966. But as the figures of Table 5–6 show, these issues made up less than half the total in those years. It is both interesting and significant that the European foreign currency bond market could handle such a rapid increase in demand, although, to be sure, bond rates were pushed up. Ultimate demand for the bonds is estimated to have come from all over the globe, including over 20 per cent continental Europe (excluding Switzerland), over 15 per cent from the Sterling Area, and half

[37] Excluding issues of the Sterling Area in Britain and of the Franc Area countries in France.

from Switzerland acting largely as a conduit for funds from elsewhere. About 10 per cent of the funds could be identified as having come from the United States and Canada.[38]

Thus in the mid-1960s, and partly as a consequence of U.S. policies, a European market began to play the same role as entrepôt for funds which New York had played earlier. The same considerations that had made the New York market attractive to both European borrowers and lenders made dollar bonds attractive in Europe; dollar issues could command wider participation, hence a wider market, even with New York temporarily inhibited in its foreign lending.[39]

TABLE 5–6   New Foreign Currency Issues
on European Bond Market
($ million)

	Denominated in			With Currency Option	Total
	U.S. Dollars	Other Currencies	Units of Account		
1957–62	—	—	10	174	184
1963	103	29	48	—	180
1964	483	92	10	44	629
1965	627	353	—	136	1,116
1966	1,200	196	76	20	1,492

Source: David Williams, "Foreign Currency Issues in European Security Markets," IMF, *Staff Papers,* May 1967, p. 54.

The Impact of International Financial Integration on Economic Policy

The degree to which national money and capital markets have been integrated with one another should not be exaggerated. Many impediments to international capital movements, both pyschological and institutional, still exist. But the potential integration already present should not be underrated either. National short-term interest rates

[38] David Williams, "Foreign Currency Issues in European Security Markets," IMF, *Staff Papers,* May 1967, p. 61.

[39] It is worth mentioning two other developments in European capital mar-

seem to have converged somewhat toward a common mean, and the covariation among them seems to have increased (Figure 5–3). The notable exceptions to this covariation occurred during periods of exchange crisis (the United Kingdom in 1961 and 1964, Canada in 1962), at which times expected changes in exchange-rate parities swamped other considerations and forward rates were at heavy discounts.

To the extent that integration of money and capital markets does occur, national monetary and credit policies are weakened. In the hypothetical limit, if all money markets were fully unified, it would be impossible for any small country alone to use monetary policy in pursuit of domestic objectives. It could control neither its money supply nor its level of interest rates. An attempt to curtail domestic demand by raising interest rates would simply invite an inflow of capital from abroad, vitiating the restrictive policy. Similarly, an attempt to ease money would stimulate capital outflow, not domestic demand. Under these circumstances monetary policy could be used to influence the balance of payments; a country could "finance" a deficit by tightening credit at home in order to induce an inflow of funds from abroad. But monetary policy could not be used by national authorities in pursuit of full employment, price stability, or economic growth.[40]

kets which represented efforts to "internationalize" them. The first is the "unit of account" bond, denominated in a composite of European currencies equivalent to one U.S. dollar. This type of bond is designed to protect lenders against currency devaluations, but not against a rise in the price of gold. The first such bond was issued for $5 million in 1961, and in 1961–64 a total of $68 million in unit of account bonds were issued in Europe. The arrangements were made largely by banks in Belgium and Luxembourg.

The second development is the so-called parallel loan, whereby a single issue is made simultaneously in several different capital markets, with the issue price adjusted to meet the requirements of each market. The first such issue was made by an Italian organization in 1965. For an analysis of these and other methods for integrating European capital markets, see Claudio Segré, "Foreign Bond Issues in European Markets," *Banca Nazionale del Lavoro Quarterly Review,* March 1964, pp. 43–87.

The unit of account loan was given a fillip when the ECSC issued $20 million of such bonds in early 1966. But neither of these techniques has enjoyed wide popularity.

[40] For a theoretical exposition of the effects of monetary policy under fixed exchange rates with freedom of international capital movements, see Marcus Fleming, "Domestic Financial Policies Under Fixed and Under Floating Exchange Rates," IMF, *Staff Papers,* November 1962, pp. 369–80; also R. A.

FIG. 5.3.

Short-Term Rates for U.S., U.K., Canada, France, Germany, Belgium, Netherlands, and Switzerland
1958-1967

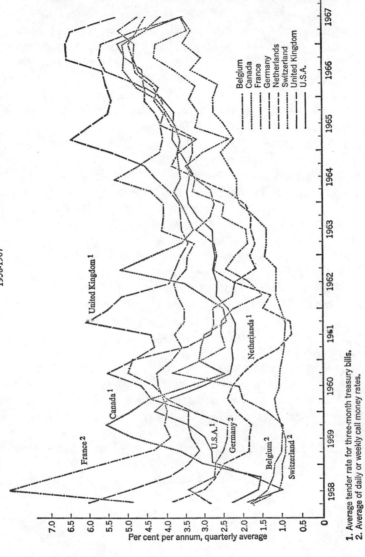

1. Average tender rate for three-month treasury bills.
2. Average of daily or weekly call money rates.
Source: IMF, International Financial Statistics.

In addition to weakening the impact of monetary policy on domestic economic objectives, higher integration of international money and capital markets subjects countries more readily to monetary disturbances from outside, arising either from misguided or deliberate monetary action by other countries or from sudden and unpredictable movements of funds for reasons other than differences in yield.

Despite the distance which remains between the present state of affairs and complete integration of capital markets, the tendency of integration to weaken, or to inhibit, domestic monetary policy can already be observed. In the recession of 1960–61, for example, the United States held short-term interest rates well above the level which domestic conditions required, quite explicitly for balance-of-payments reasons. Treasury bill rates were not permitted to fall below 2¼ per cent, despite declines to below 1 per cent in previous recessions of even less severity. Lower interest rates would have stimulated an even larger outflow of capital than took place. In the ensuing recovery, bill rates rose gradually to nearly 3.4 per cent in mid-1964, despite the presence of unemployment unacceptably high to the political party in power. When British interest rates were raised sharply in November 1964, pulling up Eurodollar rates, the U.S. discount rate was increased, money was tightened, and Treasury bill rates rose sharply from 3.6 per cent to 3.9 per cent, again explicitly for balance-of-payments reasons.

A second illustration of the influence of international capital movements on domestic monetary policy, of the opposite kind, is provided by Germany in 1960. To restrain a vigorous domestic boom, German monetary authorities permitted short-term interest rates to rise from 2 per cent in the summer of 1959 to 5 per cent in the third quarter of 1960. This increase coincided with a sharp increase in interest rates in Britain, but it also coincided with a sharp decline in U.S. interest rates. The flow of funds into Germany, mostly from the United States but also from Switzerland and other members of the EEC, was staggering. Over $1 billion in foreign funds flowed into Germany in the second and third quarters of 1960, compared with only $100 million in the corresponding period of 1959. At that time the total German money supply was the equivalent of about $11 billion. The German

Mundell, "Capital Mobility and Stabilization Policy under Fixed and Flexible Exchange Rates," *Canadian Journal of Economics and Political Science,* XXIX, November 1963, pp. 475–85.

authorities reluctantly abandoned their policy of tight money, and by the end of 1961 German short-term rates had declined to below 2 per cent. At the same time, as already noted, the American authorities prevented short-term interest rates from falling to their usual recession lows. In its annual report for 1960, the German Bundesbank observed that "the more the domestic interest-rate level rose, and the more individual credit institutions were forced to observe restraint in granting credit, the greater recourse to foreign sources of funds became. . . . In these circumstances the Bundesbank found occasion in the autumn of 1960 to revise its credit policy, and to go more by the needs of the balance-of-payments position, even though the domestic business cycle remained in a phase of boom. . . . The experiences of last year have shown clearly that one cannot keep internal economic activity within bounds through a restrictive credit policy so long as the balance of payments . . . shows large surpluses." [41] Both countries, in 1960, had been gearing monetary policy to domestic requirements, and in the following period both countries had to give greater cognizance to the international flows of funds resulting from divergences in national monetary policies.

In view of the increasing constraints which freedom of international capital movements places on autonomous national monetary policy, it is not surprising that several countries have retained their extensive system of exchange controls over portfolio capital movements, while others have groped toward new, more selective instruments of monetary and foreign exchange policy. Some are designed to restrict capital outflow, while others are directed at limiting capital inflows. Both kinds of measure serve to insulate domestic money and capital markets from foreign influence. The devices range from taxes and prohibitions on certain types of capital outflow and voluntary restraints on foreign lending to prohibition of interest payments to foreigners, special reserve requirements for deposits by foreigners, and taxes on interest earnings by foreigners. In addition, some countries have encouraged capital outflow in order to reduce domestic liquidity and give restrictive monetary policy greater effectiveness on domestic activity. Illustrations of all these practices are numerous.

The Netherlands, for instance, allows foreign issues on its capital market only if domestic and balance-of-payments conditions permit

[41] *Report of the Deutsche Bundesbank for the Year 1960* (Frankfurt a/M, 1961), pp. 41, 47.

it, and it limits the ability of its banks to accept or make deposits in foreign banks. Switzerland, which unlike other European countries has preserved currency convertibility for residents as well as nonresidents throughout the postwar period, severely limits foreign issues on its capital market, and thereby has preserved relatively low interest rates on issues floated there. The Swiss government protested vigorously when, in 1964, Denmark floated an issue denominated in Swiss francs through a consortium of London banks, for it viewed the move as a threat to its own control over capital issues.

To limit capital outflow in the face of expansionary monetary policy for domestic reasons, the United States in 1963 imposed its interest equalization tax on American purchases of stocks and bonds from other industrial countries,[42] and in early 1965 it inaugurated a program of "voluntary credit restraint" under which banks would limit their new lending to foreigners in 1965 to a given per cent of the claims outstanding at the end of 1964, and within that total would give preference to export financing and to loans to less-developed countries. Corporations and non-bank financial institutions were also asked to cut back their overseas lending, and firms were encouraged to borrow abroad for their overseas operations. These programs were extended in subsequent years.

Switzerland (in 1960), Germany (in 1961), and France (in 1963) prohibited payment of interest on foreign deposits in domestic currencies in domestic banks, in order to discourage an inflow of short-term capital.[43]

[42] The interest equalization tax was actually passed into law in September 1964, but it was retroactive to July 1963. Canada was exempt from its provisions under special arrangements, and in early 1965 Japan was given an exemption on $100 million of new borrowing.

In 1965 the United Kingdom also placed a "tax" on the outflow of investment funds. Previously, Britishers wishing to invest abroad could do so through the "security dollar" market by paying a market-determined premium on the dollar which varied in practice from 1 to 12 per cent. In 1965, investors were required to sell to the Bank of England, at the official exchange rate, a quarter of the proceeds from sales of foreign assets; and all those undertaking direct investment abroad were required to buy the necessary currency through the security dollar market, thus paying the premium, which increased sharply under the pressure of this new demand.

[43] The inflow of capital into Switzerland has been attracted not so much by high deposit rates there as by the security and anonymity which Swiss banking practices offer and occasionally by speculation on an upward revaluation of

Finally, as mentioned, both the German and the Italian central banks have on occasion encouraged the large-scale export of short-term capital by offering attractive forward exchange rates to their commercial banks; these attractive rates served both to raise the yield, measured in domestic currency, on foreign assets and to provide cover against exchange risk. In a world of high international mobility of capital, this kind of instrument may offer a more powerful influence on domestic monetary conditions than might open market operations in domestic securities. But as noted above, there are limits to the manipulation of forward exchange rates.

The number and variety of selective measures to insulate domestic credit markets from international capital flows had reached the point where the Bank for International Settlements (BIS) could report that "as a general rule, the inflows of funds prompted by domestic monetary tightness [in 1964] do not appear to have undermined credit restraint to any great extent. All countries now have at their disposal various selective controls or techniques which they use from time to time to regulate capital movements and hence bank liquidity." [44] An additional reason for the effectiveness of national monetary policy in restraining credit, however, is that *all* of the industrial countries were restraining credit and raising interest rates in 1964, some of them to limit capital outflow. Indeed, interest rates in most industrial countries rose very sharply in 1965 and 1966, reaching levels in several countries not experienced since the 1920s,[45] and led to a dramatic meeting of finance ministers in early 1967 to achieve a coordinated reduction in interest rates.

To judge from their behavior, national governments are evidently reluctant to accept the consequences of integrated capital and money markets. Countries with deficient domestic demand do not want to give up monetary policy as a measure for stimulating output and employment, while countries with inflationary pressures have been unwilling to abandon monetary policy as a restraining device.

Governments have been partially but not wholly successful in their attempt to preserve some domestic autonomy in matters of monetary

---

the Swiss franc. But prohibition of interest payments increased the opportunity cost of holding an anonymous Swiss account.

[44] BIS, *Thirty-Fifth Annual Report,* cited, p. 45.

[45] U.S. Treasury bill rates reached 5.4 per cent in October 1966, and 3-month Eurodollar rates exceeded 7 per cent.

policy. Funds are fungible. So long as some capital movements are permitted, domestic credit conditions will be linked to some extent. Both unimpeded direct investment and the Eurodollar market—even if its lending were limited to foreign trade—would afford investors and borrowers the opportunity to vary their placement of funds or their source of funds according to credit conditions. It is the marginal borrower and the marginal lender who determine interest rates, and the existence of alternative (external) sources of funds or alternative (external) investment opportunities will influence these marginal transactions.

So long as some links do exist, a question of key importance to economic policy is: how does the level and structure of interest rates get determined for the community of nations as a whole?

This question cannot be answered simply. The level of interest rates in a community of interdependent nations apparently making their own decisions depends closely on the level and distribution of international reserves and on provision for extending international credit to countries in deficit. If reserves are low (or if countries are unwilling to use the reserves they have), and if provision for international credit is meager, then the level of interest rates will have an upward bias to it. Any country which raises interest rates for domestic purposes or to induce an inflow of funds from abroad will tend to force other countries to raise their rates in self-defense. But the process is not symmetrical. Each country will hesitate to lower its interest rates for fear of precipitating an outflow of funds. Exceptions to these generalizations arise when a country with a weak balance-of-payments position raises its rates, or a country with a momentarily strong position lowers them, thereby, in each case, inducing equilibrating flows of funds. In general, however, the situation is closely analogous to an oligopolistic industry with high interaction among decisions leading to a "kinked" demand curve facing each firm. Raising prices will lead to a great loss of sales to competitors, but lowering prices will simply induce competitors to lower their prices too. Lowering interest rates will lead to capital outflow, but raising them will induce neighboring countries to do likewise. Under these circumstances collusion on monetary policy is a natural (and in this case desirable) outcome. Otherwise the community of nations runs some risk of ending up, through a process of action followed by defensive reaction, with a level of interest rates which is inimical to the domestic policy objectives of *all* of its members.

If international reserves or liberal lines of credit are available to countries, however, the links between national interest rates will be looser and the risk of self-defeating defensive tightening of credit is correspondingly reduced. It is true that reserves or lines of credits will eventually be exhausted if a country persists in pursuing a much easier monetary policy than its neighbors (or if a large country pursues a much tighter monetary policy than other countries do). But the existence of ample liquidity will give countries a breathing space which at least affords monetary authorities the time and possibility of reducing rates in the hope that their neighbors will also do so.

CHAPTER SIX

National Economic Policy in an Interdependent World Economy

During the past decade there has been a strong trend toward economic interdependence among the industrial countries. This growing interdependence makes the successful pursuit of national economic objectives much more difficult. Broadly speaking, increasing interdependence complicates the successful pursuit of national economic objectives in three ways. First, it increases the number and magnitude of the disturbances to which each country's balance of payments is subjected, and this in turn diverts policy attention and instruments of policy to the restoration of external balance. Second, it slows down the process by which national authorities, each acting on its own, are able to reach domestic objectives. Third, the response to greater integration can involve the community of nations in counteracting motions which leave all countries worse off than they need be. These difficulties are in turn complicated by the fact that the objective of greater economic integration involves international agreements which reduce the number of policy instruments available to national authorities for pursuit of their economic objectives. This chapter touches on all of these facets of higher economic interdependence among industrial nations, both as fact and as objective, but its principal focus is on the third complication—the process of mutually damaging competition among national policies.

The three preceding chapters attempt to show that both institutional and economic changes have increased economic interdependence among the industrial countries since the late 1940s. Import quotas in industrial countries have been virtually abolished on trade

148

in manufactured products; tariffs have been reduced; and transportation costs have fallen relative to the value of goods. At the same time, the accumulation of capital and the spread of technology have made national economies more similar in their basic characteristics of production; comparative cost differences have apparently narrowed, suggesting that imports can be replaced by domestic production with less loss in national income than heretofore. Whether a country imports a particular good or exports it thus becomes less dependent on the basic characteristics of the economy, more dependent on historical development and on relatively accidental and transitory features of recent investment decisions at home and abroad. An invention in one country may lead to production there for export, but the new product will relatively quickly be produced abroad—or supplanted by a still newer product—and possibly even exported to the original innovating country.

Enlargement of the decision-making domain of the world's great producing firms results in the rapid movement of capital and technical knowledge across national frontiers, thereby contributing to the narrowing of comparative cost differences; but their activity will also quicken the speed with which trade adjusts to new sales opportunities because they have direct knowledge of foreign markets and access to distribution channels.[1]

Monetary disturbances, too, are likely to be much more quickly translated into changes in the volume of exports and imports than they were formerly. Under fixed exchange rates, greater than average monetary inflation in one country will invite a more rapid deterioration in the balance on goods and services than was true in the past.

Finally, as financial markets become more closely integrated, relatively small differences in yields on securities will induce large flows of funds between countries. Banks will increasingly number "foreign" firms among their prime customers; the advantages of inexpensive credit to firms in countries with ample savings and well-functioning financial markets, such as the United States, will be shared increasingly with firms elsewhere.

All these changes in the characteristics of the international economy during the past decade—and it should be emphasized again that economic integration is still far from complete—are crucial to the

[1] A quick response assumes the absence of collusive agreements on prices, market-sharing, and the like.

functioning of the international payments system and the autonomy which it permits in the formation of national economic policy. These changes mean that in normal periods prospective imbalances in international payments—imbalances that would arise if countries did not respond to reduce them or did not adjust policy measures to forestall them—are likely to be more frequent and of larger amplitude than they have been in the past. "Disturbances" arising from new innovations, from generous wage settlements leading to price increases, and from excess or deficient domestic demand will affect the balance of payments more perceptibly. Whether or not imbalances also last longer depends upon the relationship among the "disturbances"; if they are well distributed among countries and tend equally toward deficit or surplus, the duration of imbalances may well be less than in the past; otherwise it may be longer.

These changes suggest that prospective balance-of-payments difficulties are likely to be more common, and that they will worsen as the structural changes continue in their recent trend. By the same token, however, correction of imbalances in international payments should be easier in the future. Trade flows will respond more sharply to small "disturbances"; but the flows should also respond more quickly to policy measures designed to influence them. If a small relative increase in the price level will lead it into greater balance-of-payments difficulties than before, a relatively small decrease should undo the difficulties. Similarly, international capital flows will respond more readily to small differences in national credit conditions; but small differences in national credit conditions directed to correcting the imbalance can induce equilibrating flows of capital. Thus if the national authorities can recognize disturbances early, are willing to use some of the tools at their disposal for correcting imbalances in international payments, and can act reasonably quickly in doing so, then the increased sensitivity of payments to various disturbances need cause no undue difficulty, provided that policy instruments are properly chosen and adequately coordinated among countries.

Interdependence before 1914

There is a natural inclination to compare the international economy of today, especially in the claim that it is becoming more integrated, with the international economy before 1914, when, it is often said, the world economy was highly integrated. In the four decades before World War I, most of the major countries were customarily on the gold standard (implying fixed exchange rates), capital was free to move into or out of most countries, trade was impeded only by comparatively moderate tariffs, and quotas were generally absent. Even labor was generally free to migrate from country to country without visas, security checks, and immigration quotas.

In one important sense, however, the comparison is not at all apt. Today national governments are much more ambitious about the objectives of national economic policy than they were in the nineteenth century. As noted in Chapter 2, governments have taken on the responsibility for assuring high levels of employment and, increasingly, a rapid rate of growth; and they attempt actively to influence the allocation of resources and the distribution of income to a much greater degree. These new tasks place greater burdens on the available instruments of policy. Before 1914, by contrast, preoccupation with "defending the currency" was dominant, and the (admittedly more limited) policy instruments at hand were more willingly devoted to that end.[2] Thus, the intrusions of international economic integration on national economic policy was more readily accepted because national economic policy was far less ambitious in its aims

In addition to this important difference, economic relations among industrial countries are probably potentially much closer today than they were even before 1914, despite the characteristics of the pre-1914 world noted above. True, British and French capital moved overseas readily and British investors built railroads around the world. The proportion of Britain's annual savings which went abroad was, in fact, staggering by modern standards.[3] Nonetheless, communications were far less perfect than they are today and foreign investors ran greater commercial risks arising from imperfect knowledge (except in the case of colonial bonds that in effect had the sponsorship of the home government).

Despite the freedom of capital to move, it did not in fact move in

[2] Between 1880 and 1913, for instance, the British Bank Rate was changed 195 times—once every two months on average—and largely to protect the Bank of England's reserves.

[3] A. K. Cairncross, *Home and Foreign Investment, 1870–1913* (Cambridge: Cambridge University Press, 1953), pp. 104–6, estimates that in 1907 no less than 40 per cent of British national saving went to foreign investment.

sufficient volume even to erase differences in short-term interest rates. Over the period 1876–1914, short-term interest rates in New York averaged more than one percentage point higher than corresponding rates in London, and there was only a weak correspondence in movement between short-term rates in the two financial centers. Short-term interest rates in London and Paris were much closer together and the correspondence in their movement was higher but still far from perfect. Long-term interest rates showed similar divergence in their levels and movement. Response to new investment opportunities, when it came at all, was often slow.[4]

While tariffs were generally low, barriers to trade in the form of transportation costs were very substantial, although they declined sharply after the introduction of the ocean steamship. Large differences in comparative costs meant trade was socially very profitable, but the composition and level of trade was correspondingly less sensitive to small changes in costs, prices, and quality. Finally, business organizations, far from being international, became truly national corporations in the United States only with the approach of World War I, and the process was even slower in many European countries.

Thus, the integration of the pre-1914 world economy was something of an illusion. While the pre-1914 world was integrated in the sense that government-imposed barriers to the movement of goods, capital and people were minimal,[5] those imposed by nature were much greater and economic integration was not high in the sense used here: quick responsiveness to differential earning opportunities resulting in a sharp reduction in differences in factor rewards.

[4] See Oskar Morgenstern, *International Financial Transactions and Business Cycles* (Princeton: Princeton University Press, 1959), for an exhaustive study of interest rate movements in the 19th century. The correlation coefficient between monthly averages of the commercial paper rate in New York and the open market discount rate in London was only +.45; the correlation between open market discount rates in London and Paris was +.67. Same, p. 109.

Morgenstern considers it "remarkable" that such permanent differences could be maintained for hundreds of months; "the interaction of all these highly organized money and capital markets and the vast flows of funds back and forth was not strong enough to overcome fundamental institutional and risk differences." Same, p. 470.

[5] This is the definition Balassa used in his *The Theory of Economic Integration,* cited, p. 1.

Countries today are gradually entering a new environment, not merely returning to a condition that once existed. They confront new problems arising from the combination of more ambitious national and international economic objectives and a potentially higher degree of economic interdependence than has ever existed before. How are they to maintain international equilibrium under a regime of fixed exchange rates and at the same time achieve their national objectives? We return to the central problem posed in Chapter 1. It is now necessary to specify more precisely how conflicts may arise and to indicate some of the ways in which governments have responded to those conflicts.

Economic Objectives and Policy Instruments

A well known proposition in the theory of economic policy requires that the number of policy instruments be at least as great as the number of objectives (target variables) if all objectives are to be achieved.[6] If the number of instruments is fewer than the number of targets, it will not be possible to reach all of the targets; in that case at least some targets must be given up, and the authorities must choose among them.[7]

[6] A useful framework for the discussion of economic policy has been provided by the Dutch economist, Jan Tinbergen. He draws distinctions among three types of economic variables: target variables, instrument variables, and data. Target variables are those to the values of which we attach some social importance *per se*, e.g., unemployment or the growth in per capita income. Instrument variables, or policy instruments, are those which the public authorities can manipulate directly in order to influence the target variables. Data are the other economic variables which influence the target variables. If an economy starts from a position "on target," that is, with all of its target variables where the authorities want them, then changes in the data are "disturbances" and call for some adjustment in the policy instruments in order to restore the desired values of the target variables. See J. Tinbergen, *On the Theory of Economic Policy* (Amsterdam: North Holland Publishing Co., 1952); and *Economic Policy: Principles and Design* (Amsterdam: North Holland Publishing Co., 1956).

[7] In general, it will be desirable to have more instruments than there are targets. This is especially true where the relationships between instruments and targets are not well known. More often than not, policy-makers are quite confident about the *direction* in which a given change in a policy instrument will affect the target variables, but they are not at all confident about the extent of

A simple example can illustrate the need to have at least as many instruments as targets. Suppose the government of an isolated country has two economic objectives: it would like to assure full employment of its labor force at all times, and it would like its national product to grow at a specified rate each year. It can vary the over-all size of the budget deficit or surplus (fiscal policy) to assure full employment. But full employment of resources can be met with a variety of combinations of investment, consumption, and government expenditure. Without some other instrument, the desired growth rate cannot be assured. If, however, investment is stimulated by a low rate of interest and higher investment leads to more growth, then monetary policy and fiscal policy together can be manipulated to achieve the two objectives. The higher the growth rate desired, the lower should be the rate of interest. Fiscal policy can then be adjusted to assure full employment. This very simple model apparently influenced thinking in the early years of the Kennedy administration.

Viewing economic policy as a problem in specifying targets and finding sufficient instruments to reach them helps to illuminate many policy problems confronting national authorities. It was noted in Chapter 1 that the objective of greater economic integration has led many officials to reject both flexible exchange rates and frequent variations in fixed exchange rates as instruments for maintaining balance-of-payments equilibrium. A number of other instruments of policy have been ruled out by international agreement on the same grounds, or on the grounds that their use was likely to lead to retaliation and counter-retaliation that would leave countries worse off than they were at the outset. Most types of export subsidy, tariff discrimination among countries, increases in tariffs, and discriminatory exchange regulations fall into this category. A number of provisions of the GATT are devoted to these exclusions and prohibi-

---

the influence. This may be due to simple ignorance about an economy with fairly stable structural relationships, or it may be due to a rapid change in the structure of the economy.

In the presence of this uncertainty, it is desirable to have as many policy instruments as possible. None of them will be superfluous, for all can help to keep the target variables as close as possible to their targets. Each instrument variable should be used in proportion to the confidence held in its relationship to the target variables. For a formal analysis of this problem, see William C. Brainard, "Uncertainty and the Effectiveness of Economic Policy," *American Economic Review,* LVII, May 1967, pp. 411–25.

tions; with specified exceptions, such as the formation of customs unions or free trade areas, trade discrimination is proscribed,[8] as are many types of export subsidies and discrimination in domestic taxation between home and foreign goods. The IMF Articles of Agreement make similar prohibitions with respect to currency arrangements. As noted in Chapter 2, the extensive use of these measures in the past, especially in the 1930s, led to widespread retaliation and mutual recriminations, and they acquired a bad name among outward-looking officials. But the price of international rules of good behavior as set forth in the GATT and the IMF Articles has been a reduction in the range of instruments available to national policy-makers.[9]

Some policy instruments may be used, as a practical matter, only within a limited range. In the United States, changes in the discount rate of the Federal Reserve System and (since 1962) deliberate deficits or surpluses in the government budget are both regarded as legitimate tools of economic policy; but in normal times the public is not likely to countenance a discount rate of 20 per cent or a budget deficit of $50 billion. These exceed the range of acceptability; policy instruments have "boundary conditions." In the abnormal situations when such limits become operative, an instrument is withdrawn from use. Sometimes these limits are not fully known until they are tested; then we discover that we have more targets (or fewer instruments) than were previously apparent.

It goes without saying that to be attainable, economic objectives must be consistent. If they are not consistent, no number of policy instruments will suffice to reach the objectives. One illustration in the forefront of discussion in most industrial countries involves the relationship between employment and price stability. Given the institution of private collective bargaining, is the target of "full employment" (4 per cent unemployment in the United States, under 2 per

[8] Trade discrimination is also permitted, under Article XIV of the GATT, when currency discrimination is permitted under IMF rules, i.e. when the IMF declares a particular country's currency "scarce" under its scarce currency clause. As noted in Chapter 2, no such finding has ever been made, even during the period of severe dollar shortage of the late 1940s.

[9] Freedom to use some of these instruments may in any case have been more apparent than real. As noted below, export subsidies in one country raise exports only if other exporting countries refrain from using them, or if importing countries do not offset them with higher duties. But that is precisely what happened in the interwar period.

cent in the United Kingdom, according to the standards and definitions accepted by each) consistent with "price stability," defined, say, as stability in the consumer price index? Many economists would find a conflict.

This kind of inconsistency can perhaps be overcome by developing new policy instruments.[10] Another kind of inconsistency, especially important to national economies linked through international trade and capital movements, cannot be eliminated through the development of new instruments. Examples are objectives regarding the balance of payments and the trade balance. Since one country's trade surplus is another country's trade deficit, it is impossible for all countries to succeed in running trade surpluses. The same is true for balance of payments, taking into account capital movements.[11] If there are n countries, only $n - 1$ of them can succeed in reaching their independent balance-of-payments targets; [12] at least one must accept defeat or else fail to target values for its trade position and its balance-of-payments position, thereby acting as an international residual. It has been suggested that the United States played this role until the late 1950s, by taking a relatively passive position toward its payments position after the termination of Marshall Plan aid.[13]

The requirement of consistency is not merely theoretical. In 1962, for instance, all of the major industrial countries wanted simultaneously to improve their payments positions on current account.

[10] These new instruments would involve shifting the trade-off between unemployment and price inflation—called the Phillips Curve—enough to make simultaneous attainment of the two objectives feasible. This is the thrust of "incomes policies."

[11] This assumes that national *definitions* concerning the balance of payments are all consistent, and abstracts from the additional complications created by disparate national definitions of balance-of-payments "deficit" and "surplus." See Poul Høst-Madsen, "Asymmetries Between Balance of Payments Surpluses and Deficits," IMF, *Staff Papers,* July 1962, pp. 182–201.

[12] Unless, of course, the targets all happen to be consistent, e.g., if the sum of all balance-of-payments targets happened to add to the annual addition to monetary gold stocks.

[13] J. J. Polak, "International Coordination of Economic Policy," IMF, *Staff Papers,* July 1962, p. 199. The ability of the United States to take a passive position ended around 1959, when the deficit became very large and foreign officials began to call for correction. One interpretation which can be put on the international discussions to establish machinery for creating international liquidity (see Chapter 8) is that it represents a search for a new residual supplier in the international payments system.

While mutual success was logically possible in this case, it did imply a correspondingly sharp deterioration in the current account position of the less developed countries taken together, which in turn would require ample financing from the industrial countries in the form of grants or loans. No such increase in capital outflows was targeted. Thus, national targets were inconsistent.[14]

The Speed of Adjustment

In summary, successful economic policy requires an adequate number of policy instruments for the number of economic objectives, and it requires that these objectives be consistent with one another. If either of these conditions fails, policy-makers are bound to be frustrated in their efforts. Before turning to how these frustrations become manifest, however, one further point should be made: growing interdependence can slow down greatly the process by which independently acting national authorities reach their economic objectives, even when all the targets are consistent and there are sufficient policy instruments at hand to reach them. Thus, in practice, nations may find themselves farther from their objectives than would be true with less interdependence.

High interdependence slows the speed of adjustment to disturbances if national policy-makers do not take the interdependence into account. This is because the economic authorities in one country may be working at cross purposes with those in another. An investment boom in one country may raise interest rates both at home and, by attracting internationally mobile funds, in neighboring countries. The first country may temporarily welcome the high interest rates to help curb the boom and may also tighten fiscal policy to keep inflationary pressures in check. But other countries may fear that higher interest rates will deter investment at home and take steps to lower interest rates. Unless this monetary relaxation is taken into account in framing fiscal policy in the first country, its authorities will find that fiscal policy has not been sufficiently contractionary. But more contractionary fiscal policy will tend to hold interest rates up, so that the monetary authorities in the neighboring countries will find they have

[14] Triffin has underlined the dramatic inconsistencies in balance-of-payments targets in the early 1960s. See Robert Triffin, *The World Money Maze* (New Haven: Yale University Press, 1966), pp. 118–32.

only been partially successful in lowering their rates. Even if in the end the whole process settles to a point where the various national authorities are satisfied, it will have taken longer than if there had been close coordination between the authorities in the several countries involved. The greater the interactions between the countries, the longer convergence will take if countries act solely on their own.

Sometimes, of course, actions in a neighboring country can reinforce those taken at home. If in the above example the domestic investment boom transmitted inflationary pressures to a neighboring country through enlarged imports, then contractionary fiscal policy there will complement contractionary fiscal policy at home. But in this case failure to take into account the interactions between the two countries may lead to *over*-correction and excessive unemployment. This will arise if the authorities in each country decide how much they have to act when acting alone to restore equilibrium; then when both countries act, the total effect will be excessive.

If policy decisions are truly decentralized among nations, in the sense that the authorities in each nation pursue only their own objectives with their own instruments without taking into account the interactions with other countries, then the more interdependent the international economy is, the less successful countries are likely to be in reaching and maintaining their economic objectives. This is due to the greater impact of domestic measures on foreign economies, calling forth correspondingly greater offsetting responses which in turn affect the first country. Under these circumstances, countries must either reconcile themselves to prolonged delays in reaching their objectives or they must coordinate their policies more closely with those of other nations.[15]

[15] These ideas are complex and are best stated somewhat more formally in a technical footnote.

In matrix notation, let $y = Ax$ describe the relationship between target variables (y) and small changes in policy instruments (x). The matrix $A = [a_{ij}]$, where a_{ij} indicates the impact of instrument x_j on target y_i. Arrange the variables so that all the targets and instruments of one country are grouped together, followed by those of another, etc. A can thus be partitioned, with blocks representing individual countries running along the diagonal, and blocks representing the degree of interdependence, or interaction between the instruments of one country and targets of another, lying off the block diagonal.

Suppose that the vector y^* represents the target values the economic authorities of the various countries would like to reach, that the targets are all

It has, of course, long been true that small countries must watch closely economic developments and policies in their larger neighbors and take those developments into account. For the Netherlands, forecasting German GNP and German economic policies is a critical component to forecasting Dutch GNP. But as economies grow more interdependent, the importance of *two*-way interactions increases, so that economically large countries such as Britain, Germany, and even the United States must increasingly take into account developments and *policies* abroad.

---

consistent, and that there are enough policy instruments to reach them all, giving the authorities the correct values for these instruments, $x = A^{-1}y^*$.

Suppose now that the target variables take on values different from their targets. How do the authorities react? Their reaction functions might be described by the following set of differential equations,

$$\frac{dx}{dt} = B(y^* - y) = B(y^* - Ax),$$

which says that the authorities change their instruments at a rate which depends on how far the target variables are from their targets. If they do not take into account international interdependence, B, the matrix of reaction coefficients, will be a block diagonal matrix, indicating that national policy-makers look only at their own target(s).

The solution to this system of linear differential equations takes the form:

$$y_i(t) = y_i^* + \sum_j K_{ij} e^{-\lambda_j t}$$

where the λ_j are the characteristic roots of BA and the K_{ij} are constants determined by A and by the initial disturbances. For a policy system which works in the sense that $y_i(t)$ will gradually approach y_i^*, the second term on the right is transitory. The system will be more efficient, i.e. achieve the policy targets more rapidly after any disturbance, the more rapidly this term fades away. It will fade more rapidly the larger are the λ_j.

In general, the larger the off-diagonal elements are relative to the diagonal elements; i.e. the higher the degree of ignored interdependence, the smaller the smallest root will be and the longer it will take after any given disturbance to reach the target values y^*. High interdependence which is ignored gives rise to the possibility of overshooting targets several times (the roots are complex), and it even gives rise to the theoretical possibility that targets will not be reached at all until the nature of the adjustment process is changed.

Coordinating economic policy involves not only exchanging information on targets and use of instruments, but taking this information into account when using instruments. Convergence to targets is then much faster. For a fuller exposition of this and other points concerning the theory of economic policy in an international setting, see R. N. Cooper, "Economic Policy Adjustment in Interdependent Economies," *Quarterly Journal of Economics* (forthcoming).

International Competition in Economic Policy

In an interdependent economy, governments do not have full control over the instrument variables needed to influence the trade balance or the balance of payments. Each government can affect the domestic interest rate in an attempt to influence international capital movements or can set tariffs on imports and subsidies on exports to influence the trade balance. But success in influencing capital movements or trade flows depends on what other countries are doing. It is interest rate *differentials,* not the absolute level of interest rates, which induce the movement of capital. And it is domestic tariffs *less* foreign subsidies which influence the level of imports. There are many instruments of economic policy for which relative differences affect international transactions, but the absolute value may continue to exert a strong influence on purely domestic decisions. This is true, for example, not only of short- and long-term interest rates, but also of liberal tax benefits to investment, generous depreciation allowances, lax regulation of corporate activities and a host of other measures designed to influence corporate location. It is also true of foreign trade: generous credit arrangements or credit-risk guarantees for exports may encourage total exports without improving the trade balance if other countries are pursuing similar measures.

This feature of policy instruments—that the absolute level of the instrument may have important effects domestically, but that only the level relative to that in other countries influences the balance of trade or payments—raises the question: where do the values of these instruments finally settle? International capital movements between two otherwise isolated countries will presumably be roughly the same whether interest rates are at 7 per cent in one and 5 per cent in the other or at 4 per cent in the first country and 2 per cent in the second.[16] In each case, the differential is two percentage points. But what determines whether "community" interest rates settle at the higher level or the lower one? The effects on other objectives may be very different. Economic growth will be inhibited more in the first case than in the second.

This would be of secondary importance if all countries had many

---

[16] This must be qualified to the extent that interest rates influence total savings differently in the two countries.

policy instruments at their disposal. Each country could compensate for any deleterious effects on domestic objectives arising from the value of instruments determined predominantly by the community as a whole. But as we already noted, the number of instruments and the range of values they can assume are often sharply limited by tradition or law. Indeed, it is highly likely that at any point in time a country will have as its disposal *only* the minimum number of policy instruments that it needs to satisfy important domestic political demands. Policy instruments affect the welfare of particular members of the community as well as national economic objectives. Governments are therefore unlikely to have a surplus of instruments at their disposal. Public expectation is that certain measures, while theoretically conceivable, will in practice not be used. Any attempt to invoke them, therefore, meets stiff resistance.[17]

The values that policy instruments take on in the community of nations, and the process by which those values are reached, are of strong interest to the individual nations. They may not have sufficient domestic flexibility to offset the damaging effects of policy instruments that are forced to an inappropriate level by international competition among governments. As a result, greater international integration can force choices among national objectives, all of which might otherwise be attainable.

There are situations in which most or even all members of the international community will find themselves worse off. The competitive devaluations and tariff wars of the interwar period offer the most striking example; many of the proscriptions in the GATT and the IMF Articles of Agreement are designed to avoid a repetition of those events.

But competition among policies was not thereby banished on all fronts. For example, interest rates shot upward in 1965 and 1966 to levels one to two percentage points higher than those which had prevailed in most countries in 1964. Some of the increases were designed to curb domestic demand; others were defensive, to limit capital outflow. Even after domestic economies had cooled down, it took a dra-

---

[17] The inflexibility of potential policy instruments is summed up in the adage, "Any *old* tax is a good tax." Changes in taxes not only affect marginal decisions—that may be the objective—but also capital values, which the market has adjusted to allow for the old tax. Thus changes in taxes often result in capital gains for some and capital losses for others.

matic meeting of finance ministers at Checquers, England, in early 1967, to reverse the process.

Four other types of policy instruments having these characteristics have been used in the effort to strengthen the balance of payments of various countries: restrictions on government procurement, government-sponsored export promotion, tax incentives to domestic investment, and changes in domestic tax structure. The United States, faced with large payments deficits during the early 1960s, made or considered moves in all of these areas. In each case there was ample precedent abroad for doing so.

Government purchases for government use are specifically excluded from coverage by the GATT rules governing international trade.[18] The result is that a conspicuously small proportion of government purchases, by any government, is from foreign suppliers who compete with domestic producers. In the United States the "Buy American" provision, which after 1954 officially gave preferential treatment of 6 to 12 per cent (in addition to tariffs) to domestic over foreign competitors, has existed since the 1930s. But, in 1962, a number of government agencies, including most importantly the Department of Defense, raised the preference accorded to domestic suppliers as high as 50 per cent.[19] Foreign aid expenditures by the American government are even more restricted. Starting with development loans in 1959, such expenditures were tied increasingly to purchases in the United States, until only a limited class of expenditures was not so tied, regardless of the price advantages offered by foreign suppliers.

The government procurement practices of other countries are more difficult to document, since most governments do not require open bidding on government purchases with well-publicized preferences to domestic producers, such as are found in the "Buy American" provi-

[18] GATT, Article XVII(2).

[19] The Department of Defense also introduced, and then raised, a margin of preference to American suppliers for its procurement for use by American forces abroad, which procurement was not subject to the Buy American Act. The change added an average of 26 per cent to the budgetary cost of those items shifted from overseas to domestic procurement. See the testimony of Charles Hitch, Comptroller of the Defense Department, before a Subcommittee of the Senate Committee on Banking and Currency, *Balance of Payments—1965,* U.S. Congress, 89th Cong., 1st sess., March 1965, p. 156.

sions.[20] Many countries follow the practice of tying foreign assistance, either by law or by skillful selection of projects and recipient countries, to purchases from the donor country. This is as true for those donors with fully employed economies as for those with excess capacity and unemployment, even though tying is far less effective in the former case, and merely stimulates additional imports; and it is as true for donor countries in balance-of-payments surplus as for those in deficit. Canada, Japan, and the United Kingdom tie the bulk of their foreign assistance, and France ties some expenditures. France and the Netherlands give virtually all of their foreign assistance to colonial or former colonial areas, where *de facto* aid-tying takes place through long-established trading firms. German aid ofteñ originates with requests from prospective exporters who have found projects in recipient countries eligible for foreign assistance by German criteria.[21]

Many of these practices, of course, arise not only from balance-of-payments considerations but also from protectionist sentiment. Domestic producers apply strong political pressures on their governments to buy at home, especially when the goods are to be "given away." But weakness in the balance of payments often strengthens their arguments and increases public acceptability of such restrictive measures.

Government activities are not solely restrictive of trade. On the contrary, a second range of practices involves all kinds of schemes, except direct subsidies proscribed by GATT, to promote exports of goods and services. Governments sponsor trade fairs, product exhibitions, and other advertisements for the products of their exporters; they insure commercial and so-called noncommercial risks involved in exporting; and they often help to finance exports directly. No major industrial trading nation can be found without a government or government-sponsored agency for insuring and/or extending credit for exports. Some countries, such as France and Italy, give especially

[20] When the European Common Market is finally established, member governments will be obliged to give equal access to suppliers throughout the EEC.

[21] On national practices and their economic effects, see R. N. Cooper, "External Assistance and the Balance of Payments of Donor Countries," in the United Nations Conference on Trade and Development, Vol. V, *Financing and Invisibles* (New York: United Nations, 1965).

favorable treatment to export paper in their banking systems or at their central banks. Export credit is often exempt from general credit limitations to restrict domestic demand. All of these measures really subsidize exports, although it is often impossible to identify the amount of the subsidy in any particular sale.

The United States established the U.S. Travel Service in 1961 to attract foreign tourists to the United States. European governments have been aiding tourism much longer, and each year spend substantial amounts for the purpose of attracting foreign tourists. Moreover, expenditure for the promotion of tourism has been growing rapidly, doubling every two to four years. In addition to straightforward publicity, most European countries subsidize the hotel industry either through preferential tax treatment or through low-interest or government-guaranteed loans.[22] In most countries, these programs date from the late 1950s or the early 1960s.

Subsidies to domestic investment is another area in which governments have moved to improve their international payments positions. Investment subsidies for manufacturing and agriculture improve the competitiveness of a country's products in world markets. Some countries give direct fiscal incentives to new investment in plant and equipment, such as the investment tax credit of 7 per cent adopted by the United States in 1962 and the 25 per cent investment grants in the United Kingdom. Japan permits greatly accelerated depreciation of assets. A rough impression of the influence of these arrangements can be gained from Table 6-1, which indicates the speed with which new equipment can be written off, taking into account investment allowances and tax credits. Table 6-2 indicates the substantial incentive to invest which accelerated depreciation and investment allowances provide in some countries by reducing corporate profits taxes.

Under a regime of fixed exchange rates, government subsidy for domestic investment is similar to a devaluation of the currency in that it improves the cost competitiveness both of the country's export products and of its products which compete with imports.[23]

---

[22] OECD, *Tourism in OECD Member Countries, 1963* (Paris, 1963), p. 22 and Annex I.

[23] Investment subsidies differ from straightforward currency devaluation, however, in that the improvement in competitiveness varies from industry to industry according to the capital-intensity of the productive process, and they

Subsidies to investment are obviously motivated by considerations extending well beyond the balance of payments; economic growth has become a target of economic policy in its own right, partly for political and strategic reasons (arising in part from the "economic race" with the Soviet bloc), partly because rising standards of living are universally desired. But balance-of-payments considerations do play an important role in the decision to inaugurate investment incentives. Britain for years has emphasized the need to enlarge and improve its capital stock to compete more effectively in world markets. Former U.S. Secretary of the Treasury Dillon, testifying on behalf of the U.S. investment tax credit in 1962, argued that the measure was required "if U.S. business firms are to be placed on substantially equal footing with their foreign competitors in this respect. It is essential," he said, "to our competitive position in markets both here at home and abroad, that American industry be put on the same basis as foreign industry. Unless this is done, increased imports and decreased exports will unnecessarily add to the burden of our balance of payments deficit." [24]

Changes in the structure of domestic taxation, and in particular the "mix" between direct and indirect taxes, constitutes another area in which governments have moved, or have been tempted to move, to improve their national trade positions. GATT rules prohibiting export subsidies have been interpreted to preclude remission of direct taxes on exports but to permit remission of indirect taxes. Thus taxes on corporate profits arising from export cannot be rebated, but manufacturers' excise taxes or turnover taxes can be. Similarly, countries are permitted to levy indirect taxes, but not direct taxes, on imports. Because of this asymmetry in border tax adjustment, it is possible under fixed exchange rates for a country to stimulate exports and to impede imports by shifting its tax structure from direct taxes to indirect taxes, provided that direct taxes affect prices.

The GATT rule is based on the classical economic assumption that indirect taxes are shifted entirely to the purchaser, while direct

---

encourage the use of more capital-intensive methods of production in all industries benefiting from the subsidy.

24 *Revenue Act of 1962*, Hearings before the Senate Committee on Finance, 87th Cong., 2nd sess., April 2, 1962, Part 1, p. 83. It is noteworthy, moreover, that investment incentives are usually directed at the manufacturing industries, e.g., those whose goods are important in international trade.

TABLE 6–1   Percentage of Investment in New Plant and Machinery Allowed to be Written Off for Tax Purposes

	In First Year	*By Fifth Year*	*Cumulative Total Over Asset Life*
Belgium	22	92	n.a.
Canada	30	71	100
France	25	76	100
Germany, F.R.	20	67	100
Italy	25	100	n.a.
Japan	43	68	n.a.
Netherlands	26	86	110
Sweden	30	100	100
United Kingdom [a]	55	91	130
United States [b]	29	78	114

n.a., not available.

[a] Including an investment allowance of 30 per cent, replaced by grants in 1966.

[b] Including an estimate for the effect of an investment tax credit of 7 per cent.

Sources: Report of the Committee on Turnover Taxation (London: HMSO, Cmnd. 2300, March 1964), p. 52; and *Revenue Act of 1962,* Hearings before the Senate Committee on Finance, 87th Cong., 2nd sess., April 2, 1962, p. 82.

TABLE 6–2   Statutory and Effective Corporate Income Tax Rates

	Earnings Fully Retained		*Earnings Fully Distributed*	
	Statutory Rate	*Effective Rate* [a]	*Statutory Rate*	*Effective Rate* [a]
Belgium	30	30	30	30
France	50	46	50	46
Germany, F.R.	56	53	32	30
Italy	36	32	15	13
Luxembourg	45	32	45	32
Netherlands	45	37	35	29
United Kingdom	54	39	24	18

[a] Computed on the basis of straight line depreciation on the assumption of a constant, before-tax rate of return of 20 per cent over the life of the investment and a market rate of interest of 5 per cent.

Source: Peggy Brewer Richman, "Depreciation and the Measurement of Effective Profits Tax Rates in the European Common Market and United Kingdom," *National Tax Journal,* XVII, March 1964, p. 90.

taxes are not shifted at all, being absorbed entirely (in the case of the corporate profits tax) by the firm. Recent work in the field of public finance suggests, however, that there may be much less difference in the price effects of, say, corporate profits taxes and manufacturers' excise taxes than was once thought to be the case.[25] To the extent that indirect taxes are partially absorbed by the producer, or that profits taxes are shifted forward to the consumer, the GATT rules regarding border treatment of national taxes allow some "subsidy" to exports and a country can improve its trade position by switching from corporate profits taxes to excise or turnover taxes.

Some countries have made tax changes in this direction, and others have been urged to do so. Sweden reduced its income tax and imposed a general sales tax in 1960; in mid-1964 Italy reduced payroll taxes (which are not rebatable) and, to recoup the revenue, increased turnover taxes (which are rebatable). The German government in 1967 approved a change from a turnover to a value-added tax which will improve the export competitiveness of German products; [26] and Britain has been periodically urged to increase its indirect taxes and lower the direct corporate taxes, although a special committee set up to examine the matter rejected the proposed change.[27] Similar changes have been proposed for the United States.

Once again, many considerations have influenced these proposals; in some cases there may be powerful arguments for making the

[25] Marian Krzyzaniak and Richard A. Musgrave, *The Incidence of the Corporation Income Tax* (Baltimore: Johns Hopkins University Press, 1963), Chaps. 6 and 8; and J. A. Stockfish, "On the Obsolescence of Incidence," *Public Finance*, XIV, No. 2, 1959, pp. 125–48.

[26] Because rebates under the turnover tax, due to complications in calculating the exact burden of the tax on each commodity, were lower than the values of rebates permissible under the GATT rules. For the same reason, import levies were lower than they might be.

[27] *Report of the Committee on Turnover Taxation* (London: HMSO, Cmnd. 2300, 1964). In late 1964, however, Britain did increase tax rebates on exports by extending the definition of rebatable excises to include taxes on fuels and office supplies and equipment. The rebates were estimated at about 2 per cent of the value of affected exports, and were removed in 1968, after devaluation.

In 1966, the six members of the EEC agreed to change their systems of indirect taxes to value-added taxes by 1970. At a later date, the rates of taxation will presumably be made uniform. Until the new uniform rate has been chosen and the other changes in taxes which will be necessary to leave revenues unchanged are known, it is not possible to say whether this move will tend to improve or worsen the trade position of the EEC.

change regardless of the effects on the balance of payments. But it is interesting to note that these proposals have come alive just since the late 1950s, as international competition has stiffened, and that improvement in the trade balance is often mentioned explicitly as an important reason for making the change. The Committee for Economic Development has stated, for example, that "a major advantage of a general excise tax [over a corporate profits tax] is that it would tend to improve the ability of the United States to compete with others in world markets," and it goes on to argue that the United States must "equalize" its tax structure with that of the Common Market as tariffs between the two trading areas are reduced.[28]

All of these policy measures have a common characteristic. Taken by one country alone, each represents a concealed devaluation of the currency, at least with respect to a selected class of transactions. But like devaluation, these measures are effective only if other countries do not respond in kind. To each country, tying foreign aid and giving preference to domestic producers in government procurement may appear to offer a means to improve the balance of payments; indeed, in the short run it may do so. But if all countries follow the same practices, the benefit to each is much reduced and some countries will have their payments positions worsened as a result. In the meantime, the total real value of foreign aid has been reduced by reliance on high cost suppliers, and inefficient production has been fostered.

The same thing is true of the other measures discussed. General adoption of export promotion schemes and government-sponsored tourist publicity will surely have a much greater effect on the total level of world exports and tourism than on the payments position of any one country, since the measures will largely cancel one another and leave only residual effects on the balance of payments. Similarly, if all countries adopt special tax incentives for domestic investment, the net improvement in competitiveness—which depends as much on incentives abroad as on those at home—will be haphazard and unpredictable. The principal effect may well be not on any one country's balance-of-payments position but on the total investment and the rate of growth in the world economy at large—so long as these effects are not nullified by a competitive rise in long-term interest rates! Finally,

[28] Committee for Economic Development, *Reducing Tax Rates for Production and Growth,* December 1962, pp. 39–40.

an effort to raise exports and impede imports through changes in domestic tax structure may have little over-all effect on foreign trade and leave countries with tax structures which many would prefer not to have.

At any point in time, there are often cogent and persuasive arguments for introducing one or more of these measures to improve the balance of payments. If other countries did not respond in kind, the desired improvement would be forthcoming. But if other countries act likewise, the measures largely cancel out. Not only is the purpose of the move nullified, but all countries may find themselves worse off in terms of their other objectives. As a rule, individual countries cannot act unilaterally without inviting reaction. If they are successful, they are quickly emulated by their neighbors, so that the initial gains are transitory at best. Countries often must act in self-defense, in response to the behavior of their trading partners. This is particularly so when measures to reduce one country's deficit do not reduce the surpluses of the surplus countries but increase the deficit of another deficit country or move countries in balance into deficit. These third countries then feel compelled to respond defensively and their actions in turn increase the deficit of the initial deficit country. Moreover, many of the measures thus taken are difficult to reverse; countries do not readily contract export credit programs or lengthen the periods of depreciation allowable for tax purposes.[29]

In Summary

Contemporary competition among policies is not obvious, as it was in the round of tariff increases in the late 1920s and the competitive depreciations of the early 1930s. But more subtle and sophisticated methods can substitute, albeit imperfectly, for currency depreciation. Taken in sequence by different countries, these measures produce a kind of ratchet effect. We then have a series of competitive depreciations in disguise.

This chapter has focused on how balance-of-payments difficulties,

[29] There are some exceptions. Measures which are subject to a time limitation can be allowed to lapse. As an anti-inflationary measure, Germany finally permitted its provisions for accelerated depreciation to lapse in 1960—after nine years of large payments surpluses.

actual or feared, can give rise to undesirable competition in policies. In Chapter 4 we saw how competition for the location of industry can also weaken economic policy in the areas of regulation and taxation, due to the mobility of business. To attract new firms, or to keep the firms they have, local authorities may eschew tax or regulatory measures which in their view would benefit the community as a whole, but which might drive away investment.

National governments have not yet engaged in a scramble to adjust their policies to be most attractive to foreign-owned business firms; on the contrary, a number of countries are concerned about the amount of foreign control already present. Differences in taxation and other measures relating to business activity do, however, affect international corporate location, and some beginnings of national competition for this location can be seen. Luxembourg liberalized its depreciation allowances and offered an investment allowance in 1962 in what appeared to be a deliberate move to attract foreign investment for operation throughout the European Common Market. Belgium and the Swiss cantons have also adopted tax and other features designed to attract foreign enterprise.[30]

These developments are understandable, and can be expected to become more common. In a highly integrated economic area which surpasses in size the jurisdiction of governments, each group of policy-makers is subject to such strong interactions with the surrounding area that the constraints on its actions become very severe. Indeed, in the hypothetically limiting case, these constraints determine entirely the course of action each jurisdiction must take. The region, or the nation, in a highly integrated economy becomes analogous to the perfect competitor—or at best the oligopolist—in a market economy. The range of choice it has, consistent with economic survival, is very small; for the most part it simply adapts its behavior to stimuli from outside. Awareness of the high interactions will eventually inhibit action.

A. C. Pigou and John Maynard Keynes pointed out long ago that the sum of individual decisions by consumers and producers may not always be optimal for society as a whole (and hence for its members), even though its members may be acting individually on entirely

---

[30] Furthermore, the relaxation in France's tough policy on foreign investment may have been dictated in large measure by the prospect of losing investment to other members of the EEC with free access to the French market.

rational grounds.[31] Some kind of collective action is therefore required to produce an optimal outcome.

The same can be true among nations or among regions within a nation, if the interactions among their decisions are sufficiently strong. One jurisdiction gropes around for new instruments in an attempt to improve its position. If it succeeds, others follow and there is a competition in policies which defeats everyone's objectives and in fact can even lead all participants *away* from their national or local objectives, like the members of a crowd rising to their tip-toes to see a parade better but in the end merely standing uncomfortably on their tip-toes.[32]

An invisible hand seems to be working in the area of economic policy as well as in the market place. Competition in the market place is alleged to lead to the most efficient allocation of resources. Whatever the merits of this claim, we can be much less confident that competition among policies will be optimal. Governments seek many ends, not the efficient allocation of resources alone; and the process of policy competition can certainly thwart some of those objectives.

Existing rules of international behavior as set forth in GATT and in the Bretton Woods Agreement do limit the use of direct and straightforward means of policy competition such as open export subsidies and multiple exchange rates, and they therefore slow the process of policy competition since the more subtle and sophisticated methods—loopholes in GATT and the Bretton Woods Agreement— usually involve strong domestic considerations which delay their implementation. But existing rules do not fully accomplish the aim of preventing self-defeating policy competition and of freeing domestic policy measures to pursue largely domestic objectives. Moreover, the

[31] A. C. Pigou, *The Economics of Welfare* (London: Macmillan & Co., 1932). This was also the central underlying message of Keynes' *General Theory of Employment, Interest, and Money* (London: Macmillan & Co., 1936).

[32] A recent illustration of this, drawn from the United States, is provided by the growing use by states and municipalities of their privilege to float tax-exempt securities for the purpose of raising funds for new businesses locating there. This practice was used by only three states as recently as 1956, with such issues totalling less than $2 million; but by 1966 these issues had been made in 28 states and exceeded $500 million. As the process spreads, the actual effect on the location of industry diminishes, and the net effect will simply be to erode the Federal corporate tax base and to raise interest charges on all tax-free state and municipal securities, thus in the end hurting the protagonists in the process.

pressures on domestic policy are likely to become greater as the world economy becomes more interdependent. Freedom of action in economic policy formation can be lost through the need for each country to compete in policies with its competitors in commerce.[33]

The courses of action open to minimize any adverse effects from this competition among governments in an interdependent world economy are those outlined in Chapter 1, or various combinations of them. Countries can coordinate closely their national economic policies, attempting to define and reach an optimum combination of policies for the community as a whole. This route involves extensive "interna-

[33] A simple game offers a suggestive if inexact analogy to the consequences of policy competition. Consider a "game" in which each of two persons must name an even number between two and ten. If they name the same number, each player receives half of that number. If they name different numbers, the player naming the lower number wins the number he named; the other player wins nothing. The "payoff matrix" for either player looks like this:

		Number chosen by the second player				
		2	4	6	8	10
Number chosen by the first player	2	1	2	2	2	2
	4	0	2	4	4	4
	6	0	0	3	6	6
	8	0	0	0	4	8
	10	0	0	0	0	5

Maximum joint gains are reached if both players choose "ten"; in that case each of them wins five. But for each player the choice of "eight" dominates the choice of "ten" in the sense that the payoff is sometimes higher and is never lower, no matter what the other player chooses. If the choice of "ten" is ruled out by both players on these grounds, choice of "six" then dominates the choice of "eight" by reasoning similar to that above; and so on, until both players end up choosing "two" as the only safe strategy yielding some sure payoff.

The mutual gains from cooperation are obvious in this case, and should be obvious to both players. The temptation to cheat will always be present, but if the game is played again and again the long-run loss from deviating from a jointly agreed choice of "ten" should induce both players to stick to their agreement. If, however, this kind of game is extended to include many players—

tionalization" of the process of economic policy-making, transferring this governmental function to the larger integrated area.[34]

Alternatively, countries can attempt to remove the major source of pressure on their actions—their unfavorable international payments positions—by providing each country with ample liquidity to finance any deficit and allowing it to go its own way. Or this goal can be achieved by reversing the growth in interdependence, by artificially breaking down or reducing the numerous economic links between countries. These three possibilities are taken up in the following three chapters.

---

each player wins half of any number named in common with others, but more if he names the lowest number—any one player may feel he can violate the agreed conventions to his own benefit without inducing retaliatory action by all the others. Since *all* the participants may reason in this way, all may be made worse off than necessary.

International trade and financial policies have something of this character: if all the other players adhere to the rules which benefit all, any one of them may gain by deviating from them, and therein lies the risk of unraveling. The rules will be workable only if all play by them.

[34] The same is true for regulation and taxation as well as balance-of-payments policies. A governmental unit spanning a territory which equals or exceeds the locational domain of the firm can make and enforce regulations without inviting socially undesirable relocation of industry. As the locational domains of business firms increase, it is necessary also for the jurisdictions of governments to increase correspondingly—at least in some dimensions—if subsequent "policy competition" among governments is not to result in practices and policies which are socially sub-optimal. Water and air pollution control provide topical examples. It is this, rather than the narrower question of possible misallocation of resources, which suggests that the pressure for "harmonization" of policies—i.e., joint decisions—makes sense in a highly interdependent community of nations.

PART III

Alternative Payments Systems

CHAPTER SEVEN

Economic Policy Formation
with
Internal Adjustment

In Part II, we examined certain changes in the structure of economic relations in the Atlantic economic community over the past decade or two and pointed out the implications of these changes for success in setting and achieving national objectives of economic policy. It is time now to return to the different types of arrangements which might govern economic relationships among these countries, and to see how well, taking into account the growing interdependence among countries, they solve the central problem posed in Chapter 1: how to preserve the manifold benefits of extensive international economic intercourse free of crippling restrictions, while at the same time preserving a maximum degree of freedom to pursue legitimate economic objectives of the national community.

As we saw in Chapter 1, how countries handle their balance of payments is a critical factor governing the economic relationships among them. It will be useful to refer once again to the three "polar" types of arrangement for coping with prospective payments imbalances: methods of internal adjustment, methods of external adjustment, and methods for financing imbalances. This chapter starts out with a description of an international payments system that rules out artificial barriers to the movement of goods, capital, and labor among nations for balance-of-payments reasons, but at the same time is niggardly in official finance for balance-of-payments deficits. Under these circumstances, countries must maintain balance in international payments largely through adjustments in domestic economic policy: fiscal policy, monetary policy, tax policy, and the like. We can call this kind of payments system a "gold standard" system for short, although, of course, gold may itself play quite a minor role or even no role; the key element is the adjustment of internal economic policy to the requirements of external balance.

A gold standard system with a low level of interdependence among nations and with money wages and prices very resistant to downward movement leads to trouble; substantial deflation and unemployment is required in a deficit country to eliminate a payments deficit; or, alternatively, substantial inflation is required in the surplus countries. This system was soundly and properly rejected by the designers of the postwar payments system at Bretton Woods in 1944.

What about a gold standard system when economic interdependence is high, rather than low, among the participating nations? Under those circumstances, such a system might work better than it did in the late 1920s. Indeed, this is the sort of system which prevails *within* countries. The several regions of a single country can neither change the value of their currency relative to that of their neighbors nor impose barriers to imports from the rest of the country. Yet balance-of-payments adjustment problems among regions of a country do not ordinarily cause concern; we are usually not even aware of them. As we see below, this is partly a failure of perception. But it is partly because some incipient imbalances are covered smoothly and unobtrusively by equilibrating capital movements. A key role in maintaining balance in regional payments positions is played by flows of private capital. Regions can borrow in a national capital market, or through a national banking system, to finance the excess of their expenditures elsewhere in the country.

If this system could be made to work internationally—if, as economic interdependence among nations increases, private capital movements can be made to play a strongly equilibrating role—it would go a long way toward reducing the powerful disadvantages of an old-fashioned gold standard. The emergence of the Eurodollar and Eurocapital markets are encouraging developments in this respect. But, to anticipate the conclusions, such equilibrating movements of capital would not be sufficient by themselves to solve the central problem. National policy would not be freed to pursue domestic objectives simply by virtue of the opportunity to borrow abroad. There must in addition be close cooperation among nations in two respects: in the formation and pursuit of policy objectives for the Atlantic economic community as a whole, and in providing official transfers—foreign aid, we would call it today—to regions which for some reason are not readily able to borrow on satisfactory terms in the community-wide capital market. Both of these forms of cooperation require a very high degree of political cohesion, a willingness to work together and to make compromises and even financial sacrifices in the broader interests of the community.

But, before we turn to the requirements for cooperation, it is useful to look at the operation of a gold standard system of adjustment when private capital is highly mobile.

Balance-of-Payments Adjustment in an Integrated Community

To see the effects of high capital mobility on the ability of each country to pursue its own economic objectives, consider an extreme case in which, as far as capital is concerned, the Atlantic economic community is fully integrated; that is, interest rates on securities of comparable quality are everywhere the same, and lenders judge only the financial reliability of the borrower, not his nationality.

In particular, it is assumed that exchange risk is completely absent, as it is within a single country. Under these circumstances, countries could not use monetary policy in pursuit of domestic objectives. Monetary expansion in a small country could not be effective either in increasing aggregate demand or in raising the rate of growth by stimulating investment. It would merely lead to an outflow of capital, as residents with higher money balances bought assets generally acceptable throughout the community. Similarly, monetary contraction would not restrain demand, for funds would flow in from the neighboring countries, replacing any funds withdrawn by the monetary authorities and vitiating their action as far as economic activity is concerned.

Although monetary policy would have to be abandoned as an instrument of domestic economic policy, fiscal policy would suffer no such disability. Any country could take fiscal action either to stimulate or to depress demand. It is true that fiscal stimulation, starting from a position of payments balance, would lead to a trade deficit in goods and services with the other members of the economic community, but this could be financed by floating securities in the international capital market or by borrowing through the international banking system.[1] Indeed, fiscal expansion might well result in a *surplus* in the balance of payments, as capital flowed in to finance both the additional government expenditure and any increase in the demand for money resulting from the higher level of economic activity.[2]

Just as monetary policy could not be used for stabilization, it could not be used for growth. But a country desiring to stimulate its growth in income could do so by reliance on tax and other measures to encourage the formation of capital and to promote the location of business enterprise within the country.

Moreover, integration of international money and capital markets would have one important dividend for payments equilibrium. Under the assumed integration of national economies, divergent monetary policies would diminish as an autonomous source of disturbance to international payments. Nominally independent monetary authorities would soon learn that manipulation of the rate of monetary expansion for domestic purposes would be fruitless, and would bring these rates into rough correspondence with the rate of expansion which would not give rise to autonomous imbalances in payments.

It is often suggested or implied that divergences in monetary expansion are the principal or even the sole source of imbalances in international payments.[3] In this view, once rates of monetary expan-

[1] The efficiency of fiscal policy as a stabilization weapon in an economically integrated community has been persuasively argued by James Ingram. See his "A Proposal for Financial Integration in the Atlantic Community," in *Factors Affecting the United States Balance of Payments,* Joint Economic Committee of the U.S. Congress, 87th Cong., 2nd sess. (Washington: GPO, 1962). See also Ingram's *Regional Payments Mechanisms: The Case of Puerto Rico* (Chapel Hill: University of North Carolina Press, 1962).

[2] In technical terms, this result would occur if the interest-sensitivity of capital movements and the marginal-transactions demand for money are high, relative to the marginal propensity to import and the interest-sensitivity of the demand for money.

This approach, of course, assumes that fiscal policy is in fact an active and flexible instrument of policy. This is contrary to fact in a number of countries—indeed in some countries fiscal policy is not yet recognized as a legitimate tool of economic policy, and in such cases exceptionally heavy reliance is placed on monetary policy. But use of fiscal policy is growing, and, by the time international capital markets are fully integrated, fiscal policy is likely to be widely used.

[3] This view is especially commonly held on the Continent of Europe. For example, the President of the German Bundesbank, Karl Blessing, has written that balance-of-payments disequilibria are "closely connected with monetary,

sion are brought into harmony, imbalances in payments will cease to be a serious problem. Unfortunately, except in the obvious sense that *some* degree of monetary stringency can always prevent or rectify *ex post* deficits, orderly and coordinated monetary expansion will not eliminate payments deficits. While excessive rates of monetary expansion are the principal cause of some *ex ante* deficits in international payments, other prospective deficits are caused by changes in taste and in technology, by new discoveries and exhaustion of old resources, by divergences in the rate of growth in real output from country to country, and by changes in domestic policies such as rates of taxation. The monetary contraction required to rectify these imbalances might result in serious under-utilization of resources. So long as the world economy is growing and changing, imbalances among countries and regions are inevitable.[4] Nonetheless, reducing divergences in monetary expansion from country to country would undoubtedly eliminate one important source of imbalance.

To sum up, although the tools would change, countries with ready access to an efficient international capital market and faced with a high mobility of capital would seem to be masters of their own destinies. Through fiscal policy they could set demand at the level required to assure full employment, and economic growth could be influenced through taxation and other measures to encourage investment and technological change. This of course is an idealized picture based on perfect mobility of capital. But it indicates the possibilities when capital and money markets are truly international even when financial capital is not perfectly mobile.

Three Imperfections in the "Gold Standard" Regime

There is no doubt that much could be accomplished under the kind of arrangement described in the preceding section. Sacrifices of domestic economic objectives such as those required under a gold

---

financial, and economic policies in various countries. To prevent [sic] such disequilibria it was necessary to maintain monetary discipline at home." *American Banker*, July 20, 1965, reported in IMF, *International Financial News Survey*, August 20, 1965.

4 One need only think of the impact of the Haber process on Chile's nitrate industry, of rayon on Japan's silk industry, of the discovery of oil on Venezuela's payments position, or even of the growing popularity of foreign travel on the U.S. payments position.

standard without high interdependence would not be required. Still, there are three trouble spots in the picture.

First, the qualification "small" is an important one. A small country can borrow extensively in an international capital market without perceptibly affecting interest rates, but a large one cannot. If the United States, or Germany, or any other large member of the Atlantic community faced deficient demand at home, an attempt to eliminate it through fiscal expansion financed by borrowing in the international capital market would tend to raise the community-wide level of interest rates, with the result of discouraging investment in other countries. Even in a community of small nations, it is important to know how the level of interest rates is determined for the community as a whole. Where the community is dominated by several members large enough to influence the rates, this question becomes doubly important, for unremitting fiscal expansion by one country might, by raising interest rates in the entire community, induce investment recessions and unemployment in other countries.[5] Fiscal expansion must be accompanied by some monetary expansion.

Second, *growth policy* for a nation in this kind of community involves not so much influencing the mix between consumption and investment—an aim accomplished by easy money and tight fiscal policy in a relatively self-contained economy—as bidding resources away from neighboring countries. Borrowing "abroad" permits a nation to add to the total resources available for current consumption *and* investment. This is fine if there are other countries that willingly defer consumption for the sake of foreign investment. But if all countries try to raise their rates of growth in this way, they will succeed only in raising interest rates instead and may paradoxically *lower* the rate of investment. Again, the crucial question arises: how are interest rates determined for the community as a whole? A similar point applies to tax concessions and other measures to encourage location of business enterprise; not all countries can apply these techniques successfully, and to attempt it leads to the competition in policies discussed in the previous chapter. There is a serious risk that this

[5] Realization of this possibility depends on the interest sensitivity of investment and on the degree of international capital mobility relative to the extent of trade links among countries.

The expanding country would in this case run a payments surplus so it could itself provide the required degree of monetary expansion.

competition, like interest rate escalation, will leave the entire community worse off than it was at the start.

The solution to both of these problems, of course, is to determine both the desired level of monetary expansion and the appropriate mix between consumption and investment for the community as a whole, through some kind of international policy-making machinery.[6] A growth target must be set for the community as a whole. One possible solution, but not a necessary one, is to turn these matters over to a supranational economic authority, endowing it alone with the powers of money creation. But it would be adequate for national authorities to continue to act, both with respect to monetary expansion and with respect to the structure of taxation and other matters affecting corporate location, so long as the actions are closely coordinated among the national members of the community. Coordination is the key here—neither unification nor mere cooperation.[7]

Finally, even a small country can borrow in a private international capital market for a prolonged period only if the proceeds are used for investments which are sufficiently productive not only to pay interest on the debt but also to satisfy creditors that further lending is appropriate.

A nation or a region may exhaust some resources on which it re lied heavily for exports, or it may find export demand shifted away for other reasons, leaving wages and other factor costs too high to make investment profitable in the new situation. If the profitability of investment is too low, private enterprise capital will not enter the area, and even borrowing by the public authorities in the international capital market may meet increasing resistance from lenders. Investment with low productivity will not add to future export earn-

---

[6] The same is true for policies to influence the distribution of income. National policies to redistribute income will not be possible if factors of production are highly mobile. Heavily taxed factors will move to neighboring areas, and lightly taxed factors (or factors which receive large government benefits) will move in from neighboring areas. There must be broad agreement among the members of the community on what the distribution of income should be.

[7] "Unification" of national policies would involve making them all identical. "Coordination" means that national policies are geared to common over-all objectives, but it may occasionally be desirable to have national policies pursue different courses. Thus, national interest rates or tax policies might differ according to balance-of-payments requirements. "Cooperation" implies a good deal less than coordination of policies; it is much more permissive.

ings. The substitution of capital inflow for export earnings leaves a country's payments in balance but it worsens the structure of its external debt. As its borrowing increases, a deficit country may find itself having to pay an ever larger premium over prevailing interest rates; eventually it may not be able to borrow at any reasonable price. A country's credit rating can drop, just as that of a private corporation can.[8] Thus, there are distinct limits to the expansionary fiscal policy which even a small country in an integrated economic community can pursue. If there were not, depressed areas such as West Virginia might have discovered long ago the marvels of borrowing "abroad" to finance domestic expansion.

Ultimately, a country with a payments deficit arising from an adverse shift in demand or supply which lowers the return on investment, adjusted for risk, below the cost of borrowing faces three alternatives: permanent under-utilization of its resources, out-migration of its surplus factors of production, or a decline in factor prices sufficient to maintain exports at the initial level.[9] If it wishes to avoid the first of these possibilities, labor and capital must emigrate from the country or accept a decline in real income.

A country can generally restore balance in its international payments by lowering factor incomes, hence improving the price competitiveness of its export- and import-competing products. While discussion of the need for "austerity" is usually couched in terms of labor incomes, it is not just (or even) labor income but *total expenditure* which must fall.[10] Indeed, if the propensity to import out of non-

[8] New York City provides an example. In 1965 its credit-rating dropped because of a large fiscal deficit—despite the largest revenues in its history—and it had to pay a premium of one-fourth of 1 per cent on a subsequent bond issue over the borrowing rates it would have paid at the previous credit rating. See *The New York Times,* July 21, 1965, p. 1.

[9] A fourth alternative exists and has occasionally achieved results. It involves a structural change in production induced as a competitive response to the initial adverse change. The "comeback" of a region or a firm may thus be due to induced innovation. In fact, the region or firm would have been better off if it had made these changes even without an adverse turn of events. But, like individuals, they may adopt new modes of behavior more readily under adversity.

[10] Strictly speaking, real income need not fall in absolute terms if (*a*) other countries are growing, (*b*) this growth involves some increase in demand for the products of the country in question, and (*c*) these two effects, taken

wage income is higher than it is for wage income, the decline in real income required to bring about a given improvement in the trade balance will be smaller if it is concentrated in non-wage income. (The opposite, of course, is true if the propensity to import out of wage income is higher.)

If producers can accustom themselves to earning a lower rate of return on their capital, then the deficit country can restore balance by lowering its prices even without lowering wages. But just as there are institutional barriers to a fall in money wages, there are undoubtedly also strong traditions and expectations that prevent businessmen from investing for a lower rate of return than that to which they are accustomed. And if the return to capital is lowered, the inflow of private foreign capital will be reduced.

Factor mobility is a key determinant of the burden of adjustment borne by the various factors; the most mobile factors can escape these burdens relatively easily. If labor and capital both move easily, then a combination of moderate borrowing through the sale of assets to other countries in the community followed by factor migration can provide smooth adjustment to the real disturbances to international payments which will inevitably take place. Factor immobility and inflexibility in factor prices under a "gold standard" arrangement among nations, or regions within a nation, on the other hand, will lead to under-utilization of resources in regions with incipient deficits—deficits which would emerge if the region's labor and capital were fully employed at going factor prices—and to inflation in regions with incipient surpluses. And the burden of under-utilization will fall most heavily on those factors which are least mobile.

Capital is likely to be more mobile than labor. It is argued in Chapter 4 that both capital and labor have become much more mobile in the Atlantic economic community since 1950, but that labor mobility is still quite low. Even within the United States, with its high geographic mobility of labor, capital is on balance probably more mobile.[11] When international mobility involving a change in cultural en-

---

together, are sufficiently large to restore balance within the period of time permitted by possibilities for financing the deficit.

[11] Some persons, and, similarly, some forms of capital, are more mobile than others. The young and the footloose move, the aged and the fixed capital, and of course the land, stay. Once fixed in the form of plant and machinery,

vironment is required, labor may move only under extreme duress. Thus, the greater mobility of capital may force the principal burden of adjustment in factor incomes onto labor, landlords, and other relatively immobile factors.

"Depressed areas" within a country usually reflect precisely the type of problem considered here. A region which at full employment has an incipient payments deficit, but which cannot use external instruments of policy to reduce its payments to other regions and which cannot finance this deficit indefinitely, will become "depressed" through loss of funds to the surplus regions. Total factor incomes will fall, and if factor prices (wages, profits, rents, and the like) do not fall, unemployment of labor and capital will result. Thus, a depressed area is simply a region that would run a balance-of-payments deficit at full utilization of resources and that has no instruments of policy, such as exchange rate variations or tariffs, which can be used to improve its full employment payments position.[12]

Not all regions with incipient payments deficits need become depressed. As noted above, fiscal policy can stimulate demand and the resulting trade deficit can often be covered by borrowing outside the region. But this borrowing can continue indefinitely only if investment in the region is sufficiently profitable. Unfortunately, in a highly integrated economy, it is likely that a fall in exports will often be the source of a depression in business activity, and that the same factors

---

capital is not mobile. But physical capital can be allowed to deteriorate, or be sold for salvage, and the depreciation allowances and other cash flows can be invested elsewhere.

[12] It is important here to distinguish between a "depressed area" and a low income area. A depressed area has substantial under-utilization of resources, while a low income region enjoys full employment but at low factor incomes. The latter has made the factor price adjustment necessary to maintain full employment and external balance at the same time; but it does so only with a low average standard of living. The two symptoms are often found together, of course, for if an area is depressed for some length of time its remaining factors may eventually accept the cuts in income required to maintain employment.

Depression of demand may bring into play another type of adjustment, however. Some domestic industries may be jostled out of inefficient practices or poor design or marketing judgments by new competition from foreign supplies. The now classic case is the introduction of the compact car by the American automobile industry in 1960, following the rapid growth in automobile imports in the late 1950s.

which lead to a decline in exports will also lower the return on investment,[13] making extensive borrowing from outside the region more difficult.

The likely emergence of depressed areas—which might be depressed nations—under a "gold standard" regime would impose severe strains on an interdependent community of nations, and calls for a high degree of political cohesion, or coercion, if depressed areas are not to bolt from the system and impose barriers to international transactions. The strains will be aggravated if substantial discrepancies exist between the locational domains of capital and of labor, for in that case the burden of adjustment will fall very heavily on labor.[14]

This political cohesion must be directed toward two central tasks: determining certain over-all policies such as the rate of monetary expansion and the nature of business regulation and taxation for the community as a whole; and mitigating the impact of payments adjustment on those members which, because of the nature of their difficulties, cannot readily cushion the impact through their own actions

---

[13] This conjunction of influences has been emphasized by Marina v. N. Whitman, "International and Interregional Payments Adjustment: A Synthetic View," Princeton Studies in International Finance, No. 19, 1967.

[14] Robert A. Mundell has argued that an "optimum" currency area for purposes of fixing exchange rates is an area of high labor mobility. Economic adjustment between regions linked by fixed exchange rates requires some deflation of total incomes in deficit regions and inflation in surplus regions. The degree of required deflation or inflation depends on labor mobility; the greater the mobility, the smoother will be adjustment and the smaller will be the divergence from internal stability in both deficit and surplus regions. See "A Theory of Optimum Currency Areas," *American Economic Review*, LI, September 1961, pp. 657–65.

Ronald I. McKinnon, in contrast, focuses on the desire of the residents of any area to stabilize the real value of their monetary assets, and this leads him to a definition of optimum currency area involving openness in trade and mobility of financial claims, rather than labor mobility. See "Optimum Currency Areas," *American Economic Review*, LIII, September 1963, pp. 717–25. See also "Optimum World Monetary Arrangements and the Dual Currency System," *Banca Nazionale del Lavoro Quarterly Review*, XVI, December 1963, pp. 366–96, where McKinnon examines a system with flexible exchange rates between Europe, on the one hand, and Canada, the United States, Britain, and the Sterling Area on the other, with fixed exchange rates within each area.

In the terminology used here, Mundell focuses on labor domains, while McKinnon emphasizes the domain of financial capital.

combined with borrowing in the international capital market. The remainder of the chapter is devoted to considering, first, the measures which various nations have adopted to help their own depressed regions, and then the extent of international cooperation in economic policy which has so far taken place. These explorations are designed to suggest the large distance between what is required for the effective functioning of a gold standard system and what has been achieved so far in the Atlantic economic community.

The Problem of Depressed Areas

Depressed areas within countries are helped in two ways: a central fiscal authority (and often a nationwide banking system) "automatically" cushions its adjustment problems by providing funds which would not otherwise be available; and deliberate regional policies often provide additional assistance.

It is commonplace to hear of the eventual need for monetary unification in an integrated economy; such unification is necessary, not to avoid balance-of-payments difficulties (the monetary discipline of the system will prevent greatly divergent rates of expansion), but to assure that the over-all level of monetary demand is appropriate for the community as a whole. It is less common to hear of the need for fiscal unification. Paradoxically, in one respect fiscal unification in an economic union of countries is especially desirable *before* achieving a high degree of economic integration in the sense of Chapter 1, namely, high factor mobility. In the absence of high mobility, depressed areas will emerge; but the personal hardship and economic loss of depressed areas is greatly mitigated when a central fiscal authority or its functional equivalent transfers income from rapidly expanding areas to depressed areas.

Factor mobility in the United States is high but it is not perfect, and depressed regions develop from time to time as national demand shifts away from the products of a particular region. When this happens, the fall in regional income is cushioned through both the tax and the expenditure side of Federal fiscal operations. As regional incomes fall, tax payments to the Federal government fall more than proportionately, while Federal expenditures in the area continue. This process automatically slows the fall in incomes, and, moreover, it does so in a way which reduces the region's "external" payments. Some Federal expenditures in a depressed area, such as unemployment compensation, will increase; this will buoy up local demand and will provide additional funds from outside the region. The opposite will occur in regions of high employment, where contributions to the unemployment trust fund will exceed receipts from it.

A national banking system also can cushion the fall in demand for a region's products. A region in deficit will lose "reserves," i.e., make net payments outside the region. But it will be spared the multiple contraction of credit which would otherwise take place, since the regional outpayments are to branches of the same banks located in the regions in surplus. Moreover, banks can easily extend credit to the depressed region by drawing on their depositors elsewhere—but of course they can also do the opposite, and their willingness to lend in the depressed area will depend on commercial considerations.

Deliberate *regional policies* play an important role in inter-regional balance-of-payments adjustment beyond that provided by automatic inter-regional transfers through a central fiscal system.

Regional policies involve preferential treatment of certain areas of the country, whether in the form of government expenditures, tax concessions, subsidized loans, or directed procurement. The motives for such policies are mixed. In some cases, they are designed to increase living standards in regions of low income. In others, they are designed to rejuvenate regions which are in economic decline or even regions which are growing less rapidly than the rest of the national economy. Often the programs commingle the two objectives: to raise living standards and to provide employment.

As already noted, depressed areas have a direct balance-of-payments interpretation: they are regions which at full employment and an acceptable rate of growth would run unsustainably large regional payments deficits. Balance-of-payments discipline condemns them to under-utilization and stagnation. New England and West Virginia, North England and South Wales, all became depressed areas because of structural shifts in demand away from their "export" products. Unemployment ensued, followed by some fall in factor incomes and some outward migration, but both of these last adjustments were slow. Agricultural areas often lag behind other regions in economic growth because demand for foodstuffs fails to keep pace with rising incomes. If mobility is low and workers will not move readily to the work, it may be desirable to move work to the workers.

Most European countries now have some sort of regional economic program; most of these were inaugurated in the 1950s, although in a few countries they antedate the Second World War. The instruments of regional policy are varied, but they typically involve long-term, low-interest loans to local authorities for construction of "social overhead" capital, such as roads or electric-power generation facilities, and either low-interest loans or tax concessions to private businesses locating in the depressed or low-income regions. Britain, for example, regards unemployment in excess of 4.5 per cent as *prima facie* evidence that a region should be designated a "development district." As such, the government may make grants or loans for any undertaking which will provide employment in the district; it can provide assistance for the clearance of derelict land and the provision of basic services; and it can make payments toward the removal and resettlement of workers. A standard grant of 10 per cent of the cost of acquiring and installing industrial plants and equipment is made to businesses in the district, and they are permitted to write off equipment as rapidly as they choose for tax purposes.[15]

In addition, some preference may be given to the products of development districts in government procurement. In 1962, Britain agreed to enlarge its foreign aid program to the extent that purchases with such additional assistance would be made from British industries with surplus capacity, such as steel products, ships, locomotives, and the like.[16] The United States has a related provision in its "Buy American" regulations of 1954. Under this regulation, a general preference of 6 per cent is given to domestic suppliers over foreign suppliers for all government procurement for domestic use, but regions with unemployment much higher than the national average enjoy a preference of 12 per cent. Other countries also use government procurement as a technique for transferring funds to depressed areas and generating employment there.

It is no accident that the EEC has devoted considerable attention

[15] European Free Trade Association, *Regional Development Policies in EFTA* (Geneva, 1965), Chapter IX.

[16] H. M. Treasury, *Aid to Developing Countries* (London: HMSO, Cmnd. 2147, 1963), p. 13.

to policies for regional development within the Community. With barriers to trade and most capital movements dismantled, members of the EEC leave themselves open to "regional" depression resulting from shifts in demand away from their products. Moreover, most member countries had already adopted various internal regional policies and it was necessary to assure that these programs, which deliberately attempt to attract industries into certain regions or to give preference to the products of certain regions within each country, did not conflict too sharply with the rules governing fair competition in the Community as a whole.

The EEC called for careful study of regional policies within the Community as early as 1961 and asked for recommendations regarding their retention, extension, and harmonization. The studies were directed toward methods for "restoring economic impetus in depressed industrial areas" as well as to "speeding economic development in underdeveloped areas" of the Community.[17]

Community-wide action in the EEC is at present limited to three operations. One is the European Social Fund, which was established to help retrain and relocate workers who lose jobs as a result of changing trade and production patterns in the EEC. Its operations have been very modest. Second, and on a much larger scale, the European Investment Bank has loaned funds for the establishment of industry and the construction of social overhead capital in the "underdeveloped" areas of the EEC, notably southern Italy. Its loan funds derive from initial subscriptions by all members of the EEC and from borrowing in national capital markets; it is designed very much along the lines of the International Bank for Reconstruction and Development (IBRD), and its operations have been subjected to the same criticisms: its lending policies are too tough. It does, however, provide a medium for transferring funds from the main financial centers of Europe to the depressed and underdeveloped areas of the Community through expert and knowledgeable hands; without it, capital would not move so readily to those areas.

Finally, the EEC shows the rudiments of a centralized fiscal authority in its common agricultural policy. Payments of over $400 million in the period 1967–70 are to be made from a central agricultural fund to those farmers in the Community, largely in Germany and to a

[17] For a brief summary of the resulting reports, see *European Community,* No. 74, August–September 1964, pp. 6–7.

lesser extent in Italy and Luxembourg, who will experience the greatest dislocation as a result of the harmonization of agricultural policies. Since contributions to the fund are to come from all members of the Community, there will be net payments from countries with the least dislocation to those with the most. While this arrangement is not couched in balance-of-payments terms, it reflects a process similar to unemployment compensation from a central trust fund.

Regional policies have little place in classical economic prescription. If labor and capital are unemployed in one region and in heavy demand in another, efficient use of resources calls for factor movement from the former to the latter region. Regional policies impede such movement by offering inducements to both labor and capital to stay in the depressed area, and indeed to encourage capital to move into the area.[18] They operate on the assumption that economic waste can be reduced by ignoring the dictates of static allocative efficiency through re-employing unused factors of production where they are located. When factor mobility is low this policy is often economically justifiable. It has been estimated that the net gain to the British Treasury for every man employed through regional policies is $2,500 and the gain in total output is nearly three times that amount.[19]

Only if little discount is applied to future output would it be desirable, on economic grounds, to "force" workers to migrate from depressed regions to regions of high employment through the pressure of economic necessity. Even in this case it may be socially and economically worthwhile to provide financial assistance to encourage rapid movement.

This discussion has been couched largely in terms of adjustment for a "deficit" area. Adjustment is most painful in such cases. But a

---

[18] *Regional policies* are directed at improving the economy of a particular region. Many countries also have measures to increase the mobility of labor out of depressed regions.

[19] Lionel Needleman, "What Are We to Do About the Regional Problem?" *Lloyds Bank Review*, January 1965, p. 55. Needleman's estimate is reached by adding the taxes a re-employed worker would pay ($320 per year) to the unemployment and national assistance payments he would not receive ($490), discounting the sum of these government "savings" over five years at 6 per cent (yielding a present value of over $3,400), and deducting from this the "nonreturnable costs" to the government of re-employing the worker through regional policies ($950).

"gold standard" regime is in principle symmetrical; just as deficit areas will be put under deflationary pressure, surplus areas will experience inflationary pressure. This, too, may be painful. Taxation in the surplus areas for transfers to the deficit areas, either automatically through a central fiscal system or deliberately through regional policies, will help reduce these inflationary pressures. Regional policies should thus have some appeal to surplus areas too, and indeed a number of countries do have programs to relieve increasing congestion in certain booming areas of the national economy.

Reliance on regional policies will of course be necessary only if the private market, or the region itself with the help of the private capital market, cannot make the adjustment in a reasonably rapid period of time. Well-chosen regional policies, while involving some subsidy to the depressed areas, will increase the profitability of private investment there and thus should eventually become unnecessary.

Attempts to Coordinate National Economic Policies

The second element required for a smooth-functioning "gold standard" regime is coordination of certain economic policies for the economic community as a whole. The major international agreements of the postwar era bearing on economic policies—the IMF Articles of Agreement and the GATT—represent major attempts to define the limits of economic policy and to lay down the ground-rules concerning what measures are to be permitted. These were discussed in Chapter 2. On the whole they aimed at setting bounds on government policies rather than coordinating national actions in response to particular disturbances, although the tariff reductions under the GATT involve a coordinated reduction in tariffs, and the IMF has frequently, in its dealings with individual nations, offered advice and even set down policy conditions which had to be met by the borrowing country. But these were on a case-by-case basis.

A move toward more positive coordination of economic policies among several countries was made through the OEEC, established in 1948. The United States had made as a condition of extensive Marshall Plan aid close cooperation among the European countries in allocating the assistance and, beyond that, in fostering recovery and growth in Europe. This was a new experiment in international cooperation. The OEEC looked toward "a period of cooperative activity unlike anything hitherto known in the economic relations between any group of independent states." [20]

Ironically, the cooperation was necessitated not by close and free economic transactions between European countries, but because these transactions were blocked at every turn by restrictions on trade and payments. Trade was governed by dozens of bilateral arrangements between countries. It was recognized early that European recovery would be much more rapid if countries could dismantle these restrictions in parallel and allow each country to concentrate its energies on efficient production of some goods which could then be traded for needed imports. Thus, the Marshall Plan involved not only financial assistance from the United States, but also efforts to improve the productivity in European industry and to rationalize the pattern of European trade.[21]

The mutual benefit to all from a reduction in intra-European trade barriers was unambiguously clear in the late 1940s; yet no country felt secure enough to start the process unilaterally. Cooperation leading to mutual and reciprocal reduction was therefore necessary for success. As we saw in Chapter 2, common targets of economic policy—specified percentages of trade to be freed from quota restriction within a specified period of time—were universally accepted. Escape clauses permitted countries with especially weak positions to delay removing their quotas and even, on occasion, to reimpose them, as Britain and several other countries did in the Korean commodity boom of 1951.[22] But these reversals involved international consultation and agreement.

Other efforts at coordination of economic policy under OEEC were less successful. Some attempt was made to coordinate national

[20] OEEC, *Interim Report on the European Recovery Program* (Paris, 1948), Vol. 1, pp. 11–12.

[21] See Chapter 2. An excellent contemporary history and analysis of attempts to unsnarl European payments is found in William Diebold, Jr., *Trade and Payments in Western Europe* (New York: Harper & Bros., for the Council on Foreign Relations, 1952). See also Harry B. Price, *The Marshall Plan and Its Meaning* (Ithaca, New York: Cornell University Press, 1955).

[22] Kravis has emphasized the great importance of such escape clauses in any kind of international cooperative effort. See Irving B. Kravis, *Domestic Interests and International Obligations* (Philadelphia: University of Pennsylvania Press, 1963).

investment programs with a view to eliminating unnecessary duplication of capacity in a period in which capital was scarce, but very few changes in national plans were made in response to these efforts.[23] Apart from freeing trade and payments, the activities of the OEEC were largely devoted to offering technical advice to national governments and to providing a forum in which a useful exchange of information among national governments could take place. Even this represented an enormous improvement over arrangements in previous periods, but it was still very far from international coordination of national policies.

The OEEC was succeeded in 1961 by the OECD, which added Canada and the United States (and, later, Japan) to its membership. The OECD's Economic Policy Committee brings together high-level economic policy-making officials from all twenty member countries three times a year to review the economic outlook and the measures which are being planned in each country. Member countries are committed to no specific targets of economic policy beyond general assent to "promote the efficient use of their economic resources" and to "pursue policies designed to achieve economic growth and internal and external financial stability and to avoid developments which might endanger their economies or those of other countries," [24] Rather, the Economic Policy Committee "enables each government, when framing its future policy measures, to be fully aware of the likely impact of these measures on its neighbors." It represents an exchange of information and limited opportunity for confrontation; some discussion of the appropriate instruments of policy—for example, the mix between monetary and fiscal policies—has taken place, but it has been done gingerly. "Governments are *not* expected to consult the Committee in advance on particular steps they propose to take in economic policy." [25]

[23] Price, cited, p. 90.

[24] Convention on the Organization of Economic Cooperation and Development, Article 2.

[25] Quotations from OEEC, *Twelfth Annual Economic Review* (Paris, 1961), p. 26. Italics added.

There was in fact an ill-fated attempt by the now defunct Working Party One of the Economic Policy Committee to establish an internationally agreed Code of Good Behavior in 1959–60. This effort was directed toward defining policy commitments and laying down ground rules for appropriate policy measures under a variety of circumstances, and designed in particular to prevent

Countries are more willing to abjure certain instruments of policy than to commit themselves to specified instruments or even targets of economic policy. Periodic efforts to obtain an international commitment to policies of full employment, starting with the Bretton Woods Conference, have failed. In view of this history, the agreement in late 1961 by the OECD countries to raise the gross national product of the member countries taken together by 50 per cent during the period 1960–70 marked a sharp departure. It represented a loose commitment (since member countries were not individually bound by the 50 per cent target) to strive toward a common objective of a type which has normally been regarded as a matter of *domestic* economic policy.[26]

The OECD growth target involved implicit recognition of the close

the international transmission of fluctuations in economic activity and to compel countries to gear their policies at least in part to the requirements of external equilibrium. But several member countries, and especially the United States, were reluctant to commit themselves in advance to specified lines of action.

The EPC's Working Party Three on the Promotion of Better International Payments Equilibrium considers directly the balance-of-payments objectives and policies of the larger member countries. Its discussions, however, make no attempt to coordinate these objectives and policies in any formal way, although from time to time the Working Party has made its views known informally to various member governments. Its major function is to keep high policy-making officials informed about balance-of-payments developments in other countries and about foreign attitudes toward balance-of-payments policies taken by each official's country. These discussions should thus assure a rough consistency of balance-of-payments objectives, for glaring inconsistencies in national targets will be brought to light.

[26] This target involved growth in GNP at an average rate of 4.1 per cent a year, compounded. Since most European countries had been growing at a rate considerably more rapid than that, the target was not very exacting for them. Both the United States and the United Kingdom, however, wanted to raise their economic growth from the low rates obtaining in the late 1950s, and the OECD target provided international impetus and sanction to their efforts. It also provided a focal point for the activities of the newly-formed OECD.

A second joint target concerns the level of capital flows—1 per cent of gross national product in each member country—to be extended to less developed countries in the form of economic assistance or other net capital flows. The Development Assistance Committee of the OECD has also attempted to set guidelines for the terms of foreign assistance. This effort lies outside the area of domestic economic policies.

linkages between growing economies and of the drag which a few slowly growing countries can exert on the economic growth of others. A rapidly growing country will generally experience a rapid rise in imports. Unless its exports or other receipts from foreigners are also growing rapidly, it will run into balance-of-payments difficulties. Under a regime of fixed exchange rates and absence of restrictions on trade, the rapidly growing country can slow down its economic expansion, it can borrow abroad to finance its expansion, or it can persuade its trading partners to raise their rate of economic expansion. The OECD growth target provided a joint commitment to the last alternative, at least within a limited range. Growth of the industrial West was not to be slowed by balance-of-payments difficulties created by some laggard nations.[27]

The members of the EEC have gone much farther in the direction of coordinating economic policies, although they are still very far from full coordination. The Rome Treaty states that member countries "shall consider their policy relating to economic trends as a matter of common interest." The Commission of the EEC, a supranational body, has responsibility for making proposals concerning economic policies within the Community. In the spring of 1964, the Council of the EEC adopted a number of proposals put forward by the Commission to combat inflation in the member countries, including agreement to limit increases in government spending to 5 per cent during the subsequent year, to maintain or tighten restrictive credit policies, and to finance balance-of-payments deficits through long-term borrowing. Member countries were not technically bound by the recommendations, but they were "firmly committed to do everything possible in carrying out the measures." [28] As Robert Marjolin, former Vice-President of the Commission responsible for economic and fi-

---

[27] The effect of growth on demand is only one of the links between growth and the balance of payments, of course. Rapidly growing countries will, as a rule, also experience changes in their production capabilities, which improve their export competitiveness. The degree to which this improvement occurs depends very much on the source of growth, whether it is based primarily on technological change or primarily on growth in the labor force and capital stock. See my "U.S. Economic Growth and World Leadership," in W. W. Heller (ed.), *Perspectives on Economic Growth* (New York: Random House, Inc., 1968).

[28] EEC, *European Community*, No. 71, May 1964, p. 4.

nancial policy, put it: "Inexorably, as we find ourselves in the half-light between the still extensive sovereignty of the individual states and the dawning sovereign rights of a united Europe, some measure of coordination of national economic policies is emerging from these lengthy discussions [analyzing and comparing national experiences and policy decisions]." [29] This coordination has gone much further in matters touching directly the composition of international commodity trade, such as national agricultural policies. But the difficulties in such supra-national or even international coordination of economic policies were illustrated by the sharp rebuke to the EEC Commission by the French Premier Pompidou in mid-1965, when he asserted that "France is determined to retain full control of her economy and will not accept dictation from the international civil servants working for the European Economic Community." [30] The role of the Commission remains, therefore, entirely advisory in the areas of domestic economic policy; but its ability to initiate proposals formally places it closer to a supra-national economic policy-making executive than is the secretariat of the OECD. And the forums of the EEC, like those of the OECD, provide occasion for confronting national policy-makers with international inconsistencies in national policies.

Cooperation among central banks is much more limited, even though it has a much longer history. Despite the celebrated (and bitterly resented) cooperation on interest rate policy between Montagu Norman of the Bank of England and Benjamin Strong of the Federal Reserve Bank of New York—aimed at holding U.S. rates down in the late 1920s so that Britain's rates could stimulate domestic activity without inducing a large outflow of capital—central bankers are, of all economic policy-makers, perhaps the most jealous of their rights and responsibilities. The BIS plays host monthly to high officials from the central banks of Europe, with the United States and Canada generally sending "observers." But before 1960 these meetings were apparently more social than business-like, and even since that time they have apparently avoided candid discussions of measures about to be taken. There have been occasions, as Britain's raising its bank rate to 7 per cent in November 1964, when foreign governments have been in-

[29] EEC, *European Community*, No. 78, February 1965, p. 4.
[30] Reported in *The New York Times*, July 28, 1965, p. 1.

formed of changes in monetary policy somewhat ahead of public announcement; but these occasions are rare and they represent courtesy
exchanges of information rather than attempts to work out policies in
concert.[31]

All of these developments—the OECD's Economic Policy Committee and its working parties, the EEC Commission's role in analysis
of economic developments and policies, the monthly meetings of central bankers at the BIS—represent recognition that complete decen-
tralization of economic policy-making in an interdependent world is
not optimal. But these are only rudimentary beginnings toward a system in which full coordination leading to the optimal policy for the
community of nations as a whole is achieved. Countries rarely discuss, in Walter Heller's words, "economic policy in the making." [32]
It is more usual for them to explain their policies after the decisions
have been made and publicly announced. Still, the interactions are
early visible. The need to explain and even justify national economic
measures in an international forum at frequent intervals undoubtedly
compels officials, when framing their programs, to think more than
they would otherwise about international repercussions.[33] Yet in a
world of high capital mobility they must go much farther, and take
up Kindleberger's suggestion to form an open market committee
to determine monetary policy for the Atlantic Community as a
whole.

[31] A notable exception was the meeting of several finance ministers at
Checquers, England, in early 1967, with the objective of reversing the escalation of interest rates in Europe and North America. Shortly after this meeting
a number of countries eased monetary policy substantially, in what appeared
to be a concerted move. This meeting was *ad hoc,* outside the institutionalized
forums for economic cooperation.

A second exception occurred in November 1967, when Britain informed its
major trading partners of the impending devaluation of sterling and for two
costly days sought assurances that other countries would not also devalue.

[32] Walter W. Heller, as Chairman of the Council of Economic Advisers,
was chairman of the U.S. delegation to the Economic Policy Committee during its first years under the OECD.

[33] This is borne out very strongly in the area of trade policy. See Gerard
Curzon, *Multilateral Commercial Diplomacy: An Examination of the Impact
of the General Agreement on Tariffs and Trade on National Commercial Policies and Techniques* (Geneva, 1965).

Summary: *The Importance of Political Cohesion*

Of the three regimes for coping with imbalances in international payments set out in Chapter 1, this chapter considered reliance on internal measures to eliminate imbalances. Restrictions on trade and other payments to influence the balance of payments were ruled out under this regime, and liquidity for financing imbalances was assumed to be sharply limited in supply. This kind of regime typically prevails within a single country.

Under such a "gold standard" regime, imbalances arising from monetary disturbances are unlikely, for countries will soon discover that monetary expansion or contraction for domestic purposes which deviates greatly from the over-all rate of monetary expansion in the community as a whole is pointless. The "discipline" of the balance of payments is severe. It is correspondingly important, however, to coordinate national macro-economic policies—and especially the rate of monetary expansion—to assure that community-wide objectives are not lost through national competition in economic measures.

Nonetheless, imbalances in international and inter-regional payments will still arise, and their correction will ultimately require declines in real incomes in some regions and increases in others. If reductions in factor *prices*—including profit rates as well as wage rates—are resisted, then some under-utilization of the labor force and the capital stock will result. Thus, regional depression and inflation become crucial features of the adjustment process under fixed exchange rates in the absence of flexible restrictions over trade and payments.

High factor mobility will minimize the social costs associated with adjustment to imbalances, for factors will move from depressed areas to areas with excessive demand. In the long run such movement will restore equilibrium to both types of region, although during a transition period factor movement may actually worsen the disequilibrium in depressed areas and add to excessive demand in the booming areas. But if factor mobility is low, as it typically is among nations, then the social costs of a "gold standard" regime may be very high; and if labor mobility is lower than capital mobility, the burden of adjustment will be borne by labor.

The economic costs of a regime requiring internal adjustment can be reduced through compensatory transfers from regions in surplus to regions in deficit. Private capital flows will provide adequate financing under some, but not all, circumstances. Transfers may take place automatically through a centralized fiscal system such as the national government of any country; and they may also occur as a result of deliberate regional policies financed in effect by taxing the surplus regions and subsidizing the deficit regions.

Unless such regional assistance is forthcoming, depressed areas under a "gold standard" regime may benefit by withdrawing from the system and imposing barriers to transactions with other regions. This is not, of course, a realistic possibility for a region within a country, although before present national governments solidified their control, a number of civil wars were fought to retain dissident areas within many countries. But withdrawal is a very real possibility for individual countries or groups of countries within the community of nations; unrestricted international intercourse may occasionally work powerfully to the disadvantage of certain countries if their factor prices are not flexible. The temptation to withdraw will be reduced if provision exists for assistance from other countries.

A high degree of political cohesion is therefore necessary for the effective and sustained operation of an international monetary system which relies heavily on changes in internal policy for elimination of external imbalances. Surplus regions must be willing to finance regional policies, even when the recipient regions are in other countries. Citizens in the community of nations must regard regional unemployment (or regional inflation) as undesirable even when it occurs in other regions. This comes close to the criterion for political integration, mentioned in Chapter 1, that strictly regional (or national) identifications must be relatively low compared with functional identifications (workers' common interest, etc.) and identification with the community as a whole.

Recent experience in the major industrial countries does not reveal an encouraging degree of identification with the economic problems of other countries. Preoccupation of a number of continental European countries with inflation during the early 1960s and their pleas for tighter monetary policy and higher interest rates was widely interpreted to mean that the governments in power placed a higher value on price stability than they did on full employment and that they were willing to entertain higher unemployment to reduce inflation. Yet this was not the real choice confronting those countries: the choice was between price stability *in Europe* and unemployment *in the United States*. If confronted with the direct choice at home, there is little doubt that most governments would move quickly to reduce unemployment. In their call for higher interest rates, the preference which many European officials were really registering was a preference for price stability in Europe at the expense, if necessary, of full employment in the United States.

At the same time, many American officials and others who had condemned the sharp rise in American prices in the middle and late 1950s rejoiced at the rise in European prices in the early 1960s as improving the competitive position of the United States. Smooth operation of a "gold standard" regime requires greater mutual concern for the problems of other regions than these attitudes indicate, for solution to these problems requires joint action.

One alternative to the generation of mutual sympathy and concern crossing regional and national boundaries is a process which permits regions to block joint action of benefit to other regions. This is, in fact, the political process which has usually accompanied the gradual coalescence of regions into nations: a process of regional lobbying and logrolling develops so that no region suffers too badly at the hands of others. But without a well established forum in which this process is institutionalized and the possible exchanges are numerous, it will take place largely through the threat by some nations to leave the system.

CHAPTER EIGHT

Provision for
Ample Liquidity

A system of fixed exchange rates and minimal restrictions on international transactions could work with little or no coordination of economic policies, and without explicit "regional policies," if countries are well supplied with international means of payment in the form of owned reserves or readily available lines of credit. Liberal financing at least permits reduction of imbalances to be gradual rather than abrupt. If the "disturbances" to international payments are symmetrical over time, tending alternately toward deficits and surpluses for a region, ample but not unlimited liquidity avoids the need for much adjustment.

We saw that a centralized fiscal authority does to some extent provide compensatory financing for regions within a country. Nations do not have the advantage of automatic compensation through a central fiscal authority, but much the same effect can be achieved if they have large international reserves or ready access to credit from the surplus countries. If countries can finance payments deficits for prolonged periods, they will be more able to devote the limited instruments of policy at their disposal to the attainment of domestic objectives. In this respect greater international liquidity [1] helps to preserve national au-

---

[1] As used here, "international liquidity" means officially owned reserves in the form of internationally acceptable means of payment or in assets which can be quickly converted into international means of payment at little or no cost, *plus* automatic lines of credit which yield international means of payment. Defining international liquidity involves the same difficulties as defining "money." There are many kinds of assets which approach money in liquidity, in ease of use, and in certainty of value, and where one draws the defining line for "money" is inevitably arbitrary. The same is true of "international liquidity." The United Kingdom, for example, until 1967 held in its government port-

tonomy in economic policy. A country faced with an unacceptably high level of unemployment or an unsatisfactory rate of growth could avoid the necessity of compromising its objectives in these dimensions for the sake of preserving balance in international payments if it could unabashedly devote its monetary and fiscal policies to domestic objectives and finance the resulting deficit with its reserves or by drawing on lines of credit. Even where there is no fundamental conflict between domestic and balance-of-payments objectives, in the sense that all desired objectives of policy are consistent with one another at the prevailing exchange rates, countries will need foreign exchange reserves or other forms of international liquidity to finance imbalances arising from temporary disturbances due to shifts in expenditure or portfolio behavior which are always occurring in a growing and free enterprise economy.

The Demand for Liquidity

The need to hold international means of settlement in a regime of fixed exchange rates arises from several sources. First, there is a *transactions* demand for foreign exchange. This arises from known differences in timing of receipts and payments to foreigners, under circumstances when it costs something to buy and sell foreign exchange—foreign-exchange buying and selling prices typically differ by a small margin, for example. Those engaged in international transactions will find it convenient to hold some cash balances in the foreign currencies they need, or at least to hold assets (such as time deposits) in foreign currencies which can be readily and cheaply converted to foreign exchange when needed.

As international trade grows, the larger value of transactions denominated in foreign currencies may be expected to increase the required "working balances" in foreign exchange, although perhaps not

---

folio a large volume of common stocks purchased with bonds from British citizens during the Second World War. At any time these securities could be traded for dollars—an important international means of payment—on the large and relatively efficient stock exchanges of the United States. But these securities were not counted as British "reserves" because they were not considered sufficiently liquid; and indeed, in 1965 when the British government did move to liquidate some of these holdings in order to add to its "reserves," it had to do so circumspectly for fear of disrupting the securities market.

proportionally.[2] But this growth in transactions demand for international means of settlement does not automatically increase the need for international liquidity. Most of these requirements will be satisfied by the private parties, banks and businesses, engaged in international transactions. Central banks may also have some transactions demand for foreign exchange, however, to cover (for example) known seasonal fluctuations in demand for foreign currency not fully satisfied by private holdings.[3]

Second, there is a *precautionary* demand for international liquidity arising from uncertainty about the future course of foreign exchange receipts and payments. Liquid funds are held against unforeseen demand for payment, representing insurance against the need to undertake balance-of-payments adjustment measures when they may only have to be temporary or when circumstances make adjustment unusually costly. Banks and businesses engaged in international commerce will themselves carry precautionary balances—or will have arranged for lines of credit in case of need—but the central bank must also carry such balances. Private balances are likely to be inadequate, partly because the opportunity cost of holding liquid foreign assets may be high, partly because private demands for credit in foreign currency may pyramid and place undue strains on private lending institutions. Furthermore, private balances may not be available at those times when foreign exchange is needed by the authorities, since the range of contingencies against which private precautionary balances are held is quite different from the concern of the authorities to avoid unnecessary balance-of-payments adjustment.

Despite the practical difficulty of separating these two considerations, it is quite important to separate them conceptually. The argument of Chapter 6, drawing on the evidence of the preceding chapters, is that a growing sensitivity of international transactions to economic "disturbances" combined with relative inflexibility in domestic ob-

---

[2] For theoretical work on the relationship between demands for cash and the value of transactions, see W. J. Baumol, "The Transactions Demand for Cash: An Inventory Theoretic Approach," *Quarterly Journal of Economics,* LXVL, November 1952, pp. 545–56.

[3] The opportunity cost of holding foreign exchange may differ substantially between central banks and private banks and businessmen. It may be quite sensible for a central bank to hold large transactions balances even when the private sector correctly chooses not to do so because domestic financial assets with high yield are available.

jectives and policies will lead to larger and more frequent imbalances in international payments. In addition, payments positions will be increasingly disturbed, in the absence of close coordination, by misalignments in national economic policies arising from the independent pursuit of national objectives by national authorities.[4] Both developments will call for a greater precautionary demand for reserves. This is quite distinct from the argument that international liquidity must expand because international trade and payments are growing in value, with a presumption that there should be some direct link between the total value of international transactions and the liquidity required to support it.[5]

There is no similar presumption in the case of rising demand for precautionary reserves in the face of changes in the structure of the international economy. Official reserves do not have to finance the *level* of international transactions; they must merely finance *imbalances* in international transactions. If the structure of international transactions is changing in a way which makes such imbalances, particularly unforeseen imbalances, larger and more frequent, and if national authorities are unwilling or unable to take either internal or external measures to reduce them, then the demand for international liquidity will grow *more* rapidly than the value of international transactions. Under other circumstances, of course, it would grow less rapidly.

Ample provision of international liquidity—which in effect involves lending from countries in surplus to countries in deficit—would satisfy this growing precautionary demand for reserves.

International liquidity as defined here excludes the *conditional* line of credit. As found in practice, conditionality arises in either of two ways: loans may involve fixed terms for repayment, and they may require compliance with certain conditions for foreign and domestic economic policy laid down by the creditor. Either of these conditions makes such lines of credit quite different from owned reserves or automatic lines of credit, for conditionality restricts the freedom of

[4] Lack of coordination in framing and executing national economic policies in a highly interdependent world economy can increase very substantially the need for international reserves. See R. N. Cooper, "Economic Policy Adjustment in Interdependent Economies," cited.

[5] A link of proportionality is often assumed. See, for example, *International Reserves and Liquidity,* by the staff of the International Monetary Fund (Washington, 1958).

the borrowing country. Automatic lines of credit may, of course, involve nominal maturities; but if they are truly automatic they can be renewed indefinitely. Conditionality involves a compromise between preservation of domestic economic autonomy through provision of liquidity and compelling adjustment through external or internal measures. It can be used to direct the speed and nature of adjustment.

Even unconditional lines of credit or ample reserves do not prevent all the ways in which high economic interdependence among nations impinge on the effectiveness of national economic policy. While ample liquidity can protect countries from extreme balance-of-payments pressures, it does not prevent the erosion of national regulation and the evasion of national taxation made possible by high mobility of firms and persons. Furthermore, it does not prevent the slowing down of the process of attaining national objectives as interdependence increases.[6] In these respects, the alternative of unconditional credit or ample reserves is inferior to coordination of national policies, discussed in Chapter 7. The coordination of national policies meets both these difficulties by elevating policy-making to a higher level of government. The controlled use of restrictions on international transactions, discussed in the following chapter, meets these difficulties by inhibiting and even reversing the high degree of interdependence from which they arise.

Furthermore, the ample provision of liquidity has two well-known and related dangers. Automatic financing of deficits by surplus countries is open to abuse by a deficit country by permitting it to appropriate real resources from the rest of the world [7] or to buy claims on the rest of the world. If a country can readily finance payments deficits, it may take advantage of that possibility to import heavily or to invest extensively abroad, buying high yield assets with low yield liquidity which is in ample supply.

A closely related but distinct danger is that inflationary pressures

[6] The adjustment process here involves adjustment to all national objectives, not just to the balance of payments. See Chapter 6.

[7] To judge from their behavior and statements by their officials, in normal times this is not likely to be a serious problem among industrial countries. On the contrary, all of them seem to want trade *surpluses*, pushing their goods out into the rest of the world rather than attempting to absorb resources from the rest of the world. For a dated but still illuminating discussion of modern day mercantilism, see J. M. Keynes, *The General Theory of Employment Interest and Money* (London: Macmillan & Co., 1936), Chapter 23.

in one country may be transmitted to other countries. Without balance-of-payments "discipline" a country may permit total money demand to expand at an excessive rate, and this excessive demand will spill over into other countries. Under the arrangements assumed, these other countries would be confronted with the awkward choice of inflating along with the initiator of the inflation, or of taking domestic action to offset the inflationary impact of rising foreign demand, thereby enlarging trade surpluses and transferring resources to the inflating country. The more stringent the action in the surplus countries to neutralize the inflationary impact of the prospective surpluses, the larger the realized surpluses will be.

Arrangements for ample liquidity thus permit unrestrained countries to complicate greatly the tasks of domestic economic policies in those countries which place avoidance of inflation high on their list of national economic objectives. A system making extensive use of liquidity to protect the domestic objectives of interdependent national economies, therefore, requires considerable agreement among participants on basic economic objectives and substantial mutual trust in the ability and willingness of national authorities to stick to these objectives and to pursue them diligently.

Liquidity to Finance Large and Prolonged Imbalances

Countries have never been given *carte blanche* to run payments deficits and to pursue whatever foreign and domestic policies they choose. Owned reserves have always been limited in amount. There have, however, been several occasions in which a high degree of autonomy has been encouraged by provision for ample reserves; substantial automatic lines of credit have been proposed and some have even been put into effect. In varying degrees, the Keynes Clearing Union plan, the EPU, and the IMF have involved automatic lending facilities. A number of bilateral arrangements among countries have had a similar effect.

We saw in Chapter 2 that before the Bretton Woods conference the British had advanced a proposal for a Clearing Union which went a long way toward meeting the conditions for ample international liquidity. Countries were to have quotas with the Clearing Union against which they could draw, in any two-year period, up to 50 per cent automatically and without question.[8] Beyond 50 per cent, however, the Clearing Union could require strict external measures to reduce the payments deficit, including, if necessary, currency devaluation. The quotas initially proposed, however, were large enough in amount—over $30 billion for all countries together—to afford a country substantial leeway to run deficits before encountering the strictures of the Clearing Union.

The EPU, established among fifteen countries of Western Europe in 1950, bore a family resemblance to the Clearing Union. It consolidated the payments positions of all members with each other in a central account, and the resulting net positions with the EPU itself were settled monthly. The EPU offered to member countries two types of automatic credit. *Within* each month, members received automatic credit in any required amount. At the monthly settlement dates each country would make payment to the EPU or receive payment from the EPU in accordance with a formula which depended on its cumulative creditor or debtor position with the EPU. Settlement was not generally for the full amount of the debit or credit position, however. country would make payment to the EPU or receive payment from quotas, for example, and only thereafter were they required to pay to the EPU gold or dollars equal to some fraction of the monthly deficit. This fraction increased as the cumulative debit position increased, and when the cumulative position reached 100 per cent of a country's quota, full settlement of further deficits had to be made in gold or dollars. A creditor with the EPU gave full credit up to 20 per cent of its quota, and thereafter received 50 per cent of further credits in gold or dollars, up to the full amount of the quota.[9]

---

[8] An annual interest charge of 1 per cent was to be levied on debits to the Clearing Union in excess of 25 per cent of each country's quota.

[9] These were the provisions which obtained from 1950, with only slight modification, until July 1954. From mid-1954 to mid-1955, creditors and debtors alike settled 50 per cent of their monthly imbalances with the EPU in gold or dollars. In 1955 this percentage was raised to 75, but quotas were also increased so as to preserve the amount of credit potentially available. For a fascinating analysis of the EPU, the initial objections to it, and the benefits to which it gave rise, see Robert Triffin, *Europe and the Money Muddle* (New Haven: Yale University Press, 1957), Chapter 5. Brian Tew gives a lucid description of the EPU and the way it worked in his *International Monetary Cooperation 1945–60* (London: Hutchinson University Library, 1962), Chapter 9.

Quotas at the EPU were nothing like the scale called for in Keynes' Clearing Union. The total for all member countries in 1950 was just under $4 billion, and the largest quota (for the United Kingdom) was barely over $1 billion,[10] and the next largest (for France) was only $0.5 billion. Because of the portion required to be paid in gold or dollars, credits under the EPU amounted to only 60 per cent of the quotas.

On several occasions countries did experience deficits larger than those financed by the quotas, and special credits from the EPU were arranged.[11] These credits, however, were discretionary, not automatic, and they involved commitments by the deficit countries to pursue certain financial policies. Indeed, Germany in 1951 permitted supervision of its import licensing system by a panel of three experts appointed by the OEEC.

The IMF, as we saw in Chapter 2, began operations in 1947 with total member quotas at $7.7 billion, twice as large as the total EPU quotas three years later, but also with a larger membership.[12] Its lending in the first full year of operation equalled about 6 per cent of total quotas, but thereafter lending dropped off sharply and did not become substantial again until the Suez Crisis of 1956–57 (see Table 8–1). Fund lending, however, is largely discretionary and takes place only after the Fund has satisfied itself that the borrowing country is following "appropriate" internal policies to assure elimination of the deficit. Even the gold tranche drawing rights, equal to one-fourth of total quotas, did not become easy to use on short notice until 1965; and still a service charge of one-half of 1 per cent is levied on such drawings. Stand-by facilities, introduced in 1953, provide greater ease in drawing; but the scrutiny of domestic policies simply takes place at the time the stand-by is requested rather than when the drawing occurs. Thus, while IMF drawing rights have often provided a most welcome supplement to international reserves, they fall (except

[10] Moreover, the British quota in fact was for the entire Sterling Area, which pooled its reserves in London and carried on its transactions in sterling. Payments to and from the Sterling Area by continental European countries could thus be made through the EPU.

[11] Notably for Germany in 1950–51 and France in 1958.

[12] EPU quotas, except in the case of the United Kingdom, were on average about one-third larger than the original IMF quotas of the EPU members.

TABLE 8-1 Drawings at the International Monetary Fund
In Comparison with Reserves of Borrowing Countries

	IMF Drawings During Year ($ million)	Number of Borrowing Countries	Reserves of Borrowing Countries at the end of the previous year [a] ($ million)	Drawings as a Percentage of Reserves
1947	468	8	5,371	8.7
1948	208	11	9,515 [b]	2.2
1949	102	6	6,601 [c]	1.5
1950	—	—	—	—
1951	35	2	917	3.8
1952	85	6	2,375	3.6
1953	230	6	2,079	11.0
1954	62	3	664	9.4
1955	28	2	397	6.9
1956	692	11	4,377 [d]	15.8
1957	977	20	8,834 [d,e]	11.1
1958	338	14	2,590 [d,e]	13.1
1959	180	12	1,174 [e]	15.3
1960	280	14	2,562 [d]	10.9
1961	2,478	22	8,315	29.8
1962	584	18	4,713	12.4
1963	333	15	1,243 [f]	26.9
1964	1,950	22	25,227 [f,g]	7.7
1965	2,434	23	20,395 [f,g,h]	11.9
1966	1,448	34	21,675 [g,i]	6.7

[a] Gold, foreign exchange, and gold tranche position at the IMF.
[b] Excludes reserves of Ethiopia; includes India, whose reserves included some long-term securities.
[c] Excludes reserves of Yugoslavia.   [e] Excludes reserves of Haiti.
[d] Excludes reserves of Paraguay.   [f] Excludes reserves of Liberia.
[g] Including a U.S. drawing; U.S. reserves were $16.8 billion at the end of 1965.
[h] Excludes reserves of Burundi.
[i] Excludes reserves of Burundi, Guinea, Liberia, and Rwanda.
Source: IMF, *International Financial Statistics.*

for the gold and super-gold tranches) in the category of conditional rather than unconditional lines of credit.[13]

The EPU and the IMF represent the most important lending institutions for monetary purposes in the postwar period. From time to time large bilateral credits have been made for balance-of-payments reasons, however, and these serve a similar function to the extent that they can be relied upon. In 1946, the United States lent $3.75 billion to the United Kingdom, to be amortized over a period of 50 years. Marshall Plan aid to all Western Europe was much larger in size, amounting to over $16 billion, and some part of that can be considered to have been for monetary purposes although most of it was closer in intention to development assistance: it was to finance food and a once-for-all reconstruction of the European capital stock (including working capital). In 1958, the United States, the EPU, and the IMF participated in financial loans to France totalling $655 million. Emergency balance-of-payments support was gathered in the early 1960s for Canada ($750 million in 1962), Italy ($1,000 million in 1964), and the United Kingdom ($910 million in 1961 and $1,880 million—more if needed—in 1964). These operations were

[13] The stringency of conditions increases with the proportion of the quota drawn. The IMF is "liberal" in lending the first credit tranche. It is interesting to note that IMF quotas have lagged substantially behind the growth in world trade and national incomes. Original quotas were computed on the basis of a five-part formula: the ratio of exports to national income for 1934–38 times the sum of

(1) 2 per cent of national income in 1940;
(2) 5 per cent of gold and dollar reserves in mid-1943;
(3) 10 per cent of average annual imports in 1934–38;
(4) 10 per cent of maximum variation in annual exports in 1934–38.

If this formula is applied to the period 1955–59 instead of 1934–38, total Fund quotas in 1962 would have been $38 billion instead of $15 billion. The United States quota alone would have been $11.5 billion instead of $4.1 billion. A more recent base would place total quotas above $50 billion, compared with the $21 billion to which they were raised in 1966. Larger quotas do not mean larger reserves, of course, since the Fund gold tranche in most cases merely corresponds to gold subscriptions. But conditional liquidity would be much larger.

For a discussion of the Bretton Woods formula, see Oscar L. Altman, "Quotas in the International Monetary Fund," IMF, *Staff Papers*, V, August 1956, pp. 136–42.

all *ad hoc*. The United States was the principal participant in the lines of credit to Canada and Italy, both involving the IMF. Loans to Britain were made by continental European countries under the so-called Basle Arrangements, briefly described in Chapter 2. It can be seen that these individual operations exceeded *total* lending by the IMF except in its most active years.

The United States has institutionalized short-term lending facilities in a series of bilateral "swap" arrangements between central banks, whereby at the initiative of either central bank each bank opens a drawing account for the other. These swap facilities totalled $7.1 billion in late 1967, compared with a U.S. quota at the IMF of $5.2 billion and automatic drawing rights of about $1.3 billion. They have been used from time to time by the United States, and they were used in the support operations for Canada, Italy, and Britain (in 1964) mentioned above. These facilities vary in maturity, but none exceeds 12 months. The swaps are renewable by mutual agreement, and they have been renewed on a number of occasions when it appeared that the need for them would be temporary but longer than the original maturity.[14]

The emergency loans of recent years and the apparent need of the United States for swap facilities suggest certain deficiencies in the International Monetary Fund as a source of and supplement to international liquidity. IMF lending was evidently felt to be too costly, too clumsy to arrange, too small in amount, or too visible to the public to satisfy the requirements of the countries in need. Moreover, except in the case of the United Kingdom in 1964, these *ad hoc* lending operations all took place while the borrowing countries still had large owned reserves, suggesting that even these were not adequate to the task. Italy was enormously well-supplied with reserves in early 1964, and never let them fall below $2.8 billion. Canada still had $1.7 billion in reserves when it arranged the large credit line in June 1962.

In periods of great uncertainty a decline in owned reserves—or a large drawing from the IMF—may be incorrectly taken as a sign of

[14] Transactions under the swap arrangements are described in semi-annual articles in the *Federal Reserve Bulletin*. The swap arrangements were first inaugurated in 1962. But Federal Reserve stabilization loans were made in the 1920s, and a renewal of this practice was urged in 1953 by the staff of the Randall Commission. See Commission on Foreign Economic Policy, *Staff Papers* (Washington: GPO, 1954), p. 484.

weakness, a signal to flee the currency. Yet if countries become reluctant to use owned reserves to protect their foreign and domestic policies in the face of balance-of-payments deficits, owned reserves cease to serve their most useful function. Countries may prefer to borrow to cover deficits, partly to avoid a visible decline in gross reserves, partly because such lending may itself represent a demonstration of confidence by officials of the lending countries.[15]

The interest of the United States in establishing swap arrangements was influenced by the occasional need for speed and the desire for secrecy which an IMF drawing could not provide; but it also reflected the second limitation on IMF lending mentioned in Chapter 2: a shortage of resources. The U.S. quota at the IMF is so large that a substantial American drawing might deplete the Fund's holdings of convertible currencies other than the dollar and sterling, thus impairing its other lending operations.[16] The swap facilities provide an alternative source of needed foreign exchange to the United States, albeit at short term.

Ad hoc bilateral credits are a long distance from the ample and automatic financing of deficits which is required to permit countries to maintain freedom of trade and capital movements and still to allow them to pursue objectives of domestic economic policy unfettered by balance-of-payments considerations.

Typically, the creditor cannot refrain from imposing conditions on the debtor. A celebrated case is the 1931 foreign (private) creditors' requirement that Britain cut unemployment compensation as a condition for a loan—a loan which failed to stave off devaluation in any case. The United States laid down guidelines for Britain's foreign economic policy in the postwar period as conditions for the Anglo-American Loan of 1946, including the requirement that Britain in effect waive its Article XIV rights under the Bretton Woods Agreement and declare sterling convertible within one year.[17] The United

15 Just as IMF lending to less developed countries marks foreign official approval of their stabilization programs.

16 As noted earlier, the GAB was established in 1961 to meet this difficulty; under it, the Fund could add $3 billion to its lendable currencies other than the dollar and sterling. But the GAB also, in effect, introduced another critical hurdle for the borrowing country.

17 The principal effect of these conditions was to delay convertibility rather than to hasten it, as British officials reacted to the noble but disastrous effort

States also imposed heavy conditions for financial rectitude in connection with its loan to France in February 1958.[18]

Yet the United States has a reputation as a relatively easy and generous creditor. This undoubtedly explains in part why Italy turned to the United States for funds in early 1964 rather than to its more exacting Common Market partners. The members of the EEC Monetary Committee were reported to have been much annoyed at Italy's circumvention of their authority. The IMF, as already noted, puts prospective drawers through a detailed examination and usually exacts commitments from them regarding financial policies to be taken as a condition for a large drawing. Sometimes stand-by arrangements are operative only if such policies have already been put into effect at the time the country actually wants to draw.

Very often the creditor's advice will be sound.[19] But sometimes it will not.[20] And whatever the objective merits of the conditions for financial support, they will always rankle the debtor, who will be

---

by Britain to adhere to the Agreement in July and August 1947. See R. Triffin, *Europe and the Money Muddle*, cited, pp. 138–41.

[18] *The New York Times*, January 31, 1958, p. 1, reported that "Monetary experts made it clear that France, in accepting help, had virtually signed a contract by which she was committed to carry out economic, commercial and monetary programs she had submitted in making the requests.

"She must bar inflation, maintain tight credit, keep budgetary spending and the consequent deficit down to the limits she herself set last December [Fr. 600 billion], move to lift by the middle of the year some of the quotas she imposed last year on imports, and eliminate artificial aids to exports such as subsidies."

[19] Jacques Rueff has applauded the stringent financial conditions the United States imposed on France in 1958 as just what it needed. See Jacques Rueff and Fred Hirsch, "The Role and the Rule of Gold: An Argument," Princeton Essay in International Finance, No. 47, Princeton University, June 1965, pp. 9–10.

[20] Many Latin American economists, for example, challenge sharply the "model" implicit in IMF lending conditions as being wholly inappropriate to developing economies with the economic structure typically found in Latin America. See various essays on "structuralism vs. monetarism" in Werner Baer and Isaac Kerstenetzky (eds.), *Inflation and Growth in Latin America* (Homewood, Ill.: Richard D. Irwin, Inc., for the Economic Growth Center of Yale University, 1964). Also J. Olivera, "On Structural Inflation and Latin-American 'Structuralism,'" *Oxford Economic Papers*, XVI, November 1964, pp. 321–32.

more eager to seek alternative ways to cope with the deficit, such as restrictions on trade.

Keynes' Clearing Union would have avoided the imposition of conditions except in extreme cases. Within narrower limits, the EPU and even the American swap arrangements also avoid such conditions, although drawings under the swaps must be repaid relatively quickly.

One alleged source of automatic and even unlimited balance-of-payments support has not yet been mentioned. It arises from the fact that *national* currencies are held as international reserves. Thus, the reserve currency countries would seem to have unlimited financing, for they can "print" international money which other countries are willing to hold.

Britain can buy heavily in the Sterling Area without being concerned with the *direct* impact of such buying on reserves, because Sterling Area countries simply hold their reserve accruals in sterling balances in London. France is in a similar situation vis-à-vis the members of the French Franc Area. But the constituents of both these areas are largely less-developed countries that do not accumulate reserves for any length of time; they typically convert foreign exchange earnings into needed imports rather quickly. Since neither currency area is closed and self-contained, such spending "leaks out" to the rest of the world and results in an indirect loss of reserves to the reserve currency countries, Britain and France. The less leakage there is, of course, the smaller the loss in reserves to the reserve country in any given period of time. On average, France is rather better off than Britain in this respect, since over 60 per cent of Franc Area imports come from France, while only one-fourth of Outer Sterling Area imports are from the United Kingdom. On the other hand, a larger part of Britain's import needs are satisfied from its currency area than is true for France (one-third and one-sixth, respectively).

Britain might have had access to unlimited financing in the 1920s, when sterling was the only true international currency. But the domestic deflation Britain had to undergo in order to support an overvalued currency after 1925 suggests that if it had this advantage, it did not perceive it. In fact, it had no such advantage. Some countries did indeed hold sterling in addition to—or even instead of—gold in their reserves, in response to the resolutions of the Genoa Conference of 1922 urging conservation of gold. But the United States never held sterling, and France held it only reluctantly before 1928, ceased to add to its holdings in 1928, and proceeded to liquidate its sterling holdings in 1931.

The United States in the 1950s perhaps comes closest to a country able to sustain prolonged payments deficits because of an ability to issue international money. It undoubtedly did gain some freedom of maneuver in the late 1950s and early 1960s because of the willingness of many countries to accumulate dollar balances. But the freedom was not without limits. In the first place several countries, such as the Netherlands, Switzerland, and the United Kingdom, do not as a matter of central banking practice hold foreign exchange in any substantial quantity.[21] Second, a number of countries, notably the members of the EEC, became increasingly reluctant to add dollars to their international reserves and even to hold dollars accumulated in the past. Indeed, in 1965 and 1966 the official foreign exchange holdings of the continental European countries taken as a group fell $1,920 million, while gold holdings rose $2,550 million, reflecting large conversions—mostly by France—of dollars earned in previous years.

In fact, domestic economic policy in the United States, which experienced unemployment in excess of 4 per cent continuously from 1957 to 1965, did not take the course of vigorous expansion which the freedom to print international money allegedly permitted. Fear of excessive gold losses certainly restrained monetary policy in the United States after 1959. Europeans may have felt that the United States did not go so far as it should have in tightening monetary policy, but many Americans felt it went too far. United States monetary policy obviously represented a compromise between these conflicting considerations, and eventually pressures on the balance of payments resulted in restrictions on international transactions—on government purchases abroad, on capital outflows and even on travel.

Proposals for International Monetary Reform

Generous sources of balance-of-payments financing are not to be found in practice. What about proposed reforms? After 1959, concern developed over the stability of the international monetary system.

[21] These conventions have occasionlly been violated in recent years when foreign exchange accruals were necessary explicitly to support a currency, e.g., in the Basle Arrangements for support of sterling. Such holdings have usually carried an exchange value guarantee or its equivalent.

Proposals were advanced to improve the payments systems, but none of them featured provision of liquidity sufficiently ample to permit simultaneous preservation of autonomy in domestic policy and avoidance of restrictions on international transactions. These proposals take many forms, but they can be grouped into three categories: increasing the number of reserve currencies, creating a new reserve asset backed directly by specified countries, and empowering the IMF to take on the role and functions of an international central bank.[22]

These schemes are tailored to a variety of objectives; but a principal aim of all of them is to halt and reverse a deterioration in the structure and quality of international liquidity while still providing for adequate reserve growth. As noted in Chapter 2, monetary gold stocks since the Second World War have grown barely more than 1 per cent a year, while foreign trade and other international transactions have grown at rates of 5 to 10 per cent a year. With these disparate rates of growth, a shortage of international reserves was bound to appear sooner or later unless some supplement to gold could be found. For years the U.S. dollar performed this role; the deficit in the U.S. balance of payments was both a cause and a consequence of the vast accumulation of U.S dollars in the international reserves of many countries. Moreover, U.S. gold sales totalling over $8 billion redistributed gold reserves from the United States to the rest of the world. But the sale of U.S. gold and the rise of foreign official dollar holdings both worsened the "liquidity position" of the United States and raised doubts about the ability of the U.S. Treasury to maintain the gold convertibility of the dollar. Questions were also raised about the desirability or equity of permitting a particular country to benefit from the growing demand for international liquidity. Additions to foreign dollar balances allowed the United States to import more, to purchase more assets abroad, or to undertake larger foreign aid or military expenditures than would otherwise have been the case. But the question of equity, articulated most clearly in France,[23] was generally secondary to more widespread concern

[22] A useful discussion of the second two categories of schemes, and several others, is found in Alvin H. Hansen, *The Dollar and the International Monetary System* (New York: McGraw-Hill, 1965). See also Group of Ten, *Report of the Study Group on the Creation of Reserve Assets* ("Ossola Report," after its chairman), 1965.

[23] But not exclusively in France. See, for example, the *Annual Report* of the Netherlands Bank for 1964, p. 18.

about the viability of a payments system dependent for its growth on the international use of a national currency, with reserve growth arising as more or less an accidental by-product of payments deficits run by the reserve currency country.

The proposals for reform all involved creation of a supplement—and in some cases ultimately a substitute—for gold and the U.S. dollar in international reserves; and most called for an orderly and rational decision-making process for generating reserves to replace reliance for this important matter on South African gold output, Russian gold sales, and U.S. payments deficits.

One way of accomplishing the first end, and the objective of introducing greater "symmetry" into the distribution of the alleged benefits from reserve creation, would be to enlarge the number of reserve currencies.[24] In addition to U.S. dollars, sterling, and (for the Franc Area) the French franc, countries could be encouraged to hold German marks, Swiss francs, Italian lire, Dutch guilders, and other currencies. In particular, a *surplus* in the U.S. balance of payments need not reduce international liquidity under this arrangement, since the United States could accumulate foreign currencies instead of retiring outstanding dollars. With more national currencies in the ranks eligible for international reserves, growth in international liquidity would not have to depend so heavily as it has in the past on deficits by just one country, the United States, with the attendant weakening of confidence in its currency.

A second class of proposals, allowing far less voluntarism to central banks in their choice of reserve assets, involved creating a new reserve asset backed by a number of select currencies in fixed proportions. One proposal called for a "bouquet" of currencies to be used in settlement of payments deficits, with national reserves readjusted periodically to conform to the required proportions.[25] In this the scheme differs from the multiple-reserve standard, which would per-

[24] For espousal of a multiple reserve currency system, see Friedrich A. Lutz, "The Problem of International Liquidity and the Multiple-Currency Standard," Princeton Essay in International Finance, No. 41, Princeton University, March 1963; and Robert V. Roosa, "Assuring the Free World's Liquidity," Federal Reserve Bank of Philadelphia, *Business Review*, September 1962, reprinted in his *The Dollar and World Liquidity* (New York: Random House, 1967).

[25] S. Posthuma, "The International Monetary System," *Banca Nazionale del Lavoro Quarterly Review*, September 1963, pp. 239–61. Posthuma was a director of the Netherlands Bank.

mit countries to purchase the foreign currencies they chose directly in the foreign exchange markets and to dispose of unwanted currencies in the same way. In addition, emphasis in the "bouquet" proposal shifts from the psychological discipline of the multiple reserve currency standard, imposed by the prospect of having one's currency become unacceptable to others, to a more rigid discipline imposed by fixed proportions in reserve holding and settlement of imbalances.

The notion of a "bouquet" of currencies was formalized in proposals by E. M. Bernstein and by French Minister of Finance Giscard d'Estaing. These proposals would create a new kind of international money, a composite reserve unit, which would be made up of selected national currencies in fixed proportions. Bernstein suggested that this new international currency be created through deposits of national currencies in a special account at the IMF. Each depositor would be credited for a corresponding amount of the new reserve unit and could use it freely to settle payments deficits with other participating countries.[26] Countries would agree to hold reserve units equal to at least one half of their gold holdings, but otherwise the composition of reserves would be left for each individual country to determine. The reserve unit itself would be backed by national currencies in fixed proportions, and increases in this unit could satisfy growing world needs for international liquidity.

The French plan was still less permissive. It would entirely eliminate the holding of national currencies in international reserves except those embodied in the new collective reserve unit (CRU), which would be made up of national currencies in proportions fixed according to national gold holdings as of some initial period.[27] All international settlements would be made in CRU and gold in fixed propor-

---

[26] E. M. Bernstein, "A Practical Program for International Monetary Reserves," Model, Roland & Co., *Quarterly Review and Investment Survey,* Fourth Quarter, 1963. Bernstein urges that this reform be coupled with greater automaticity in IMF lending. Robert V. Roosa has also advocated a new reserve unit in his *Monetary Reform for the World Economy* (New York: Harper & Row, for the Council on Foreign Relations, 1965).

[27] The French plan was extensively discussed long before it was finally revealed to the public in "La Politique Monétaire Internationale de la France," a speech by Finance Minister Giscard d'Estaing at the French Institute of Banking and Financial Studies, June 15, 1965, reprinted in *Exposés de M. Valéry Giscard d'Estaing sur les Problèmes Monétaires Internationaux* (Paris, 1965).

tions, thus imposing "discipline" symmetrically on all countries. International reserves would be increased by unanimous vote of the participating countries and would be allocated to them on the basis of their gold holdings. This scheme is equivalent to selective and periodic appreciations of the price of gold held by central banks, since each decision to create additional CRUs would give a "capital gain" to countries in proportion to their official gold holdings.

One of the most celebrated and controversial proposals, advocated by Robert Triffin, would transform the IMF into a true international central bank which would not only act as a "lender of last resort" to countries experiencing balance-of-payments difficulties, but would also engage, at its own initiative, in "open market operations" as required to enlarge the world's supply of owned reserves.[28] An international central bank would substitute an orderly procedure for generating international liquidity for one which is, in Triffin's view, both haphazard and dangerous. Thus, he would encourage countries to deposit their existing holdings of reserve currencies in the transformed IMF in exchange for liquid claims on that institution—claims which would be fully usable to settle international imbalances. Such deposits would remove the "overhang" of dollar and sterling liabilities which allegedly threatens the international monetary system through a crisis in confidence.

Reserve creation would take place at the initiative of the IMF by approved investments which increase national claims on itself. But reserve creation "would remain limited . . . by the wisdom of the Fund's traditionally conservative management" and by ceilings imposed on reserve creation and changeable only by special voting procedures.[29] Thus countries could rely only on modest additions to their reserves, something in the range of 3 to 5 per cent a year. The resulting claim on the IMF could either be a new unit of the CRU type or an automatic drawing right transferable among countries. In either case it would in effect involve creation of a new kind of international money.

[28] Robert Triffin, *Gold and the Dollar Crisis* (New Haven: Yale University Press, 1960), especially Part II, Chap. 4. See also "Altman on Triffin: A Rebuttal," in Seymour E. Harris (ed.), *The Dollar in Crisis* (New York: Harcourt, Brace & World, Inc., 1961), and, for a more recent version, "Updating the Triffin Plan," in Triffin, *The World Money Maze* (New Haven: Yale University Press, 1966), Chapter IX.

[29] "Updating the Triffin Plan," cited.

These various proposals for creating international liquidity culminated in agreement among the Governors of the IMF, in September 1967, to create a Special Drawing Right (SDR) for all member countries at the IMF. SDR's are to be created to satisfy a secular growth in the demand for international liquidity. Member countries agree to accept SDRs, up to stipulated limits, in exchange for their own currencies. This willingness endows the SDR with the property of "international liquidity" comparable to gold, since SDRs can in effect be used to settle all payments deficits between members of the IMF up to the holding limits of the countries in surplus. It remains to be seen how the SDRs will work in practice, and, in particular, whether countries will feel free to use them to settle payment deficits. Their use may be restrained by the requirement that each country must hold an average of 30 per cent of its allocations over the first five-year period after the SDRs are put into use. In terms of the provision of ample liquidity, however, the amount of new SDRs created is as important as its nature; and discussions thus far suggest that the amounts created are likely to be very small, at least initially.

It should be clear from this brief summary that none of these proposals for international monetary reform provide for extremely generous balance-of-payments financing, leaving to each country full discretion over its domestic economic policies. Each of them—except possibly the multiple reserve currency system, which is subject to many of the limitations of a system based on a single reserve currency—could do so technically, if the amounts of new liquidity created were sufficiently large. But most of the proposals have been put forward with a view to preserving or even tightening the "discipline" of the balance of payments. The French CRU proposal is explicitly designed to introduce greater pressures on the deficit countries to gear their internal policies to the requirements of external balance. Even the allegedly radical proposals, such as Triffin's plan for the creation of an international central bank, are moderate or even conservative by the standards required to finance large and prolonged deficits. Their radicalism is institutional, not conceptual.

Triffin's plan would not change substantially IMF lending procedures for countries in balance-of-payments deficit. On the contrary, such lending "should be subordinated" to agreement between the Fund and the drawing member on "the broad economic and financial policies followed by the member to ensure long-run equilibrium in its international transactions without excessive recourse to trade and exchange restrictions." [30] Triffin is wary of increased automaticity in IMF lending, except for moderate amounts and with short maturities. [31] Thus, the criteria for borrowing from the Fund would not be changed. Fund lending could be modified, of course, to substitute claims on the Fund for the national currencies now used in IMF lending operations, but that would represent a technical adjustment, not a substantive change.

Finally, the new SDRs may well represent a satisfactory substitute for gold in providing secular growth in international reserves, as new gold production is drawn increasingly into private uses, without in any way relaxing the conventional discipline of the balance of payments.

A Summing Up

EPU swing credits and Federal Reserve swap arrangements go much further than the proposals for major monetary reform in permitting automatic financing of balance-of-payments deficits, but they were and are limited to short-term financing. Something analogous is needed for a longer period of time—say, five to ten years. Among the major proposals which have been advanced to date, Keynes' Clearing Union (described briefly in Chapter 2) still stands out as allowing the greatest degree of freedom for domestic policy in a world of liberal trade. "Overdraft rights" at the Clearing Union were very large [32]

[30] *Gold and the Dollar Crisis,* cited, p. 115.

[31] Triffin sharply criticizes Bernstein's proposals as involving "far more revolutionary and unprecedented surrenders of sovereignty by prospective lenders" than do his own proposals by virtue of the "vast and automatic" access to credits which Bernstein's proposals seem to give to deficit countries "regardless of the wisdom or folly of their own policies, and of their acceptability to the lenders and to the international community itself." Yet this criticism exaggerates the generosity of Bernstein's proposed scheme. R. Triffin, "The Bizarre Proposals of Dr. Bernstein for International Monetary Reform," *Kyklos,* XVII, 1964, Fasc. 3, pp. 338–39, reprinted in *The World Money Maze,* cited pp. 327–40.

[32] At one point, the British proposal suggested that quotas should equal 75 per cent of average annual "trade turnover"—the sum of imports and exports—during the preceding five years. World trade averaged over $130 billion a year during 1960–64, so this rule would have resulted in quotas for all countries together totalling $198 billion in 1965. Under Keynes' proposed plan, each

and they were virtually automatic. Nothing as generous has been proposed since 1943.

The focus of most proposals for creating new forms of international liquidity on the level and quality of international reserves rather than on the ability of countries to finance ever larger deficits suggest that there may be two quite distinct aspects to the relevant level of international liquidity.

First, as their economies and foreign transactions grow, countries may want to *hold* steadily increasing reserves. International money, like domestic money, may be a "luxury good" which countries want to increase disproportionately as their total wealth increases.[33] Countries may rationalize this growing demand as reflecting increased transactions or precautionary demand for reserves, but it may in fact simply reflect the "expansive feeling" of a wealthy country.[34] But if the stock of acceptable international reserves (e.g., gold) is limited, growing countries may paradoxically find themselves taking measures to slow the rate of growth in output because reserves do not seem sufficiently large. Under these circumstances, as noted in Chapter 6, it is not generally possible for all countries to set target reserve levels (or balance-of-payments targets calling for additions to reserves) independently of one another. Unless world reserves grow as rapidly as the targets require, some countries will fail to achieve their targets.

Introduction of a reserve-creating mechanism which accommodates the global level of reserves to the independent demands of countries can eliminate the possible inconsistencies in nationally determined targets. In a world of n countries such a mechanism provides an $(n + 1)^{\text{th}}$ source or use of international reserves. Triffin's proposal has the IMF perform this role, expanding or contracting world re-

---

country could use half its quota before being obliged to make a major adjustment in policies, implying readily accessible drawing rights of nearly $100 billion, compared with total IMF quotas of $21 billion in 1966.

[33] The Netherlands Bank has argued, for example, that all domestic liquid assets in excess of 30 per cent of national income should be fully "covered" by international reserves. If domestic liquid assets rise more rapidly than national income, this would imply a growing demand for international liquidity quite apart from balance-of-payments needs. See the Netherlands Bank, *Annual Report* for 1964, p. 82.

[34] And it may, indeed, reflect a decline in the rate of return on real assets. It is said that less-developed countries cannot "afford" reserves because of their acute shortage of capital, i.e., the high opportunity cost of holding reserves.

serves as needed. The CRU proposal accomplishes the same end, though the institutional and decision-making arrangements differ sharply. Either process is analogous to that performed by a properly functioning national central bank, which provides the additional cash that the public desires to hold or takes up any cash that the public finds superfluous. A central banks' central bank could perform the same function for central banks, adjusting the level of world reserves to their independently determined demand for reserves to hold.

The second dimension of liquidity is liquidity for *use*, for financing balance-of-payments deficits. Either owned reserves or liberal borrowing facilities which can be invoked at the initiative of the deficit country can serve the purpose. Such financing must be more generous than in the past if countries are to avoid undesirable internal and external measures in the face of larger prospective payments deficits. If shifts in expenditure patterns and in portfolio holdings increase roughly in proportion to the increase in national income, then international reserves must grow more rapidly than income because the growing interdependence among nations will, with sensible domestic policies, translate these disturbances into still larger reserve losses. If reserves do not grow sufficiently, policy instruments will have to be diverted from domestic objectives to the balance of payments, or else external measures will be taken to reduce the interdependencies.

These two dimensions of international liquidity are obviously not totally separable. A higher level of owned reserves can be used to finance larger deficits, and indeed the prospect of larger deficits will very likely provide one reason for wanting larger reserves. But if that is so, countries must be willing to use their larger reserves, not merely to hold them. Reserves and IMF drawing rights do not exist to be defended; they exist to be used to defend national economic policies in the face of balance-of-payments deficits. But the observed tendency to "defend" reserves suggests that reserves to hold and liquidity to use are at least partially separable. For many countries there may be a kind of ratchet effect, with the level of *desired* reserves rising when actual reserves are observed to rise but not falling when they fall. Countries seem to worry about balance-of-payments deficits no matter how large or prolonged the preceding surpluses.

Ample provision of liquidity for use implies some change in judgment about "deficits." It recognizes that some deficits may be desirable, or in any event the least of possible evils. It is clear from the discussion above, however, that most of the debate over the need for international monetary reform and better arrangements for generating international liquidity is not merely a disguise for loosening the balance-of-payments "discipline," as is sometimes charged.

Ample liquidity to finance payments deficits, necessary to protect domestic economic autonomy in the face of rising economic interdependence with unrestrained international transactions, carries with it the two related dangers of abuse already mentioned. With ample liquidity, some countries could foist unwanted inflation on their trading partners, or they could appropriate an unfair share of the output of their partners. A monetary system giving large scope to deficit financing therefore depends to an exceptional degree on mutual confidence in the judgment of trading partners both with regard to their choice of objectives and with regard to their choice of technique in pursuing objectives. As with coordinated decision-making discussed in the preceding chapter, political cohesion must be high for such a system to continue to work effectively. But here a rather different kind of political cohesion is required: sufficient mutual trust to leave each other alone, despite high interactions between national economies and the actions of national authorities.

International monetary discussions and actions during the early and mid-1960s, while cordial and often productive, did not reflect this kind of mutual trust. On the contrary, there were chronic complaints on both sides of the Atlantic about the economic policies of other members of the community. Suspicions of abuse hindered even the modest efforts required to provide some additional liquidity, much less a regime of ample liquidity; and, indeed, some participants voiced the view that there already existed too much scope for financing deficits and that new liquidity should not be used to finance deficits at all.

The mutual trust required for the kind of arrangement discussed in this chapter may grow in the course of time. There have been some hopeful signs. Mutual support between central banks to combat speculative crises reached unprecedented heights in the 1960s. But growing interdependence will still leave certain intrusions into domestic policy, complicating both the path of adjustment to macroeconomic disturbances and the regulation and taxation of residents. The following chapter, therefore, considers a third broad course of action, the deliberate slowing down or even reversal of growing economic interdependence.

CHAPTER NINE

Controlled Restraints
on International Transactions

Provision of liquidity in amounts sufficient to permit countries to run large and prolonged deficits is not likely to find a sympathetic hearing among most financial experts. Triffin undoubtedly reflects the views of most officials when he says, "it would be revolutionary and utopian to expect the lenders to accept large automatic commitments to finance blindly the future deficits of all and any country, without regard for the wisdom or folly of the policies which may be at the root of these deficits." [1] Indeed, discussions from 1964 to 1967 among members of the Group of Ten countries indicate that even this limited group of countries, with common interests and common problems, have not developed the mutual trust required to underwrite payments deficits for prolonged periods.

Part of the reason is that payments imbalances may arise in a variety of ways. It is helpful to classify imbalances into two broad groups, according to whether they are due to (a) excessive or deficient monetary expansion, or (b) structural changes. The first involves upward or downward movements in the level of monetary demand, relative to other countries, and hence pressure on the general *level* of prices.[2] The second involves, in effect, all other changes, in-

[1] "The International Monetary System," *Moorgate and Wall Street,* Summer 1965, p. 35; reprinted in *The World Money Maze,* cited, Chapter IX.

[2] Actual price changes may not be observed if the economy in question is heavily engaged in international trade, for prices will be determined on the world market. But the tendency toward price change will affect profits and trade flows. Robert Triffin and Herbert Grubel have pointed out that the more "integrated" two regions are economically, the more will inflationary pressures in one region be observed as a growing import surplus rather than as a rise in prices. See their "The Adjustment Mechanism to Differential Rates of Mone-

cluding changes in the pattern of demand, shifts in government expenditures overseas, autonomous changes in international capital flows, and the like. It is often argued that ample provision of liquidity would permit excessive monetary expansion and would thereby aggravate payments imbalances rather than merely permit orderly adjustment.

Yet, if ample liquidity would fail to impose enough discipline on national economic policies, policy coordination is likely to impose too much discipline, given present sensitivities about national "sovereignty" which pervade most major countries. When we have neither ample liquidity nor agreed policy-coordination, we are likely to find a pervasive groping toward selective methods for influencing international transactions. Some of these methods will represent "loopholes" in the present GATT and IMF rules governing international trade and payments; others will involve outright violations of these international undertakings. But the competitive use of external measures, like the competitive use of internal measures, can damage such social objectives as allocative efficiency and economic growth. It is, therefore, necessary to consider the various classes of external measures which might be used with least damage to these objectives and which, moreover, can be widely enough accepted to avoid retaliation.

We shall consider three broad classes of external measures for influencing the size of international payments and receipts: limited flexibility in exchange rates, policy restraints on trade and other current account transactions, and policy restraints on international capital movements. The cost of restraints are then compared with the costs of internal measures as correctives to the balance of payments.

Limited Flexibility in Exchange Rates: Wider Margins

As a compromise between systems of fixed and flexible exchange rates, it has been suggested that exchange parities remain fixed but

---

tary Expansion Among Countries of the European Economic Community," *Review of Economics and Statistics,* XLIV, November 1962, pp. 486–91. Similarly, pressures for change in price structure between two highly integrated areas will be observed as a change in the composition of trade rather than as an actual change in price structure. "Integrated" here means closely linked product markets.

that permissible variations in rates around parity be broadened from the plus or minus 1 per cent allowed by the IMF to 3, or 4, or even 5 per cent.[3]

Widening exchange rate margins allegedly offer two advantages. First, movements in exchange rates contribute to the elimination of payments imbalances by setting in motion corrective movements of foreign trade and long-term capital. As a country begins to run a payments deficit, its exchange rate will depreciate and its exports will become more competitive in world markets (or, if the country is so small that it takes all world prices as given, its producers will find it profitable to divert sales from the domestic market to the export market). By a similar process, imports will become less competitive with domestic products. Finally, if the change is thought to be permanent, the increased profitability of export- and import-competing industries will induce new foreign equity investment in the country or deter national investment abroad. Thus, on all three counts, the payments position will be improved.

Second, widening exchange margins would introduce a greater element of uncertainty into the returns from short-term capital transactions, where relatively small differences in the yields influence the placement of large sums. These small differences could be swamped by movements in the exchange rates. It is possible to insure short-term holdings in another country against exchange loss by selling the foreign currency in the forward market. But larger exchange margins would increase the cost of such forward cover, and thus would discourage some movement of short-term funds.

At the same time, a system of fixed parities with wider margins allegedly differs from completely flexible rates by setting outer limits to

[3] See George N. Halm, "The 'Band' Proposal: The Limits of Permissible Exchange Rate Variations," Princeton Special Paper in International Finance, No. 6, Princeton University, 1965. See also William Fellner, "On Limited Exchange-rate Flexibility," in William Fellner *et al., Maintaining and Restoring Balance in International Payments* (Princeton, N.J.: Princeton University Press, 1966), Chapter 5. The proposal to widen exchange margins should not be confused with a similar proposal for widening the margins on purchases and sales of *gold*, designed to discourage speculation on a one-step increase in the price of gold. See Robert A. Mundell, "The Gold Herring," testimony before the Joint Economic Committee, 88th U.S. Cong., 1st Sess., November 15, 1963; and same, *The International Monetary System: Conflict and Reform* (Montreal: The Private Planning Association of Canada, 1965), pp. 37–43.

exchange rate variations, so that currency speculation and destabilizing wage-price spirals cannot get out of control. There is still an exchange parity for the monetary authorities to defend, thus preserving some measure of monetary discipline.

The proposal for a broader band around parity has much to be said for it. According to the argument of Chapter 3, widening exchange margins should be very effective at keeping payments close to balance. If the structure of comparative costs does not differ much from country to country and if barriers to trade are low, then price elasticities of export supply and import demand, especially for manufactures, will be quite large, particularly after enough time has elapsed to permit new marketing arrangements. Thus, relatively small changes in exchange rates should be sufficient, after a lapse of time, to eliminate quite large deficits and surpluses in payments.

Moreover, wider exchange margins would separate national money markets, permitting greater divergences in short-term interest rates. Even though they are not officially supported, forward exchange rates will not normally move outside the margins for spot rates. So long as par values are not expected to be changed, the speculator will buy a currency forward if the forward rate falls below the lower support point of the spot rate; he has a "sure profit" by doing so, for he knows the monetary authorities will not let the spot rate in the future fall below the lower support rate.

But if forward rates are in practice confined within the same narrow band as spot rates, differences in national short-term interest rates on comparable assets are similarly confined. Greater divergences in interest rates will evoke large-scale international movements of short-term capital completely free of exchange risk, for the forward rate cannot adjust to compensate for the difference in interest rates.[4] At present, forward rates lying outside the official intervention points

---

[4] What is relevant here is the forward rate *relative* to the spot rate. If the spot rate is already close to the floor for one currency, and if no change in parity is expected, then the forward rate cannot be at a large discount on the spot rate and hence interest rates in that country can rise very little above interest rates elsewhere without inviting a large and persistent inflow of capital, or without forcing other countries to raise their interest rates. Monetary policy cannot under these circumstances be used to curb domestic inflation.

If the flow of capital grows very large, of course, it may push the spot exchange rate up and thereby permit a larger forward discount and difference in interest rates.

indicate speculation on a change in the parity of a currency. At such times, interest rates cease to be the main determinant of short-term capital movements in any case.

In sum, wider exchange margins might help both to correct imbalances through the effects of exchange variations on trade flows and to reduce possible sources of imbalance by discouraging interest-sensitive short-term capital flows.

Wider margins cannot, however, solve problems of extreme maladjustment, where the exchange rate would be prevented from going through the floor or the ceiling only by official support operations.[5] Moreover, widening exchange margins would still leave some countries open to the possibility of destabilizing wage and price adjustments, although perhaps less so than unrestrained rate flexibility. These destabilizing movements may arise in two ways. First, workers and other residents in a country whose currency has depreciated may attempt to preserve real income by compensating any rise in the prices of imported and exportable goods by a rise in wages or other incomes. Since restoration of international balance typically calls for a decline in total expenditure, attempts to preserve real income (and expenditure) will frustrate the currency depreciation, higher wages will lead to higher prices leading to further currency depreciation, and so on in an endless cycle. This prospect is the more likely, the more important traded goods are in the economy.

Second, even if no conscious attempt is made to preserve the level of real income, depreciation may be frustrated in eliminating a payments deficit if the various segments of society are highly sensitive to the distribution of income. Exchange rate changes generally affect trade flows by influencing the distribution of income. Currency devaluation, for example, raises exports because export sales are more profitable—rewards have increased more than costs. In the first instance, profits measured in domestic currency rise in the foreign trade sector, while money wages remain unchanged (and real wages fall because of higher domestic prices for imported goods). Thus, the distribution of national income initially shifts in favor of profits and

---

[5] Wider margins could be combined with gradual changes in parity—say, 1 per cent a year—when an exchange rate rested persistently at either its ceiling or its floor. This would permit long-term adjustment of exchange rates without inviting heavy speculation on large changes in parity. See John H. Williamson, "The Crawling Peg," Princeton Essays in International Finance, No. 50, 1965.

against wage income. In a small country, whose economic activity is heavily influenced by foreign trade, shifts in income distribution resulting from currency devaluation can be very substantial.

Currency devaluation may thus induce a round of wage increases not only because of higher domestic prices for imported and exportable consumer goods, but also because higher profits enlarge labor union bargaining demands. More comfortable profits may in turn weaken the resistance of employers to new wage demands. Some evidence suggests that profit rates do play an important role in wage settlements, at least in the United States and Britain.[6]

The shift in income distribution, like the rise in the cost of living, will depend in degree on the "openness" of the country in question.[7]

[6] See Otto Eckstein and Thomas A. Wilson, "The Determination of Money Wages in American Industry," *Quarterly Journal of Economics,* LXXVI, August 1962, pp. 379–414; N. Kaldor, "Economic Growth and the Problem of Inflation—Part II," *Economica,* November 1959. R. G. Lipsey and M. D. Steuer have questioned this relationship for Britain. See their "The Relation Between Profits and Wage Rates," *Economica,* May 1961, pp. 137–55.

For currency devaluation to generate the maximum improvement in the trade balance requires that the various steps in adjustment be in the right order. Ideally, devaluation will raise profits in the foreign trade (export- and import-competing) industries, attracting both capital and labor into these industries and away from purely domestic industries. Output will expand in the foreign trade sector, money wages will be bid up, and the initial profits appearing after devaluation will be reduced. The final distribution of income need not be shifted toward profits, and in some cases will even be ultimately shifted toward labor.

If, however, there is a substantial time lag in the installation of new capacity in the foreign trade sector, high profits will persist there and the following adverse sequence may develop: organized labor, spying the high profits, may demand and get higher wages in all industries. Purely domestic industries, where profits have not risen, may respond by raising prices and/or releasing labor. The result will be (*a*) higher money wages, reducing the devaluation-induced incentive to expand the foreign trade sector, and possibly (*b*) unemployment, as workers are released from the domestic sector before they are taken up by the foreign trade sector. If authorities respond to the emergence of unemployment by expanding monetary demand, the effect of the devaluation will be further weakened. Thus the success of a currency depreciation depends crucially on the speed of the foreign trade sector in enlarging capacity versus the response of union bargaining to higher profits.

[7] This is one of the factors which determines the "optimal currency area" described in Chapter 7.

If imports are heavily represented in personal consumption, devaluation may be self-defeating. Thus, even at best, widening the margins is not desirable between all currencies, but only between certain blocs of countries which are not intimately connected by economic ties of trade and investment.

Wider margins even between blocs of countries may meet the same opposition from practical people as flexible rates, however. Bankers and financial officials seem strongly opposed to increased rate flexibility, and indeed have tended in the other direction, with monetary officials holding rates within a range narrower than that permitted by the IMF.[8] They are apparently willing to pay a substantial price, in foregoing a potentially efficient adjustment mechanism, for the accounting convenience of having a fixed parity between currencies. This judgment may well be correct, but the price of this decision should be borne at least in part by those who benefit directly from it; they should accept "looser discipline" or some flexible restrictions on international transactions, rather than pass the cost entirely to others in the form of an agonizing choice between lowering money incomes or accepting involuntary unemployment of labor and productive capacity.

Flexible rates are also said to be undesirable because they impede economic and political integration. In 1964 the German government stated (in response to a proposal by five government-appointed experts that the German mark be allowed to float): "Fixed exchange rates are an indispensable element in a world committed to integration; with a system of flexible rates the existing readiness to cooperate and integrate might be destroyed at the first appearance of serious difficulties since flexible rates would offer such an easy opportunity for isolated action."[9] But "opportunity for isolated action" is precisely the objective sought here. If countries are not willing to coordi-

---

[8] A recent statement by Robert V. Roosa, former Under-Secretary of the Treasury for Monetary Affairs and subsequently a partner in an investment banking firm, illustrates these strongly felt but not fully articulated objections to flexible rates. He holds that exchange rates "degenerate into disorderly chaos if they do not have some fixed point of reference," and that flexible rates "create a sense of rubbery unreality concerning the validity of all prices." *Monetary Reform for the World Economy* (New York: Harper & Row, for the Council on Foreign Relations, 1965), pp. 27–28.

[9] Quoted in Mundell, cited, p. 47.

nate their policies effectively, then changes in exchange rates will often be preferable to *ad hoc* and disorderly adjustments in internal and external policies.

One advantage of wider margins around parity over unfettered floating rates is that the width of the band can be narrowed as institutional arrangements evolve for coping effectively with the consequences of *de facto* integration, discussed in Chapter 6. In the meantime, somewhat greater flexibility in rates will have slowed down the process of integration to the pace of institutional evolution. But flexible rates, even limited by bands, do not automatically foster the type of cooperation in policy formation which many observers desire. Flexible use of controls over trade and capital movements lend themselves more readily to the continuous international consultation which may eventually produce close policy coordination in a world which is not yet ready for it.

Variable Restrictions on Trade and Other Current Transactions

Some of the effects of flexible exchange rates can be achieved more selectively by use of variable restrictions on trade or other international transactions. By relaxing restrictions over trade or capital movements, a country can deliberately reduce a payments surplus; by tightening restrictions, it can reduce a payments deficit.

We have already seen the restrictions often imposed by governments on their own international transactions. After 1959, the United States progressively tied its foreign assistance expenditures to purchases of American products, and the Department of Defense progressively raised the differential accorded to American suppliers over their foreign competitors. Both moves were governed by the large and persistent deficit in the U.S. balance of payments.[10]

[10] It is noteworthy that American government transactions were influenced by balance-of-payments considerations even when the United States was in surplus, illustrating a symmetry in behavior not often found between countries in surplus and countries in deficit. Under the European Recovery Program (ERP), funds were often deliberately spent in Europe under the "offshore procurement program," despite higher costs there than in the United States. The object was to get double duty out of the Marshall Plan assistance, to improve the payments positions of several European countries, and to encourage intra-European trade.

West German procurement of U.S. military equipment under the military "offset" agreements of the early 1960s also had something of this character.

Restrictions on government procurement abroad are often determined by mercantilist considerations rather than by balance-of-payments requirements. Political pressures are brought to bear on governments to protect this or that domestic industry by purchases at home. When these pressures are strong, tightening and relaxing procurement restrictions for balance-of-payments reasons becomes more difficult. Many European countries in balance-of-payments surplus not only tie their foreign aid expenditures to domestic procurement but also limit the opportunity of foreigners to compete for other government business by having little or no advance publicity of planned government procurement, giving exclusive preference to domestic firms, and enforcing regulations which preclude foreign bidding on government contracts.

But government buying accounts for only a small part of imports into most countries. The balance of payments can be influenced to a much greater extent if a wider range of transactions, such as total imports, is covered. Surplus countries can reduce their surpluses by reducing artificial barriers to all imports.

This technique was used to great effect by European countries in the 1950s. As noted in Chapter 2, the *timing* of trade liberalization under the OEEC liberalization targets was heavily influenced by balance-of payments considerations. The Managing Board of the EPU urged the large surplus countries to proceed rapidly with their liberalization; Belgium, France, Portugal, and the United Kingdom all responded to this request in 1950.[11] Countries in deficit, by contrast, moved very slowly to liberalize. And after liberalization had gone some way, a number of countries actually reversed course and reimposed quotas when they encountered balance-of-payments difficulties. Britain deliberalized in 1951 and then removed the new quotas in 1952–53; France reimposed quotas in 1951, tightened them further in 1953, liberalized again after 1954, and suspended all liberalization in 1957; Germany deliberalized in 1951, but in 1954 abandoned entirely the use of quantitative restrictions on intra-European trade for balance-of-payments reasons. In contrast, the Netherlands, Norway, and Sweden accelerated the pace of liberalization in 1951, but later slowed it again.

Import quotas were used flexibly to help maintain balance in international transactions. So long as the collective goal is total elimina-

11 Robert Triffin, *Europe and the Money Muddle,* cited, p. 187.

tion of such restrictions, however, use of the *rate* of reduction in restrictions is limited; once the restrictions are gone, this ceases to be a useful instrument of control. The rate of tariff reduction might also be used to promote balance-of-payments equilibrium. Countries in surplus could reduce tariffs more rapidly than those in deficit—again so long as some tariff reduction remains to be undertaken. Unfortunately, however, GATT procedures have militated against the flexibility required to vary tariff reduction for balance-of-payments purposes. Here, too, the principle of "reciprocity" has governed the negotiations. But in this case the participating countries have not been committed to specific over-all targets, as they were under OEEC trade liberalization. Before the Kennedy Round of 1963–67, tariff negotiations were on an item-by-item basis. The bargains struck had to have the appearance of symmetry, for otherwise it would look as though one of the bargaining partners had been "taken." [12]

Item-by-item tariff negotiations do not readily lend themselves to flexible manipulation of tariff reductions for balance-of-payments reasons. It is worth recalling, however, the close analytical similarity between tariff changes and exchange-rate changes. Imposition of uniform tariffs on imports and the granting of uniform subsidies to exports have the same effect on foreign trade as does an equivalent depreciation of the currency. Across-the-board changes in tariffs have profound monetary effects; they cannot be convincingly isolated from broad balance-of-payments considerations as being merely a change in "commercial" policy.[13] Thus tariff negotiations of the form taken by the Kennedy Round, with across-the-board reductions in tariffs by an amount specified in advance (50 per cent), might well be regarded

[12] A partial exception existed when, in the early 1950s, the United States exchanged tariff reductions for foreign "bindings"—agreements not to raise tariffs. This kind of exchange served to restore payments balance at that time.

[13] Under certain circumstances the stimulus to exports from across-the-board reductions in foreign tariffs will exactly balance the stimulus to imports from a reduction in home tariffs; but this would be a rare coincidence. Across-the-board tariff cuts are not quite the same thing, of course, as a reduction in uniform tariffs. Uniform tariffs—say, 15 per cent on all imports—affect allocation of production and consumption in a very different way than do existing tariff structures which average roughly 15 per cent (when the many items on duty-free lists are excluded). Across-the-board tariff cuts have some differential effects which uniform cuts in uniform tariffs would not have.

as an instrument of balance-of-payments policy; the commitments to tariff reduction could be fully reciprocal, but the actual reduction of tariffs could be more rapid for countries in surplus than for countries in deficit.

Tariffs have occasionally been used for balance-of-payments reasons. In a program of "konjunkturpolitische Zollsenkungen," Germany, in 1956 and 1957, unilaterally lowered tariffs by about 50 per cent on virtually all industrial goods in order to combat inflation and reduce its large and persistent balance-of-payments surplus. France in 1961, and again in 1963, unilaterally lowered some tariffs on a limited range of commodities—largely, it is true, to combat domestic inflation, but also to contribute to a reduction of France's large payments surplus at those times.

Tariffs have also been used to reduce deficits. Canada, in June 1962, imposed "import surcharges" of 10 to 15 per cent on a wide range of manufactured commodities. These surcharges were accompanied by exchange-rate stabilization at a depreciated level, and were removed in April 1963, when it became clear that the new exchange rate could survive. In November 1964, Britain imposed import surcharges at a uniform rate of 15 per cent on virtually all manufactured products. These were lowered to 10 per cent in April 1965, and removed in November 1966. Both Britain and Canada exempted foodstuffs, fuels, and industrial materials from the surcharges, although Britain simultaneously raised its excise tax on gasoline for domestic consumption.

The Canadian introduction of surcharges represented the first attempt since post-1958 convertibility by a major trading country to limit imports by the use of an external measure. Both the Canadian and the British moves clearly violated the GATT, and both evoked pained outcries from other countries—more vocal, in the case of Britain, from private parties than from officials, for officials could see more clearly the necessity for action and the limited number of alternatives available. The British move was especially galling to other members of the EFTA, however, because they were not consulted prior to announcement of the surcharges, which represented a significant step backward from the direction of free trade within the area and disturbed a central feature of the association, the apparent certainty and irreversibility of reductions in trade barriers.

The GATT permits imposition of quantitative restrictions for balance-of-payments reasons, but not increases in tariffs. The rationale for this distinction is presumably that quantitative restrictions help the balance of payments quickly by reducing imports at once. Moreover, they are a visible and constant irritant calling forth strong pressure for removal as soon as the balance-of-payments needs have passed. The furor raised by the British and Canadian surcharges suggests, however, that pressure for reducing temporary tariffs can be just as great as that for removing quantitative restrictions. Moreover, surcharges do not require the administrative favoritism implicit in allocating quotas; any importer willing to pay the surcharge can import from any source.[14]

There is an important argument for preferring surcharges to quotas in a case such as that of Britain, even apart from the merits of market controls as opposed to direct controls. New tariffs and new quotas both raise domestic prices on the products covered. In the case of tariffs, some of the resulting quasi-rents accrue to the government in the form of tariff revenues. With quotas, by contrast, higher profits accrue either to the foreign sellers or to the importers favored with quotas, depending upon the degree of international competition for the products in question. For differentiated products with little international competition, foreign sellers will raise their prices in the importing country to the level permitted by the artificial scarcities created by the new quotas, and the reduction in payments for imports will be correspondingly less.[15] For products sold competitively on the world market, the higher profits would accrue to the importers, thereby contributing to domestic income and domestic demand. Yet

[14] Interestingly, this reliance on the "market" apparently did not appeal to foreign exporters in the case of the British surcharges; many of them announced a preference for quotas based on historical market shares, which, they argued, would at least have permitted them to retain their "good will" in the British market through token sales. The surcharges allegedly made such sales so unprofitable that they were not worthwhile. The collective behavior of foreign exporters does not bear out this claim, however. British imports covered by the surcharges remained quite high until Britain deflated domestic demand.

[15] In some circumstances, the import bill might actually rise, so that quotas would worsen the balance of payments. This result would follow if domestic demand for the foreign product were inelastic and if the international industry were oligopolistic in structure, with enough recognition of joint interest among sellers to raise prices in response to the quota but not enough to have raised prices in absence of the quota.

improvement in the balance of payments calls for reducing domestic demand, and this is what tariff revenues tend to do.[16]

As a temporary emergency measure, tariff surcharges may also be superior to devaluation, for they can exclude those goods which might have a large and highly visible effect on the cost of living—with its attendant risk of setting off a wage-price spiral—per dollar of improvement in the balance of payments. They can also exclude those goods that respond only sluggishly to changes in profitability.

The elasticity of import demand is determined both by the elasticity of demand for the products in question *and* by the elasticity of domestic supply for those products. Import demand is likely to be most elastic when domestic supply can respond quickly to the higher prices and profits permitted by the tariff surcharges. For products such as foodstuffs and many industrial materials, domestic demand is not likely to be very sensitive to price changes and domestic output is likely to be relatively fixed in the short run. Under these circumstances, it may be desirable to avoid the transitional costs of resource reallocation by excluding such products from the list of goods covered by surcharges. In addition, across-the-board application of import surcharges could have the perverse effect of raising production costs and thereby discouraging exports.

The danger with this strategy, of course, is that the payments imbalance may prove not to be temporary; in that case it would be desirable to encourage the long-run reallocation and the stimulus to exports that devaluation would provide but that selective surcharges do not provide.

Moreover, when an economy is running at full capacity, domestic supply for virtually all products is inelastic in the short run. Neither devaluation nor import surcharges under these circumstances will produce much reduction in imports unless they are accompanied by a reduction in total domestic expenditure. The initial response of British imports to the introduction of surcharges in late 1964 was disappointing largely because domestic demand continued at a high level. By excluding industrial materials and foodstuffs, the British program of surcharges was properly geared to a manufacturing economy. But with a high level of domestic demand, the surcharges could

[16] The added protection to domestic industry would, of course, raise domestic demand. But this would occur with quantitative restrictions as well as higher tariffs.

not be expected to be very effective in reducing imports. It is note-worthy that the British authorities emphasized as much the demand-reducing effects of the surcharges (over £200 million at an annual rate) as they did the expected switch in home demand from foreign to domestic goods.

Canada, in contrast, had ample domestic capacity to make the demand-switching effects of its 1962 surcharges work. But it is also a substantial producer of raw materials and foodstuffs. Exclusion of these products from the commodity list subjected to surcharges left Canada open to the charge that it was really trying to protect its industry, not its currency.[17]

Before turning to variable restraints over capital movements, brief mention should be made of measures to influence current account transactions other than merchandise trade. Many countries have limited the amounts of money which their residents could spend in any year on foreign travel (Table 9-1). Over the years, these travel allowances have risen greatly in most European countries, and a number of countries have eliminated such allowances entirely.[18] Like trade liberalization, the pace at which travel allowances were enlarged was influenced by balance-of-payments considerations. France and Spain, both with strong payments positions, liberalized such allowances greatly between 1960 and 1963. Portugal and Sweden both tightened their regulations governing travel allowances in 1964, largely to limit capital outflows masquerading as travel expenditures. The United States allows unlimited funds for travel abroad, but it has twice reduced the duty-free allowance which tourists enjoy on returning to the United States, from $500 to $100 in 1961, and to the equivalent of about $70 on the same basis in 1965. Britain sharply

---

[17] The coverage of Canada's surcharges may have been governed more by legal restrictions than by economic logic. The Canadian government apparently could not impose surcharges without going to Parliament, except on those products on which Canada had negotiated tariff reductions in the past. Since these included almost exclusively industrial products, that limited the eligible list and also explains the lack of uniformity of the surcharges.

[18] Travel allowances are inconsistent with the IMF Articles of Agreement, which require full convertibility for all current transactions (including travel) for any country which has accepted the obligations of Article VIII. France, Sweden, and several other countries, however, maintain nominal allowances to prevent concealed capital flight. Unlimited funds are available for legitimate travel expenditures.

TABLE 9–1 Basic Travel Allowances [a]
(U.S. dollar equivalent)

	1956	1957	1958	1959	1960	1961	1962	1963	1964	1965
Austria [b]	200	275	275	385	385	385	577	577	1000	1000
France [b]	200	100	0	306	306	500	700 [c]	1000 [c]	1000 [c]	1000 [c]
Greece [b]	200	200	200	150	150	150	150	200	200	200
Italy	480	480	480	430	480	800	[d]	[d]	[d]	[d]
Netherlands [b]	263 [c]	263 [c]	263 [c]	529 [c]	796	796	[d]	[d]	[d]	[d]
Norway	98	210	280	280	280	280	280	500	500	700
Portugal	[d]	[d]	[d]	[d]	[d]	[d]	[d]	[d]	1740 [c]	1740 [c]
Spain [b]	n.a.	n.a.	n.a.	50	50	275	275	500	500	700 [c]
Sweden [b]	580	966	966	966	1160	1160	1160	1160	1160 [c]	1160 [c]
United Kingdom	280	280	280	700 [c]	700 [c]	700 [c]	700 [c]	700 [c]	700 [c]	700 [c]

n.a., not available.
[a] Per year. Most countries permit specified additional amounts of national currencies to be taken on each journey; these can usually be spent abroad.
[b] Per journey.
[c] Nominal limit to prevent resident capital flight. More currency is available on request for bona fide travel expenditures.
[d] No limit.
Source: OECD, Tourism in OECD Member Countries; and OEEC, Tourism in Europe.

reduced allowable travel expenditures (outside the Sterling Area) from £250 to £50 per person in 1966.

In 1962, the United States changed its tax laws governing earnings of foreign subsidiaries of American corporations, partly to remove distortions to allocation of foreign investment, partly to induce earlier repatriation of earnings. Britain in 1965 also took moves to encourage earlier repatriation of foreign investment earnings.

Finally, at any point in time, most governments face a variety of decisions regarding international shipping, subsidies to airlines, expenditure for the promotion of tourism, inauguration of new government programs abroad, and so on. Balance-of-payments considerations inevitably intrude into these decisions and often influence their outcome. A country in payments deficit will lean against new expenditures abroad and in favor of subsidies which will increase receipts or reduce payments to foreigners. A country in surplus will be pressed by other countries to avoid such measures and to take on new expenditures abroad.

Variable Restrictions on Capital Movements

As with trade and other current account transactions, restrictions can be imposed on capital movements for balance-of-payments reasons. Indeed, in practice, controls over capital movements are found much more frequently than controls over trade. Since the Second World War there has been an evident reluctance by most countries to permit the free flow of capital across national boundaries. Such flows were extremely disruptive both in the 1920s and in the 1930s. As a result, few countries dismantled their wartime controls as peacetime economic intercourse was restored. Table 9-2 indicates the extent of controls obtaining in the early 1960s.

These controls serve a number of purposes. Some are protective in nature.[19] More frequently they are precautionary rather than protectionist, reflecting a desire to avoid potentially disruptive movements

[19] Both Sweden and Japan, for example, require permission for foreign direct investment in their countries, and both have established formidable administrative or legal obstacles to such investment. Foreigners are not permitted to own mining property in Sweden. Japan often requires joint ventures with local firms as a condition for foreign investment. Switzerland has prohibited the foreign purchase of real estate, and a number of countries limit or sharply discourage foreign ownership in certain industries, such as banking.

of capital, especially financial capital. This caution applies both to speculative movements of capital and to movements which interfere with the pursuit of domestic objectives in the ways already discussed.[20] While these controls are essentially precautionary, their manipulation can lead to movements of funds designed to reduce imbalances in payments. For example, both the Netherlands and Switzerland limit the issuance of foreign securities on their capital markets according to the ability of the market to "digest" issues and according to the state of their international payments.

In addition to manipulation of pre-existing controls over capital movements, after 1960 several countries introduced a wide range of new measures with the two-fold objective of influencing capital movements for balance-of-payments reasons and of separating national money markets from one another in order to weaken the integrating force of international capital movements, i.e., to preserve some domestic autonomy in monetary policy.

Measures have been adopted to influence capital movements in all directions: to reduce inflows and to induce outflows, to reduce outflows and to induce inflows.[21] Measures taken by countries in surplus range from prohibition of interest payments to foreigners (Switzerland, Germany, France), through special reserve requirements on foreigners' deposits and special taxes on interest paid to foreigners, to prohibitions on borrowing abroad by residents.[22]

Both Germany and Italy have encouraged the export of short-term capital through the use of forward "swap" transactions, whereby the central bank offers commercial banks attractive terms on forward sales of the U.S. dollar, thus increasing the covered yield to commercial banks on investments denominated in dollars. In early 1962, the Italian monetary authorities had over $600 million and the German Bundesbank had $1 billion in outstanding forward swaps. Two-thirds

---

[20] In Chapters 4–6.

[21] Recent measures influencing capital movements are described in the annual reports of the Board of Management of the EMA. See, for example, EMA, *Seventh Annual Report, 1965* (Paris: OECD, 1966), pp. 54–85.

[22] In August 1963, France began to require specific approval for any French resident (including firms) to borrow abroad more than one million new francs (about $200,000), or to pay more than 4 per cent interest to foreigners, or to borrow for more than two years. These provisions in particular ruled out borrowing in the Eurodollar market, where prevailing interest rates were more than 4 per cent.

TABLE 9–2 Summary of Controls Over Capital Movements Exercised by Major OECD Countries [a]

Country	Convertibility of Currency on Capital Account	Type of Capital Movement					
		Direct Investments Abroad	Portfolio Investment Abroad	Commercial Credits 5 Years and Under	Financial Loans	Deposits in Foreign Banks
Belgium-Luxembourg	External	Control via free market	Control via free market	Control via free market	Control via free market	Control via free market
Canada	Full	Free	Free	Free	Free	Free
France	External	Liberalized	Free	Liberalized	Individual licensing & banking laws	Generally not permitted
Germany, F.R.	Full	Free	Free	Free	Free	Free
Italy	External	Largely liberalized	Generally not permitted, with some exceptions	Credits under one year liberalized	Individual licensing	Generally not permitted
Japan	External	Individual licensing	Generally not permitted	Liberalized	Generally not permitted	Generally not permitted
Netherlands	External	Liberalized	Control via free market	Liberalized	Individual licensing	Generally not permitted

Type of Capital Movement

Country	Convertibility of Currency on Capital Account	Direct Investments Abroad	Portfolio Investment Abroad	Commercial Credits 5 Years and Under	Financial Loans	Deposits in Foreign Banks
Switzerland	Full	Free	Free	Large credits controlled under banking laws	Large loans controlled under banking laws	Free
United Kingdom	External	Individual licensing & control via free market	Control via free market	Controlled over six months	Controlled under both banking & exchange control laws	Generally not permitted
United States [c]	Full	Subject to voluntary restraint	Free but subject to tax	Subject to voluntary restraint	Voluntary restraint	Voluntary restraint

Note: The notation "liberalized" indicates that prior authorization is required, but is freely given. The notation "control via free market" indicates that transactions are permitted, but that the call on foreign exchange to finance them is restricted by channeling them through a free market, the supply of foreign exchange to which is limited. Tendencies for outflow to increase result in changes in the free-market exchange rate rather than in an increased outflow of foreign exchange.

Source: U.S. Treasury, A Description and Analysis of Certain European Capital Markets, prepared for The Joint Economic Committee, U.S. Congress (Washington: GPO, 1964), p. 33.

[a] As of mid-1963.
[b] Payments to bilateral account countries not listed here are also under special controls.
[c] As of mid-1967.

Table 9-2 (Continued)

	Type of Capital Movement			
Country	Flotation of Securities Issues by Nonresidents	Repatriation of Direct Investments by Nonresidents	Repatriation of Portfolio Investments by Nonresidents	Areas Where Special Regulations Apply [b]
Belgium-Luxembourg	Banking laws and free market exchange rate	Control via free market	Control via free market	None
Canada	Free	Free	Free	None
France	Controlled under both banking & exchange control laws	Liberalized	Free	French Franc Area
Germany, F.R.	Free	Free	Free	None
Italy	Controlled under both banking & exchange control laws	Liberalized	Liberalized	OECD EEC
Japan	Controlled under exchange control laws	On approved investments permitted after 2 yrs. and controlled via free market before 2 yrs.; otherwise generally not permitted	On approved investments permitted after 2 yrs. and controlled via free market before 2 yrs.; otherwise generally not permitted	None

Type of Capital Movement

Country	Flotation of Securities Issues by Nonresidents	Repatriation of Direct Investments by Nonresidents	Repatriation of Portfolio Investments by Nonresidents	Areas Where Special Regulations Apply [b]
Netherlands	Controlled under both banking & exchange control laws	Liberalized	Control via free market	Guilder area
Switzerland	Controlled under banking laws	Free	Free	None
United Kingdom	Controlled under both banking & exchange control laws	Free on approved investments	Control via free market	Sterling Area EFTA
United States [c]	Free but subject to tax	Free	Free	Less-developed countries, Canada

Note: The notation "liberalized" indicates that prior authorization is required, but is freely given. The notation "control via free market" indicates that transactions are permitted, but that the call on foreign exchange to finance them is restricted by channeling them through a free market, the supply of foreign exchange to which is limited. Tendencies for outflow to increase result in changes in the free-market exchange rate rather than in an increased outflow of foreign exchange.

Source: U.S. Treasury, A Description and Analysis of Certain European Capital Markets, prepared for The Joint Economic Committee, U.S. Congress (Washington: GPO, 1964), p. 33.

[a] As of mid-1963.
[b] Payments to bilateral account countries not listed here are also under special controls.
[c] As of mid-1967.

of short-term foreign investments by German banks were covered by these swaps. The Bundesbank let the swap contracts run off in early 1963, but resumed them a year later for purchases of U.S. Treasury bills—a limitation designed to discourage deposits by German banks in the Eurodollar market, deposits which might be re-lent to German firms and thus flow back into Germany.

Measures taken by countries in deficit involve tightening tax laws governing foreign investment earnings, exempting foreigners' investments from certain regulations and taxes, channeling investment flows through a penalty market, taxing foreign borrowing, and urging restraint in lending to foreigners.

Most of these devices were *ad hoc* measures taken to meet particular needs, and little attention was paid to the possibilities for their general and flexible use or to systematic coordination of such measures among countries. It is obvious that measures by one country to induce capital inflows, for example, can work at cross purposes with measures by another country to reduce capital outflow. Yet some of these measures, such as the German forward swap facilities for commercial banks, have become highly effective and frequently used instruments of economic policy. And serious conflicts between national measures have not generally arisen, since countries discouraging capital inflow have generally been in surplus, while those discouraging capital outflow have been in deficit. Conflict has arisen, however, when the measures of one deficit country, the United States, have deterred capital outflow to other deficit countries or to countries without exceptionally strong payments positions. The American program of voluntary credit restraint, inaugurated in early 1965, aggravated the weak position of sterling during the following months, for the major external source of short-term funds to Britain was virtually eliminated. Three years later, the mandatory restrictions placed on U.S. capital outflows and other balance-of-payments measures announced in January 1968 partially offset the favorable impact of the November 1967 devaluation of sterling on Britain's balance of payments and retarded restoration of confidence in sterling. Similarly, the interest equalization tax weakened the payments position of Japan—perhaps discouraging needed expansionary measures in 1964—and it would have weakened Canada's position except for Canada's exemption from some provisions of the tax.

The Costs of Restrictions

Restrictions over international transactions have an extensive record as a method for rectifying imbalance in international payments. Indeed, variations in restrictions have been a major method for coping with external imbalance in the postwar period, despite a general presumption that they are objectionable.

The reason is not hard to find. Means for financing payments deficits are severely limited, and national authorities have been reluctant to deflate their domestic economies to correct external deficits. Countries have increasingly shunned changes in exchange rates—the solution offered by the Bretton Woods Agreement to fundamental disequilibrium—partly because such changes give rise to disruptive capital movements both before and afterward. Over-correction is usually necessary to quell speculation, but over-correction, such as resulted from the French devaluation of 1958, merely shifts the deficit to other countries.

Unhappily, domestic deflation usually results in unemployment and unutilized capacity. It wastes economic resources, not to mention the human hardship and loss of personal dignity which accompanies involuntary unemployment. Prices and wages are not flexible enough to preserve full utilization of economic capacity in the face of monetary deflation. Deflation just sufficient to remove excess domestic demand is often not sufficient, by the time the need for action is recognized, to allay speculative distrust of the currency—including distrust by foreign monetary officials who are the prospective creditors in any international currency support operation. Hence, the resort to restrictions.

Measuring the costs of misallocation of resources resulting from man-made restrictions is no easy task. But the outstanding characteristic of whatever attempts have been made is the small loss attributable to misallocation. Table 9-3 summarizes the results of six different studies, two on the misallocative effects due to monopoly in the United States, four on the misallocative effects of tariffs in various European countries.[23] If these figures can be accepted as indicating

---

[23] In the mid-1950s, John H. Young estimated the "cash cost" of Canada's tariffs to be 3.5–4.5 per cent of gross *private* expenditure. But Young overestimated the welfare costs by including in his estimate rents accruing to do-

the correct order of magnitude of the loss in GNP resulting from the specified misallocation, then flexible use of import surcharges or restrictions on capital movements will result in a very much smaller loss than a deflation which results in even a modest increase in unemployment.[24] This is no reason for ignoring allocative efficiency when policy tools are available for assuring full use of resources at all times. But when the two objectives—full employment and allocative efficiency—conflict in a modern industrial economy, the latter should clearly yield if one is interested in maximizing total output.

There will, however, be important differences in the relative costs of internal and external balance-of-payments measures according to the size and openness of the economy in question. Restrictions on trade are likely to be more costly to small and open economies, and domestic deflation relatively less costly, than will be true for relatively self-contained economies. The reason for this lies in the degree of deflation required to achieve a given improvement in the balance of payments (relative to GNP) for the two types of economy as compared with the degree of restriction over trade required to achieve the same improvement. Precisely because of its extensive foreign trade, a relatively open economy will not have to deflate very much to achieve a specified reduction in imports; it has a large marginal propensity to

mestic producers in the protected industries. See J. H. Young, *Canada's Commercial Policy* (Ottawa: Royal Commission on Canada's Economic Prospects, 1957). For a critique, see H. G. Johnson, "The Cost of Protection and the Scientific Tariff," *Journal of Political Economy*, LXVII, August 1960, pp. 327–45.

[24] It should be noted that an increase in the unemployment rate by one percentage point will typically reduce GNP by much more than that, since other workers will have been put on part-time and still others will retire early and thereby leave the labor force, or delay entry into the labor force. Furthermore, some workers still on the payroll will not be working at full capacity—a disguised unemployment which is recorded as a fall in productivity. Okun has estimated for the United States that a 1 percentage point decline in unemployment in the early 1960s would have increased GNP by 3.2 per cent. See Arthur Okun, "Potential GNP: Its Measurement and Significance," *Proceedings of the American Statistical Association*, 1962, reprinted in an adapted form in A. Okun (ed.), *The Battle Against Unemployment* (New York: W. W. Norton & Co., 1965). A similar estimate applies to the United Kingdom. See R. N. Cooper, "Britain's Balance of Payments," in Richard E. Caves (ed.), *Britain's Economic Prospects* (Washington: The Brookings Institution, 1968).

import. For a large, relatively self-contained economy, the deflation required for a given reduction in imports (relative to GNP) will be much greater; hence, the loss of output will be much greater if demand was not excessive at the outset.[25]

TABLE 9–3   Calculated Loss in Gross National Product Attributed to Specified Misallocations of Resources

	Source of Misallocation	Country	Year	Calculated Loss (Percentage of GNP)
(1)	Monopoly	U.S.A.	1929	.07
(2)	Monopoly	U.S.A.	1954	.01
(3)	Tariffs	EEC	1952	.05
(4)	Tariffs	Germany	1958	.18
(5)	Tariffs	Italy	1960	.10 (maximum)
(6)	Tariffs	U.K. exports to EEC	1970	1.00 (maximum)

References:
(1) A. C. Harberger, "Monopoly and Resource Allocation," *American Economic Review*, XLIV, May 1954, pp. 77–87.
(2) D. Schwartzman, "The Burden of Monopoly," *Journal of Political Economy*, LXVIII, December 1960, pp. 627–30.
(3) T. Scitovsky, *Economic Theory and Western European Integration* (Stanford: Stanford University Press, 1958).
(4) J. Wemelsfelder, "The Short-term Effect of the Lowering of Import Duties in Germany," *Economic Journal*, LXX, March 1960, pp. 94–104.
(5) L. H. Janssen, *Free Trade, Protection and Customs Union* (Leiden: H. E. Stenfert Kroese, 1961).
(6) H. G. Johnson, "The Gains from Freer Trade with Europe: An Estimate," *Manchester School of Economic Studies*, XXVII, September 1958, pp. 247–55.
Source: H. Leibenstein, "Allocational Efficiency versus X-Efficiency," *American Economic Review*, LVI, June 1966, p. 393.

In contrast, trade restrictions in the latter type of economy are likely to be more effective because the relatively small volume of imports can be more easily satisfied out of domestic production. In a small and open economy, on the other hand, trade restrictions will probably induce import substitution only at much higher cost than is true for the larger country. The open country is likely to be more spe-

[25] See the Annex to this chapter for a numerical illustration of the relative costs of deflation and import restrictions in the two types of economy.

cialized, and, hence, may find import substitution more difficult. This will be especially so if economies of scale are important.

It is not surprising, in view of these important differences in characteristics among countries, to find large countries showing a marked preference for external measures to improve their own payments positions when in need of doing so, and small countries showing a preference for greater internal "discipline." Such differences in preference correspond to different assessments of the relative costs of alternative measures, in each case based on insular assumptions reflecting local characteristics. But even allowing for these differences, persistent under-utilization of labor and capital will generally be a less efficient method for correcting payments imbalance than well-designed restrictions on international transactions, even for relatively small countries.[26]

The more general and uniform are restrictions over trade, the less is the likelihood of substantial misallocation. As noted above, uniform tariffs on all imported goods, combined with uniform subsidies on all exports, are analytically equivalent in their effect on production and trade to a devaluation of the currency by the amount of the tariff-*cum*-subsidy. Uniform tariffs alone, therefore, distort production somewhat by drawing resources away from all export industries to all import-competing industries. More selective tariffs, adequate to achieve the same effect on the trade balance, would generally introduce greater distortions into the price system.[27]

If restrictions on international transactions are to be used, restrictions over capital movements will raise fewer outcries than restrictions on trade. They do not affect so many people directly, and they are probably less damaging to the level of economic output, although this is a difficult judgment to document. We saw in Chapter 4 that international capital movements are often influenced more by tariffs

---

[26] A possibly important exception to this conclusion arises when economic adversity is required to induce innovation—the adoption of new techniques of production and management and the acquisition of new labor skills. These are sometimes alleged to be dynamic benefits from periodic economic recession, and this sort of consideration undoubtedly influenced Britain's 1961 bid for entry into the EEC, which was to result in a "cold shower" of competition for British industry. The argument assumes that business is not maximizing profits over time when demand is sufficient to utilize fully short-run capacity.

[27] If tariff surcharges are added to an existing tariff structure, however, selective surcharges may reduce the distortions introduced by the tariff system as a whole.

and differential national tax rates than by variations in the "real" rate of return. Blocking some capital movements would even raise world output, not lower it.[28] This is true of restrictions on capital movements motivated by deliberate differences in national monetary policies. Indeed, one reason for focussing restrictions on capital movements is that such restrictions would strike more directly at a principal source of disturbance to national economic policies than would restrictions on trade. They would help to separate capital and money markets in different countries.

Restrictions on either trade or capital movements may be imposed directly or they may be imposed indirectly, through the market. Direct controls involve quotas and licensing; "market controls" involve taxes, tariffs, and subsidies. There is much to be said, partly on general grounds of allocative efficiency, partly on grounds that there is less room for favoritism, for preferring the latter to the former. Market controls permit those who badly want to undertake a transaction to go ahead with it, paying the required tax. They permit new entrants to a given market and do not freeze trade and investment patterns. Preference for direct controls over international transactions has rested on the assumption that market controls could not work quickly enough, nor with the same degree of assurance in limiting payments to foreigners, as direct controls. Indeed, the "elasticity pessimism" of the immediate postwar period implied that market controls might not be effective at all. But the increased responsiveness of trade and investment to relative price changes, already discussed, suggests that market controls should be quite effective in correcting imbalances in payments, except perhaps in the very short run.

Any *nondiscriminatory* reduction in imports or other foreign pay-

[28] One indication of the pull of foreign tariffs on American capital is offered by the response of 169 American firms to a questionnaire asking how a free-trade area among the United States, Canada, and Europe would affect their operations. More than one-fourth of the respondents indicated that they would contract their overseas operations or would abandon expansion plans, implying that European tariffs offer the principal motive for locating there. See Mordechai E. Kreinin, "Freedom of Trade and Capital Movement—Some Empirical Evidence," *Economic Journal*, LXXV, December 1965, pp. 749–50. Nearly half of the respondents stated that their overseas investment plans would not be affected by a free trade area, many indicating that transportation costs overwhelmed tariffs as an impediment to trade; and just fewer than one-fourth indicated that they would expand their foreign operations for sale in the United States, implying that U.S. tariffs deter such overseas production today.

ments, particularly if undertaken by a large country, will reduce the foreign exchange receipts of other countries which are themselves in balance or even in payments deficit. They may have to respond with their own restrictions or deflation. Thus, there are unwanted "feedbacks," and the degree of restriction required to produce a given net improvement in the balance of payments is larger than would seem to be the case from the initial improvement. Similarly, the degree of deflation ultimately required to achieve a given improvement in the trade balance will be larger—sometimes considerably larger—than what seems to be required without allowing for the impact of import reduction on the behavior of other countries. If substantial feedbacks are not allowed for, the convergence toward equilibrium will be greatly slowed. The gap between gross and net improvement will generally be larger, the more important is the country imposing the restrictions. A small country can improve its balance without worsening the positions of other countries enough to evoke defensive response from them.

The presence of feedbacks resulting from deleterious effects on countries other than the countries in surplus suggests that some form of systematic discrimination may be desirable in the use of balance-of-payments restrictions on international transactions.[29] International transactions will be less restricted if other deficit countries are exempted from the restrictions of any one deficit country.

A case in point is the effort to limit U.S. capital outflows. Canada would have been most severely hit, so it was exempt from the interest equalization tax on American purchases of new foreign securities, and it was to be given preference in bank lending under the program of "voluntary foreign credit restraint" inaugurated in early 1965. Similarly, Sterling Area members are permitted to borrow in the London market, which is generally closed to other foreigners. Both of these exemptions can be justified, in part, on grounds that reducing payments from the United States to Canada, or from Britain to the Sterling Area, would have strong repercussions on U.S. and British ex-

[29] This suggestion was offered for trade by R. Frisch, "On the Need for Forecasting a Multilateral Balance of Payments," *American Economic Review,* XXXVII, September 1947, pp. 535–51, and has been developed at some length by James E. Meade in *The Theory of International Economic Policy,* Vol. 1, *Balance of Payments* (London: Royal Institute of Economic Affairs, 1951), Chap. 30; and Marcus Fleming, "On Making the Best of Balance of Restrictions on Imports," *Economic Journal,* LXI, March 1951, pp. 48–71.

port receipts.[30] The mandatory controls on U.S. direct investment outflows instituted in early 1968 also attempted, in a crude way, to recognize the differential effects on the U.S. balance of payments—and on the economies of capital-importing countries—of cutting capital outflows to other countries. It differentiated among three groups: investment in less-developed countries was treated most generously and investment in Western Europe least generously, with investment in Australia, Britain, Canada, Japan, and several other countries falling into an intermediate category.[31]

The difficulty with maintaining systematic discrimination for long in a world of convertible currencies and relatively free international economic intercourse is that it invites geographical arbitrage—e.g., European borrowing from the United States through Canada. This suggests that the countries *in surplus* should take a major role in reducing the imbalances by encouraging imports, discouraging inflows of capital, and the like. Restrictions on capital movements would have offered a more effective balance-of-payments tool in the mid-1960s if the European surplus countries, in a coordinated effort with the United States, limited their capital inflow rather than having the United States limit its outflow. This is because an overwhelming proportion of the capital flowing into the EEC as a group came directly or indirectly from the United States, and much of the remainder came from the United Kingdom, also in deficit, while capital outflows from the United States went to many parts of the world, including many countries themselves in payments balance or deficit. Reducing payments imbalances with a minimum of damage to international intercourse requires cooperation between deficit and surplus countries, and may on occasion call for the surplus countries to take the major action.

Conclusions

We have considered in this chapter the third of the three polar alternative methods of coping with payments imbalances set out in

[30] Japan was also affected by the U.S. limitations on capital outflow and indeed (but only partly for this reason) entered a period of "recession" which limited American exports to that country. It subsequently received a limited exemption from the interest equalization tax.

[31] Canada was subsequently exempt entirely from the mandatory program, after an exchange crisis and rumors of impending devaluation.

Chapter 1: relying on measures which bear directly on external transactions, rather than getting at the imbalances indirectly through the level of economic activity or financing them through official capital flows. Two things are to be noted. First, restrictions on external transactions—both current and capital transactions—have been heavily relied on by members of the Atlantic economic community to keep balance-of-payments positions under control despite general commitments to avoid such techniques as much as possible. There has perhaps even been some increase in their use since the late 1950s. Second, a cost-benefit comparison between broad-gauged restrictions on international transactions and demand deflation as a major weapon to maintain external balance in the face of conflicting objectives points strongly to restrictions as the preferable approach.

Variable restrictions on international transactions are likely to be increasingly effective in improving the balance of payments as the structural changes described in Chapters 3–5 take place. They can take many forms, however, with widely different implications both for efficient resource allocation in the countries using them and for other countries. Since restrictions are apparently going to be used in the absence of strong moves toward a radically different payments system from the one we have, it is important that those restrictions adopted do as little damage as possible for the balance-of-payments gains they yield. There is probably a preference for the restricting capital movements rather than trade flows when an imbalance can be corrected by operating on the capital account. More important, however, is the need for external measures to be undertaken cooperatively, both to avoid recriminatory retaliation and to adopt the least-cost courses of action. There will be occasions when removal of restrictions by surplus countries will help reduce imbalances, and that will generally be preferable to the imposition of new restrictions by deficit countries. And there will even be occasions when the imposition of restrictions by the surplus countries is preferable to the introduction of restrictions by the deficit countries. The last chapter will take up the possibilities for cooperation in this area, and compare them with the possibilities for other forms of international economic cooperation in the Atlantic community.

ANNEX TO CHAPTER NINE

Some numerical illustrations may help to clarify the points made in this chapter regarding the economic costs of deflation and restrictions as alternative measures to reduce a deficit in the balance of payments. We will consider in turn a relatively self-contained economy and one which is highly dependent on foreign trade.

1. Suppose Country A is running a deficit on goods and services equivalent to 1 per cent of total national expenditure: $X - M = Y - E = -.01E$, where X stands for exports (assumed given and unchanged), M for imports, Y for national product, and E for national expenditure. The country is absorbing 1 per cent more than it is producing. Suppose further that $M = .10E$, i.e., imports amount to 10 per cent of total expenditures, and that the marginal propensity to import is also .1, indicating a relatively self-contained economy.

(a) To eliminate the 1 per cent deficit through pure demand deflation would require a total reduction in expenditure of 10 per cent, since imports change by 10 per cent of any change in expenditure. If prices and money wages are sticky, this will involve a 9 per cent decline in national product, the difference between the decline in expenditures and the decline in imports. (If prices decline under deflation of this magnitude, the loss in output would be less, due to a price-induced switch away from imports.)

(b) Alternatively, impose a tariff on imports averaging 10 percentage points (this increase would not quite double the tariffs now levied by most countries in Europe and North America). The 1 per cent deficit will be eliminated if the price elasticity of demand for imports is two or greater, provided total expenditure is reduced by 1 per cent (the tariff revenues alone would accomplish 40 per cent of this required reduction). An improvement in the terms of trade resulting from the tariff would permit an even lower elasticity.

In this case, there is no loss in output through unemployment, since the tariff has switched demand away from imports to domestic products. But there is a loss of efficiency due to the protection of import-competing industries. The extent of this loss will depend on the structure of tariffs before the proposed increase, on the character of the tariff increase, and on the flexibility of demand and output in the economy. The loss will generally be lower, the more uniform is the tariff structure after the imposition of the duty.

A crude idea of the loss can be gained from some calculations based on theoretical work done by Harry Johnson. These calculations suggest efficiency losses in this case of slightly more than 0.3 per cent of the free-trade GNP. [1]

2. Suppose Country B is also running a deficit on goods and services equivalent to 1 per cent of its total expenditure, but in this case $M = .4E$, i.e., the country is substantially more dependent on foreign trade than Country A.

(a) To eliminate the deficit through pure demand deflation would require a fall in expenditure of 2.5 per cent in this case, leading (with constant prices) to a fall in national product of roughly 1.5 per cent.

(b) A tariff of ten percentage points would eliminate the deficit if the price elasticity of demand for imports is one-third or greater (it could be even lower if allowance is made for improvement in the terms of trade). The elasticity depends in part on the ability of the economy to substitute domestic production for imports, and this will generally be lower the larger the ratio of trade to total output. Current estimates of import elasticities for industrialized countries often place them above two, and certainly well above one-third.

Again the loss of efficiency will depend on the precise nature of the tariff structure and the tariff increases, as well as the characteristics of the economy and its consumers. Making the same assumptions about consumer demand as in the previous case, but allowing for the greater importance of foreign trade and the lower flexibility of the economy, calculations based on Johnson's formulae yield a loss of 0.2 per cent of free trade output.

Actually, for the model underlying these calculations, an import surcharge of 10 per cent would over-correct the balance of payments. Smaller surcharges would eliminate the deficit, and these smaller surcharges would have even lower efficiency costs. Moreover, the surcharge required to eliminate the deficit would be lower for Country A (1.5 per cent) than for Country B (3 per cent), the smaller size of the foreign trade sector in Country A implying a higher price elasticity of import demand and hence a smaller required change in relative prices.

[1] See H. G. Johnson, "The Costs of Protection and Self-Sufficiency," *Quarterly Journal of Economics*, LXXIX, August 1965, pp. 356–72. In Johnson's notation, I have assumed $m = 2/3$, $\sigma = 1$, to describe the degree of substitutability in production and consumption for country A and $m = 0$, $\sigma = 1$ for country B.

Taking this further difference into account, the relative costs can be summarized as follows:

Cost of Eliminating a Deficit
Equivalent to One Per Cent of Total Expenditure

	Country A	Country B
	(*per cent of total output*)	
Deflation	9.0	1.5
Tariff surcharge	0.004	0.011

Deflation is six times more costly for Country *A* than it is for Country *B*, while surcharges are about three times more costly for *B* than they are for *A*. In both cases the costs of surcharges are minuscule compared to the costs of deflation.

This kind of calculation cannot be taken too literally. But the differences in magnitude tend to corroborate the two generalizations made in the text: (1) in purely economic terms, deflation is a far more costly method of adjustment than restrictions on trade, and (2) the cost of deflation relative to restriction will be higher for relatively self-sufficient economies than for economies highly dependent on trade.

Deficits equivalent in terms of total trade rather than total expenditure would increase the costs of both techniques in Country *B* relative to Country *A*, since trade is relatively more important in Country *B*.

As the long-run changes in cost structure and growing interdependence described in Chapter 3 progress, the costs of adjustment under either alternative will decline; but deflation will remain the more costly alternative.

This illustration does not imply, of course, that deflation should be avoided when the economy is over-heated in terms of domestic objectives. In that case restoration of internal and external balance *both* call for deflation.

CHAPTER TEN

Mixed Solutions for
the Atlantic Community

There is a nostalgic tendency, among policy-makers as well as scholars, to look back to the days when the international payments system worked well. A number of observers have even called for a return to the principles of the nineteenth century gold standard, at least as they interpret those principles. Others reject the gold standard as a relic of the past, but argue that the "dollar exchange standard" as it has developed since the Second World War is as satisfactory an arrangement as one could hope for, and should not be tampered with.

Both these schools ignore the fact that the world economy is changing rapidly and irreversibly. There is no question of recapturing the "good old days," even if it could be established conclusively that the old days were in fact good. The old standard passed out of general favor long ago, and recently existing monetary arrangements have been called into question.

It is time to summarize the argument and draw some conclusions for international economic policy. For a number of reasons developed in Chapters 3, 4, and 5, economic interdependence among industrial countries has increased sharply in the last several decades, and this increase is likely to continue unless it is deliberately checked. There has been a great reduction in the natural, artificial, and psychological barriers to foreign trade and international capital movements. National economies are increasingly "open," not only in the sense of having higher ratios of trade to total output, but in the more important sense of greater exposure to disturbances in the balance of payments.

The vast accumulation of capital and the international transmission of knowledge have reduced inter-country variation in comparative cost structure from the days when differences in climate and in natural resources provided the principal basis for foreign trade. This narrowing of cost differences has been complemented by the reduction of transportation and communication costs and, since 1949, by the policy-guided reduction in tariffs and other artificial barriers to trade. All these factors increase international competition among the industrial countries.

At the same time, the psychological and institutional barriers to international capital movements among industrial countries have eroded rapidly, especially since 1958. Capital tends increasingly to move in great volume from country to country in search of small yield differentials. Businesses have become much more international in outlook, just as American business became truly national in outlook around the turn of the century. They now scan a wide area encompassing many countries in choosing a market area or a place to locate. In the terms introduced in Chapter 4, their decision-making domains have increased.

This greater economic interdependence has three consequences for national economic policy. First, it increases the number of "disturbances" with which national policy-makers must cope. Changes in incomes, prices, costs, and interest rates abroad are more rapidly transmitted into changes in the demand for domestic output or funds than they used to be, and these changes in turn affect domestic income, employment, prices, interest rates, and international reserves.

Second, the enlarged interactions among national economies will generally slow the speed with which traditional measures of economic policy take effect on the level of domestic employment, output, and interest rates, for each move will "spill over" into other economies and will evoke policy reactions there which will often weaken the influence of the measures initially instituted. Monetary policy provides an obvious illustration. Tighter money to restrict domestic demand will be weakened in its effect by an inflow of funds from abroad. If foreign monetary authorities attempt to prevent monetary tightening in their countries, the inflow will continue indefinitely until either the monetary authorities who initiated the tightening give up their task as hopeless or the other countries exhaust their ability to finance deficits created by capital outflow.

Third, competition by one nation with another in the use of national policies can leave the community of nations worse off than it need be. Regulatory action or taxation may be thwarted by the prompt movement of regulated businesses beyond the jurisdiction of the regulating nations or by the shifting of profits through intra-corporate pricing. These are common phenomena within the United States; they may become more common within the Atlantic Community, especially in matters of taxation and antitrust regulation, as the decision-making domains of business grow larger. This again threatens national autonomy.

In sum, as national economies become more closely integrated, national freedom to set national economic objectives and to pursue them effectively with national instruments of policy is increasingly circumscribed.

This growing interdependence confronts the Atlantic Community with three broad alternatives:

(*a*) to accept the integration and the consequential loss of national freedom, and to engage in the *joint* determination of economic objectives and policies;

(*b*) to accept the integration but attempt to preserve as much national autonomy as possible by providing financial accommodation for prolonged payments deficits;

(*c*) to reject the integration by deliberate imposition of barriers to the integrating forces, freedom of foreign trade and international capital movements.

The first would involve making certain decisions regarding economic policy at the level of the Atlantic Community rather than at the national level; this would prevent some of the most damaging consequences of increased interdependence. This solution requires a reasonably high degree of labor mobility among members of the community; to make it attractive to all members in the absence of such mobility, provision would have to be made for extensive regional assistance—in effect, foreign aid programs within the Atlantic Community.

The second solution would involve liberal extension of credit to members of the community in payments deficit, so their domestic economic objectives would not be threatened by balance-of-payments difficulties. This solution is an incomplete one, however, since it does not protect members fully against certain forms of policy competition, particularly in the areas of regulation and taxation.

The third solution would involve the *orderly* use of restrictions on international payments, combined with limited means of financing deficits, in order to keep payments in reasonable balance. The emphasis here is on close international cooperation in the use of restrictions, so they are imposed only to protect the balance of payments, not special interests within each country. A flexible but well-defined "code of good behavior" could be worked out for application by members of the Atlantic Community, but under close international scrutiny, such as is now given on certain matters in the GATT. Wider margins for exchange rates might represent one variant of this solution, although as we will see below it has the disadvantage, from the viewpoint of fostering international cooperation, of *not* affording an occasion for close international consultation.

Failure to accept consciously some combination of these alternatives and to work toward its efficient operation would seem at first an apparent acceptance of increasing economic integration. But it would have all the weaknesses of high, uncoordinated interdependence, including competition in national policy analogous to, but more subtle than, the competitive depreciations of the 1930s. Ultimately it would probably result in an indiscriminate rejection of international economic integration, involving uncoordinated and unsystematic use of restrictions on international transactions. This would be politically corrosive as well as economically costly.

The conclusion we reach is not a very tidy one; nor, at first glance, is it very optimistic. It is that the Atlantic economic community is not yet ready to adopt the first solution. The implied infringement of national sovereignty—an infringement which is mourned too late, since increased interdependence will erode national freedom of action in any case—and the degree of responsibility required with respect to *other* members of the community are both higher than nations are at present willing to undertake.

The second solution does not involve the same degree of commitment as the first, but it does involve a high degree of confidence in the ability of other members of the community to manage their economic affairs responsibly. There are some indications that members of the Atlantic Community are willing to extend substantial amounts of credit to one another, at least under certain circumstances and for short periods of time. But they are not willing to go far enough to make this the principal solution to the problems created by increased interdependence.

The third solution, therefore, seems to win by default.

The nonacceptability of the first, and most desirable, solution derives from two economic facts, both ultimately psychological: the low geographical mobility of labor between nations, and the unwillingness to countenance the transfers of real income between industrialized nations, transfers which would be necessary to compensate for the low mobility of labor.

Full integration of national economies and of economic policies could avoid most of the costs involved in loss of national freedom to pursue national economic goals independently by giving all parties access to an efficient, community-wide capital market and by providing special programs of governmental financial support tailored to regional needs. But the process of integrating the Atlantic Community may involve taking away the national autonomy first and provide the countering benefits only after a substantial time lag. This lag results largely from the more far-reaching political commitments which are required to generate the benefits: for example, the establishment of a central fiscal system or a common banking system supervised by a monetary authority covering the whole of the integrated area. In the terms of Deutsch and his colleagues, there is a race between "loads and capabilities," between the need for concerted action and the willingness to undertake it, and here the loads may outrun the capabilities for a prolonged period of time.[1] Widespread reluctance to make the required political commitments reflects in part a confusion between formal sovereignty and real freedom of action. Autonomy may have been lost long before the public recognizes it and is prepared to yield the sovereignty which can actually restore a certain freedom of action.

Optimum Mixes of Adjustment and Liquidity

It should be clear from what has been said up to this point that the appropriate mix among the alternative methods for coping with imbalances in international payments depends very much on the economic and political relationships among the regions or countries in question. We can distinguish five broad types, or stages, of coopera-

---

[1] Karl Deutsch *et al.*, *Political Community and the North Atlantic Area* (Princeton: Princeton University Press, 1957).

tive arrangement among the members of an interdependent economic community, taken in ascending order of closeness.

1. The first involves periodic international discussion about problems of common interest, reviews of developments in each member country, explanations of the actions that have been taken. But each nation basically fends for itself. It must decide, in any given case, whether to take action to correct the imbalance and, if so, what action should be taken. Its ability to avoid action is limited by its own gold and foreign exchange reserves plus its ability to borrow in private capital markets abroad. A shortage of reserves and borrowing facilities will invite the use of restrictions over international transactions.

This level involves relatively little mutual confidence, although the periodic discussions do serve to give all members of the community a greater understanding of the problems besetting each, and to keep the interests of the international community at large before each member. They also help to ward off actions which would generate recrimination and invite retaliation. Broadly speaking, this is the type of economic cooperation which occurs in the OECD, although some parts of this organization's work involve the next higher level of cooperation.

2. The second level of cooperation also involves periodic discussion of problems of common interest, but it goes beyond the first in requiring consultation on certain kinds of measures to be taken and in calling for international justification of policies involving restrictions on international transactions. Thus, the use of restrictions is subject to a greater degree of international supervision than at the first level of cooperation. Variable restrictions governed by international consultations and even rules would permit considerable national autonomy in setting and pursuing economic objectives and would keep restrictions within the limits required to permit this autonomy without undue damage to international commerce.

In addition, some mutual financial support may be made available, but on a discretionary and conditional basis. Potential creditors feel that discretion is needed in granting credit in order to distinguish desirable from undesirable deficits and, even more important, avoidable (policy-induced) deficits from unavoidable deficits. By withholding credit, they can perhaps induce the deficit country to change those policies which contribute to the deficit.

As already noted in Chapter 8, however, the creditors are not always the best judge of what are appropriate policies for a deficit country. Indeed, they are too often prone to apply pat rules to all deficit countries regardless of the source of the deficit or of the costs and benefits of alternative measures for dealing with it. One important function of forums such as the OECD, where economic policy-makers meet regularly to discuss national economic developments and policies, is to develop mutual appreciation of the objectives of each country and of the obstacles which they face in achieving their objectives *before* they are in need of external assistance. The atmosphere of a formal creditors' meeting in which the supplicant nation is placed on the witness stand to explain and justify its actions is not conducive to development of mutual understanding and confidence required for effective international economic cooperation. This kind of confrontation occurs too late, after the need for support is clearly evident rather than while signs of it are first emerging. Further, it lacks symmetry, which would focus equal attention on the payments surpluses which are the natural counterpart to any payments deficit. On some occasions policy changes are more appropriate in the surplus countries than in the deficit countries.

In certain respects, this level of cooperation has already been reached by the IMF and the GATT. Certain measures which restrict international transactions are subject to justification in the GATT or the IMF, and the IMF offers conditional financial support to countries in payments deficit. But in both cases the focus of attention is strongly on the country in deficit and taking the action, not on the course of action which would be most beneficial for the community as a whole, including possible actions by surplus countries.

3. National economic policy-makers may develop sufficient confidence in the policy judgments of their counterparts in other members of the Atlantic Community to make them willing to go to considerable lengths to support their decisions by providing ample liquidity whenever those countries run into payments difficulties. The financial support may be given without strings, or with only the loosest kind of requirements; the "discipline" of this system rests not on formal requirements, but on the good judgment of the decision-makers of the deficit countries. Properly understood, this type of arrangement could permit a great deal of national autonomy in pursuing national economic objectives. "Responsible" officials need not gear their whole

attention to the requirements of external balance. On the contrary, the trust in their judgment by their foreign counterparts would imply only that their national objectives were in themselves reasonable (although not necessarily the same objectives, with the same weights as might be found in other members of the community), that the policy measures they used to pursue these objectives were acceptable within their own countries, and that they had full control over the use of these policy measures in pursuing their objectives. It would be necessary, however, that the objectives of the deficit countries be broadly consistent with those of the surplus (lending) countries. For example, the system would be unworkable if the former purposely foster inflation while the latter strongly eschew it.

This sort of arrangement requires more political cohesion than international consultations on restrictive measures. A basic assumption of the extensive financial support implied here is either that the deficits are themselves desirable from the viewpoints both of the lending and the borrowing countries, or, more probably, that the imbalance will be reversed in the course of time as the result of structural changes in demand and supply or other factors.

4. Where regions have quite close economic ties and considerable mutual sympathy for each other's objectives, and where factor mobility is reasonably high, greater reliance may be placed on factor mobility among the members of the community to correct imbalances in payments. The requirements for liquidity may be quantitatively less than in the preceding case, since domestic economic policies will be more closely coordinated at the community-wide level. It will be necessary to have effective regional policies designed to mitigate the economic hardship which would otherwise result from deflation in deficit regions. Regional policies to "move work to the workers" and simultaneously provide compensatory finance from the surplus to the deficit regions would be an example. This sort of arrangement requires a degree of political cohesion or other compelling motivation sufficiently high to permit close coordination of domestic policies and to overcome political resistance to inter-regional fiscal transfers. Regional economic objectives need not themselves be identical, but there must be considerable respect for the objectives of other regions. This set of circumstances is most frequently found, of course, *within* nations which are not themselves optimal areas. It is rare to find sufficient political cohesion *between* nations to generate interna-

tional transfers of the character involved in regional policies. These typically involve sustained grants or other indefinite preferential treatment, so long as a region is "depressed." [2]

5. For regions which have very close economic ties, where capital and labor as well as commodities move freely and where there is a high degree of agreement on economic objectives, close coordination of domestic economic policies will serve to reduce one principal source of imbalance—divergences in these policies—and will guide the region as a whole to its global economic objectives. Balance among the regions will be maintained by modest and temporary movements in income and interest rates which will set in motion corrective factor movements. In this case of an optimal currency area, to revert to a term introduced in Chapter 1, balance of payments "discipline" is very severe but it exacts only a small price for its effectiveness, since labor and capital both move readily among regions in response to small differences in rewards. This is a state which is rarely found even within nations.

The relationship between the stages of cooperation and the principal method used to cope with difficult imbalances in international payments is summarized in Table 10-1. Each of the five types of cooperative arrangement among nations is appropriate under certain circumstances—circumstances which depend in part on the character of the economic relationships between the regions in question, in part on the political realtionships among them, i.e., on the degree of mutual understanding and mutual trust.

The technical arrangements for implementing each of them are important, but they are less important than clarity about the ground-rules governing the relationship. With a clear understanding of these ground-rules, many technical arrangements are possible, e.g., for generating ample liquidity or for providing discretionary (conditional) balance-of-payments support.

[2] As noted in Chapter 4, Karl Deutsch and his co-authors attach great importance to high mobility of persons as a prerequisite or accompanying feature of successful political integration. The analysis in Chapter 7 may indicate why this is so important; absence of high mobility can give rise to acute regional economic distress which would strain the political cohesion of any loose or voluntary grouping.

The EEC has made some tentative moves toward international financing of "regional" policies and toward the close coordination of domestic policies involved in this stage of cooperation.

In the absence of cooperation, needless to say, countries will correct payments imbalances non-cooperatively, which is likely to be competitively. If factor mobility between countries is high, the competitive responses will lead to a certain conformity in national policies, by the process described in Chapter 6, even when that is not desired. And the results of this competition in policies is likely to be less favorable to the national objectives of all than would policies reached through conscious coordination. Paradoxically, therefore, some autonomy in policy-making may be preserved under conditions of high economic interdependence by yielding some national sovereignty.

The Atlantic Community in the mid-1960s was still engaged in the first type of cooperation, with important but limited ventures into the second. But there were also signs of mutually undesirable competition in policies. As economic interdependence increases, a more decisive move into the second stage—or even beyond—becomes imperative.

Need Imbalances Always Be Corrected?

While the principal characteristics of the system for coping with imbalances must depend on the nature of economic and political relationships linking national economies, even a system which relies on restrictions on international transactions will not rely exclusively on them. On the contrary, the nature of the imbalance will often call for other measures: for domestic inflation or deflation, or for temporary financing. What course of action is taken depends on the expected duration of the imbalance and on the relation of the imbalance to other objectives. Temporary disturbances should be financed. Lasting disturbances to the balance of payments which also violate other policy objectives—such as non-inflationary growth at full employment—should be corrected without resort to restrictions. Lasting disturbances which contribute to international welfare should be financed.

Virtually all discussion of international imbalances takes it for granted that they *must* be corrected. All payments deficits are regarded as "bad" and should be eliminated; the only differences of opinion concern the speed and the method. In a cooperative international environment, however, it ought first to be asked *whether* a given imbalance should be eliminated, and then, only if it is determined that it should be, how fast and by what means.

One reason we do not ask often enough whether a given deficit should be eliminated is merely a semantic one. Over the course of time certain kinds of deficit have become accepted; we realign the transactions so that the country is in "balance." It is clear that a trade deficit is often desirable; it may be the counterpart in goods of a movement of savings from a capital-rich to a capital-poor country. It is usually argued that such shifts should be financed by long-term cap-

TABLE 10–1   Cooperation and Adjustment

Stage of Cooperation	Economic Conditions: Inter-country Labor Mobility	Political Conditions: Degrees of Mutual Trust	Principal Method for Coping with Difficult Imbalances
0. Competitive Independence	Low-High	Low	
1. Cooperative Independence	Low	Low	External
2. Restrained Independence	Low	Moderate	
3. Accepted Independence with Similar Objectives	Low	High	Ample Financing
4. Coordinated Domestic Policies	Moderate	Moderate	
5. Uniform Domestic Policies	High	High	Internal

ital movements, which are considered "receipts" by the country with a trade deficit and thus offset the deficit, yielding "balance" on trade and long-term capital account. Sometimes such "long-term" capital takes on a short-term disguise, such as the bank lending to Japan which rose year after year, always turning over but generally increasing in aggregate.[3]

---

[3] As is well known, defining a reasonable and generally acceptable "deficit" or "surplus" for the United States poses formidable problems. The extensive financial relations of the United States with the rest of the world generate a number of transactions which blur greatly the distinction between "autonomous" and "compensatory" transactions. As we saw in Chapter 5, the United States plays an important role as financial intermediary for many other countries. If financial institutions kept their books as the United States kept its balance-of-payments accounts during the past decade, they would be in "defi-

Imbalances in international payments which are not defined away may nonetheless be beneficial. Two cases illustrate the point. The first concerns world economic growth in the postwar period; the second, European economic integration. American deficits (and European surpluses) contributed to both, and were therefore beneficial to the extent that growth and economic integration are regarded as desirable objectives.

The contribution of American payments deficits to postwar economic growth arises both from providing a stimulus and from removing a restraint. The stimulus was demand for European exports. Export demand for European products was largely at the expense of American (and British) products, as indicated by the steady decline in the American share of world exports of manufactures after 1950. Undervaluation of the European currencies with the devaluations of 1949 assured a steady demand for European products as productive capacity became available. This assured demand provided a powerful stimulant to the creation of new capacity. At the same time, relative overvaluation of the U.S. dollar did not impede American domestic investment (at least until the late 1950s) because of the predominantly domestic orientation of American firms.[4]

American payments deficits removed a restraint to European growth by keeping most European countries in a comfortable balance-of-payments position most of the time. Without assured export demand, economic growth might have been impeded by restrictive policy moves.[5]

---

cit" most of the time, since, like the United States, they accept liquid liabilities and make relatively long-term investments.

For a discussion of these issues, see R. N. Cooper, "The Balance of Payments in Review," *Journal of Political Economy*, LXXIV, August 1966, pp. 379–95, a review of a report by a blue-ribbon panel of experts, *The Balance of Payments Statistics of the United States*, Report of the Review Committee for Balance of Payments Statistics (The "Bernstein Report," after its chairman, Edward M. Bernstein) (Washington: GPO, 1965).

[4] For an elaboration of this argument, and of the importance of asymmetrical response to over- and undervaluation of the dollar and other currencies, see R. N. Cooper, "Dollar Deficits and Postwar Economic Growth," *Review of Economics and Statistics*, XLVI, May 1964, pp. 155–59.

[5] Britain's failure to benefit from this process derives largely from preoccupation (in the early 1950s) with the reserve currency role of sterling and the failure to fund the short-term sterling liabilities. A weak foreign asset position made sterling more subject than other currencies to speculative attack. Peri-

The contribution of American deficits to economic integration in Europe is essentially the same as its second contribution to growth: removal of a balance-of-payments impediment. The large payments surpluses of the Continental European countries in the late 1950s and early 1960s spared the EEC its potentially most disruptive challenge during this formative period. Of the members of the EEC, France had the weakest external position at the signing of the Rome Treaty. Devaluation of the franc at the end of 1958, combined with stringent financial policies, re-established confidence in the franc and laid the foundation for large French payments surpluses in the following years. Its improvement was not so much at the expense of its Common Market partners, however, as of the United States and Britain. The members of the EEC could lower tariffs willingly without great concern for their payments positions, which were all strong. Where monetary cooperation and mutual balance-of-payments support lagged far behind close collaboration in commercial policy, tariff reduction might have faltered if some members had incurred large deficits.

Finally, mention should be made of the contribution of the controversial reserve currency role of the dollar—a role which, with large gold reserves, permitted but also contributed to prolonged U.S. deficits. Dollar deficits undoubtedly left the world with fewer restrictions on international commerce than would have been found if the world economy had relied on gold alone for additions to international reserves. There is serious question whether any national currency should play the role of surrogate gold; but the fact is there was no practical alternative, and it was natural (for the reasons given in Chapter 2) for the dollar to fill the gap. Thoroughgoing monetary reform involving the creation of international money will reduce the need to use national currencies as a component of growing foreign exchange reserves.

In sum, it should not be taken for granted that payments deficits and surpluses are undesirable and that steps should be taken rapidly to eliminate them. They should be assessed on their merits. Deficits do have well-known costs: they involve the transmission of inflationary pressures from the country in deficit to other countries; they may involve an arbitrary appropriation of world output by the country in

odic crises of confidence in sterling called for periodic restrictions on domestic investment.

deficit. But any deficit should be examined for possible benefits it may carry, and a confrontation of costs and benefits should be made with a view to determining which deficits—even long-lasting ones—should perhaps be financed rather than eliminated.[6]

Controlled Restraint on International Transactions

Restrictions over international transactions are needed to eliminate imbalances where income adjustment is inappropriate and financial support is unavailable. As noted in the previous chapter, restrictions over capital movements are more acceptable than restrictions on trade and other current transactions, at least outside the United States. But even restrictions over trade may have to be countenanced. The GATT already permits the imposition of import quotas for balance-of-payments reasons, but prohibits the use of surcharges. Import surcharges, however, are much more appropriate to the working of a free market and on the whole are apt to lead both to fewer distortions of competition and, after a lapse of time, to more effective assistance to the balance of payments.

External measures should not be used indiscriminately. They should be subject to certain broad guidelines which would establish presumptively appropriate measures under specified circumstances, deviations from which would require special justification. The purpose of these external measures would be to protect the currency, not to protect particular industries. Import surcharges or export subsidies, for example, should generally be uniform and of broad coverage, with exceptions governed by the objective of minimizing the distortions to trade and production for the required improvement in the balance of payments. Moreover, countries in surplus would be expected to contribute to the process of adjustment by removing any restrictive measures which they had previously placed in force for

---

[6] An obvious candidate for financing is the deficit of a country which has adopted a policy of expansion during a period of world recession. On the choice between adjustment and financing, see the discussion in F. Machlup and B. Malkiel (eds.), *International Monetary Arrangements: The Problem of Choice* (Princeton: Princeton International Finance Section, 1964), pp. 48–53; also see Walter S. Salant "Does the International Monetary System Need Reform?" in J. C. Murphy (ed.), *Money in the International Order* (Dallas: Southern Methodist University Press, 1964), pp. 17–21.

balance-of-payments reasons, and indeed to go farther by reducing barriers to capital outflows and to imports in accordance with long-term objectives of the international community.

The use of restrictions should, moreover, be limited to cases in which a country finds itself confronted with a "policy dilemma," a conflict between the policy requirements for the domestic economy and the requirements for restoring external balance. Restrictions are unwarranted in those cases in which pursuit of domestic economic objectives and restoration of external balance both call for the same measures. A country in balance-of-payments surplus which also has unemployment and unutilized capacity should adopt expansionary policies, the mix of policies to be determined in part by its objectives regarding the structure of its balance-of-payments position as between current and capital account. Countries experiencing excess domestic demand and running payments deficits should adopt deflationary policies.

In addition to being of broad coverage, external restraints on trade and capital movements should be subject to close international consultation. They should not be left exclusively to national discretion. This is advantageous for several reasons.

First, it should assure that balance-of-payments targets respecting both current account and the capital account positions are consistent among all members of the Atlantic economic community. These countries cannot, as a rule, all run balance-of-payments surpluses under present arrangements; they can all run current account surpluses only if, collectively, they are willing to provide the corresponding outflow of capital to the rest of the world, notably to the less developed countries.

Second, consultation would avoid retaliation on restrictive measures which might otherwise evoke sharp reaction from trading partners. If the nations to be affected participate in the discussions leading up to the decision to impose restrictions, giving them a better understanding of the situation and offering them some chance to influence the course of action taken, they are much less likely to respond with countermeasures.

Third, it will keep any country using restrictions under pressure to remove them when they cease to be necessary and to structure them in a way which is designed to achieve maximum impact on the balance of payments, not on the protection of particular industries or other interests. The prospect of having to justify their decisions in an international forum will tend to induce officials to take a course of action which is in fact justifiable.

Fourth, close consultation among closely linked countries constantly keeps before them the relationship between surpluses and deficits, and the relationship between liquidity and adjustment. Deficits cannot be eliminated without eliminating surpluses; and eliminating surpluses will also eliminate deficits. There may be occasions in which the interests of the Atlantic Community are best served through actions—removing restrictions on outpayments or even imposing restraints on inflows—by the countries in surplus.

Finally, if countries in surplus sufficiently dislike the measures of adjustment which either they or the deficit countries must take, they always have the alternative of financing the deficits. International consultation affords the opportunity to distinguish between deficits which are thought to be desirable—or at least less harmful than the measures required to correct them—and deficits which are not so regarded.

The controlled use of restrictions over trade and capital movements admittedly negates some of the value of a system of fixed exchange rates. In a sense, it simply introduces variable exchange rates by the back door. Like floating exchange rates, variable restrictions create uncertainty in international transactions arising from factors outside the particular industries involved in trading or investing. However, unemployment and unutilized capacity are far more costly in economic and social terms than are reasonably uniform restrictions on broad classes of international transactions. And, unlike changes in exchange rates, variable restrictions primarily affect new transactions, not, directly, the value of existing assets. Thus, the huge capital gains and losses, and the incentive to speculate on them, which are so prominent a feature of changes in exchange rates play a much smaller role in the case of variable restrictions on transactions.[7] Finally, in-

---

[7] Speculation would, of course, still take place in a regime of controlled restrictions. Importers would try to anticipate the imposition of surcharges, and capital exporters the imposition of charges on outflows. But the gains from speculation would not generally be so great in the case of capital movements as they would be under discrete changes in exchange rates; and the costs of

ternational consultation is both called for and is natural in the use of restrictions, whereas exchange-rate changes do not lend themselves as readily to such consultation; greater secrecy is required before a change in exchange-rate parity, and there is less scope for modifications afterwards; floating rates require consultation only to avoid competitive official intervention in the exchange markets.

In the context of a long-range objective of greater integration in the Atlantic Community, the need for consultation is an advantage, not a disadvantage. Over the course of time, the process should evolve up the ladder of economic cooperation sketched earlier. As mutual confidence increases in the abilities of national authorities to manage their domestic economies sensibly, there should be a gradual and increasing substitution of financial support for the use of restrictions, and this in turn would evolve into greater coordination of policies along with mutual financial support. It is not, of course, necessary to go through every stage; some stages may be skipped if the political and economic prerequisites are met.

The degree of commitment to cooperation and mutual consultation in the use of restrictions on international transactions should not be underrated. It involves, if not prior consultation on measures actually taken, at least prior discussion of the requirements for action and strong justification after the actions are taken.[8] In time, prior consultation might develop.

---

speculating in commodities are substantially higher than the costs of speculating in currencies. On both counts, speculation could be expected to be less under controlled restrictions.

Restrictions are at a disadvantage to floating exchange rates in one important psychological respect: they may arouse greater opposition from a public which does not appreciate the basic similarity between changes in exchange rates and across-the-board use of tariffs and subsidies. Whereas a change in floating rates results from impersonal forces of supply and demand, imposition or withdrawal of restrictions is a willful act by authorities, which affects the competitive position of domestic producers vis-à-vis foreigners. This weakness also applies to discrete changes in fixed parities, and, most important, it applies to *uncontrolled* use of restrictions. In the course of time the public would become accustomed to this as it has to changes in monetary policy.

[8] Such discussions already take place today under the GATT, in the IMF, and in the OECD on certain kinds of action. The proposal here is more positive in its approach. It would *encourage* the use of restrictions in certain circumstances, and would attempt to make such use an international undertaking.

There are two reasons for believing that close international coordination of external measures might be successful even when coordination of internal policies is politically unacceptable. First, choices involving the distribution of income and the rates of unemployment, price change, and growth in output undoubtedly touch national preferences more deeply than do choices involving external measures. Second, external measures more obviously affect other countries directly, and are therefore more likely to involve retaliation unless subject to international coordination and control.

The conclusion that controlled restraints over international transactions will be necessary is not a happy one. But what are the alternatives? Unhappily, the principal contender to controlled use of restrictions is uncontrolled use of restrictions. In terms of Figure 1–2, the world economy in the late 1960s seemed to be veering back toward greater reliance on restrictions on international commerce—and on artificial stimulants, such as tax rebates on exports—applied at the national level, with a minimum of prior consultation.

The coordinated use of restrictions need not be so bad as it may sound to those who have watched the difficult struggle to remove restrictions throughout the postwar period. In the first place, restrictions are far less costly to economic welfare than the alternative of gearing internal activity to the balance of payments in all circumstances, especially if the restrictions are imposed uniformly over a wide range of transactions. Secondly, the cooperative application of restrictions would keep constantly before nations both the alternative of financing deficits and the joint responsibility of surplus countries and deficit countries, so that surplus countries could be urged to remove restrictions before deficit countries were called upon to impose them.

The central problem posed in Chapter 1 concerned the preservation of national freedom successfully to pursue domestic objectives of economic policy in an increasingly interdependent international economy, while still enjoying the benefits of international commerce without crippling restrictions. Close international cooperation is required to prevent the controlled use of restrictions from negating the principal benefits from trade.

If this cooperation is not forthcoming—if the members of the Atlantic Community lack even the political cohesion required to engage in this kind of cooperation—the term Atlantic "Community" is a misnomer. In that case, it would be far better to break this group of countries into smaller units which are of sufficiently like mind to co-operate closely in these matters, and to allow exchange rates between these units to vary much more than they do now, than to accept the alternative of unrestrained restrictions and unwarranted pressures on national objectives.

A Final Word

The rather pessimistic appraisal of present possibilities for an Atlantic Community without restrictions on foreign commerce should not be misunderstood. The case against a community without restrictions rests on the fact that the decision-making domains of business are increasingly outreaching governmental jurisdictions, and we are not yet prepared politically to extend those jurisdictions and to provide the financial transfers among nations which are required to make the system work efficiently with a minimum of economic loss. The "loads" are outrunning the "capabilities."

The tendencies toward higher economic interdependence should therefore be restrained; but they should not be reversed. There are tangible economic and political benefits from closer cooperation and even coordination of national policies. Too harsh a reversal of the trends toward integration would block pressures for greater coopera-tion and might sour the political atmosphere which has been carefully fostered among the western industrial countries during the past two decades. This would be particularly true of restrictive measures which were adopted unilaterally and in violation of explicit or tacit under-standings governing official action in the field of foreign economic policy.

Moreover, there is often a two-way interaction between institutions and attitudes. We have focussed mainly on lack of readiness to ac-cept extensive coordination of national economic policies; but recep-tivity to such coordination is partly influenced by the existence of in-stitutions which have been performing such functions successfully. As noted in Chapter 1, there must be a minimum degree of prior ac-ceptability for any cooperative enterprise to work, but the successful operation of cooperative efforts in turn fosters acceptability. This two-way interaction must be borne in mind in framing institutional ar-rangements for cooperation among nations.

The argument here is for easing the loads, but for simultaneously improving the capabilities; for restraining the growth of decision-making domains of banks and businesses, but also for enlarging the jurisdictions of government in those areas of economic policy which bear most directly on international transactions.

Recent plans for improving the international monetary system are mildly encouraging with respect to international economic cooperation, despite the efforts of France to restore the primacy of gold, necessarily at a higher price. If these reforms materialize and new forms of international liquidity are produced, the results will be beneficial even if, as pointed out in Chapter 8, the new liquidity is not well suited to the financing of prolonged payments deficits among industrial countries. For the deliberate process of creating international liquidity will bring together high officials from many nations to *make decisions*. Decision-making involves a more direct confrontation of conflicting national interests than does mere discussion, and it should cultivate a high degree of responsibility toward the community of nations as a community, not merely as separate constituents.

In the field of international public health, it took two major epidemics in the 1890s to quell divergent national interests and induce cooperative efforts to control the spread of contagious disease which followed the great nineteenth century growth in foreign travel. There has already been one great international epidemic in economic affairs, and it pushed countries in the opposite direction, away from cooperation and back into their national shells. Re-emergence from the defensiveness created by the Great Depression has been a slow and painful process, taking over two decades. We are still learning how to anticipate world economic strains and to meet them efficiently, which means cooperatively. If we succeed, we will ultimately preserve greater freedom for divergences in national economic objectives than if we follow alternative, non-cooperative routes.

Index

Index

PUBLICATIONS

FOREIGN AFFAIRS (quarterly), edited by Hamilton Fish Armstrong.
THE UNITED STATES IN WORLD AFFAIRS (annual). Volumes for 1931, 1932 and 1933, by Walter Lippmann and William O. Scroggs; for 1934–1935, 1936, 1937, 1938, 1939, and 1940, by Whitney H. Shepardson and William O. Scroggs; for 1945–1947; 1947–1948 and 1948–1949, by John C. Campbell; for 1949, 1950, 1951, 1952, 1953 and 1954, by Richard P. Stebbins; for 1955, by Hollis W. Barber; for 1956, 1957, 1958, 1959, 1960, 1961, 1962 and 1963, by Richard P. Stebbins; for 1964, by Jules Davids; for 1965 and 1966, by Richard P. Stebbins.

DOCUMENTS ON AMERICAN FOREIGN RELATIONS (annual). Volume for 1952 edited by Clarence W. Baier and Richard P. Stebbins; for 1953 and 1954 edited by Peter V. Curl; for 1955, 1956, 1957, 1958 and 1959 edited by Paul E. Zinner; for 1960, 1961, 1962 and 1963 edited by Richard P. Stebbins; for 1964 by Jules Davids; for 1965 and 1966 by Richard P. Stebbins.

POLITICAL HANDBOOK AND ATLAS OF THE WORLD (annual), edited by Walter H. Mallory.

HOW NATIONS BEHAVE: Law and Foreign Policy, by Louis Henkin (1968).

THE INSECURITY OF NATIONS, by Charles W. Yost (1968).

PROSPECTS FOR SOVIET SOCIETY, edited by Allen Kassof (1968).

THE AMERICAN APPROACH TO THE ARAB WORLD, by John S. Badeau (1968).

U.S. POLICY AND THE SECURITY OF ASIA, by Fred Greene (1967).

NEGOTIATING WITH THE CHINESE COMMUNISTS: THE U.S. EXPERIENCE, by Kenneth T. Young (1967).

FROM ATLANTIC TO PACIFIC: A NEW INTEROCEAN CANAL, by Immanuel J. Klette (1967).

TITO'S SEPARATE ROAD: America and Yugoslavia in World Politics, by John C. Campbell (1967).

U.S. TRADE POLICY: New Legislation for the Next Round, by John W. Evans (1967).

TRADE LIBERALIZATION AMONG INDUSTRIAL COUNTRIES: Objectives and Alternatives, by Bela Balassa (1967).

THE CHINESE PEOPLE'S LIBERATION ARMY, by Brig. General Samuel B. Griffith II, U.S.M.C. (ret.) (1967).

THE ARTILLERY OF THE PRESS: Its Influence on American Foreign Policy, by James Reston (1967).

ATLANTIC ECONOMIC COOPERATION: The Case of the O.E.C.D., by Henry G. Aubrey (1967).

TRADE, AID AND DEVELOPMENT: The Rich and Poor Nations, by John Pincus (1967).

BETWEEN TWO WORLDS: Policy, Press and Public Opinion on Asian–American Relations, by John Hohenberg (1967).

THE CONFLICTED RELATIONSHIP: The West and the Transformation of Asia, Africa and Latin America, by Theodore Geiger (1966).

THE ATLANTIC IDEA AND ITS EUROPEAN RIVALS, by H. van B. Cleveland (1966).

EUROPEAN UNIFICATION IN THE SIXTIES: From the Veto to the Crisis, by Miriam Camps (1966).

THE UNITED STATES AND CHINA IN WORLD AFFAIRS, by Robert Blum, edited by A. Doak Barnett (1966).

THE FUTURE OF THE OVERSEAS CHINESE IN SOUTHEAST ASIA, by Lea A. Williams (1966).

THE CONSCIENCE OF THE RICH NATIONS: The Development Assistance Committee and the Common Aid Effort, by Seymour J. Rubin (1966).

ATLANTIC AGRICULTURAL UNITY: Is it Possible?, by John O. Coppock (1966).

TEST BAN AND DISARMAMENT: The Path of Negotiation, by Arthur H. Dean (1966).

COMMUNIST CHINA'S ECONOMIC GROWTH AND FOREIGN TRADE, by Alexander Eckstein (1966).

POLICIES TOWARD CHINA: Views from Six Continents, edited by A. M. Halpern (1966).

THE AMERICAN PEOPLE AND CHINA, by A. T. Steele (1966).

INTERNATIONAL POLITICAL COMMUNICATION, by W. Phillips Davison (1965).

MONETARY REFORM FOR THE WORLD ECONOMY, by Robert V. Roosa (1965).

AFRICAN BATTLELINE: American Policy Choice in Southern Africa, by Waldemar A. Nielsen (1965).

NATO IN TRANSITION: The Future of the Atlantic Alliance, by Timothy W. Stanley (1965).

ALTERNATIVE TO PARTITION: For a Broader Conception of America's Role in Europe, by Zbigniew Brzezinski (1965).

THE TROUBLED PARTNERSHIP: A Re-Appraisal of the Atlantic Alliance, by Henry A. Kissinger (1965).

REMNANTS OF EMPIRE: The United Nations and the End of Colonialism, by David W. Wainhouse (1965).

THE EUROPEAN COMMUNITY AND AMERICAN TRADE: A Study in Atlantic Economics and Policy, by Randall Hinshaw (1964).

THE FOURTH DIMENSION OF FOREIGN POLICY: Educational and Cultural Affairs, by Phillip H. Coombs (1964).

AMERICAN AGENCIES INTERESTED IN INTERNATIONAL AFFAIRS (Fifth Edition), compiled by Donald Wasson (1964).

JAPAN AND THE UNITED STATES IN WORLD TRADE, by Warren S. Hunsberger (1964).

FOREIGN AFFAIRS BIBLIOGRAPHY, 1952–1962, by Henry L. Roberts (1964).

THE DOLLAR IN WORLD AFFAIRS: An essay in International Financial Policy, by Henry G. Aubrey (1964).

ON DEALING WITH THE COMMUNIST WORLD, by George F. Kennan (1964).

FOREIGN AID AND FOREIGN POLICY, by Edward S. Mason (1964).

THE SCIENTIFIC REVOLUTION AND WORLD POLITICS, by Caryl P. Haskins (1964).

AFRICA: A Foreign Affairs Reader, edited by Phillip W. Quigg (1964).

THE PHILIPPINES AND THE UNITED STATES: Problems of Partnership, by George E. Taylor (1964).

SOUTHEAST ASIA IN UNITED STATES POLICY, by Russell H. Fifield (1963).

UNESCO: ASSESSMENT AND PROMISE, by George N. Shuster (1963).

THE PEACEFUL ATOM IN FOREIGN POLICY, by Arnold Kramish (1963).

THE ARABS AND THE WORLD: Nasser's Arab Nationalist Policy, by Charles D. Cremeans (1963).

TOWARD AN ATLANTIC COMMUNITY, by Christian A. Herter (1963).

THE SOVIET UNION, 1922–1962: A Foreign Affairs Reader, edited by Philip E. Mosely (1963).

THE POLITICS OF FOREIGN AID: American Experience in Southeast Asia, by John D. Montgomery (1962).

SPEARHEADS OF DEMOCRACY: Labor in the Developing Countries, by George C. Lodge (1962).

LATIN AMERICA: Diplomacy and Reality, by Adolf A. Berle (1962).

THE ORGANIZATION OF AMERICAN STATES AND THE HEMISPHERE CRISIS, by John C. Dreier (1962).

THE UNITED NATIONS: Structure for Peace, by Ernest A. Gross (1962).

THE LONG POLAR WATCH: Canada and the Defense of North America, by Melvin Conant (1962).

ARMS AND POLITICS IN LATIN AMERICA (Revised Edition), by Edwin Lieuwen (1961).

THE FUTURE OF UNDERDEVELOPED COUNTRIES: Political Implications of Economic Development (Revised Edition), by Eugene Staley (1961).

SPAIN AND DEFENSE OF THE WEST: Ally and Liability, by Arthur P. Whitaker (1961).

SOCIAL CHANGE IN LATIN AMERICA TODAY: Its Implications for United States Policy, by Richard N. Adams, John P. Gillin, Allan R. Holmberg, Oscar Lewis, Richard W. Patch, and Charles W. Wagley (1961).

FOREIGN POLICY: THE NEXT PHASE: The 1960s (Revised Edition), by Thomas K. Finletter (1960).

DEFENSE OF THE MIDDLE EAST: Problems of American Policy (Revised Edition), by John C. Campbell (1960).

COMMUNIST CHINA AND ASIA: Challenge to American Policy, by A. Doak Barnett (1960).

FRANCE, TROUBLED ALLY: De Gaulle's Heritage and Prospects, by Edgar S. Furniss, Jr. (1960).

THE SCHUMAN PLAN: A Study in Economic Cooperation 1950–1959, by William Diebold, Jr. (1959).

SOVIET ECONOMIC AID: The New Aid and Trade Policy in Underdeveloped Countries, by Joseph S. Berliner (1958).

NATO AND THE FUTURE OF EUROPE, by Ben T. Moore (1958).

INDIA AND AMERICA: A Study of Their Relations, by Phillips Talbot and S. L. Poplai (1958).

NUCLEAR WEAPONS AND FOREIGN POLICY, by Henry A. Kissinger (1957).

MOSCOW-PEKING AXIS: Strength and Strains, by Howard L. Boorman, Alexander Eckstein, Philip E. Mosely, and Benjamin Schwartz (1957).

RUSSIA AND AMERICA: Dangers and Prospects, by Henry L. Roberts (1956).

About the Author

RICHARD N. COOPER is a professor of economics at Yale University. Previously he has been Deputy Assistant Secretary of State for International Monetary Affairs, and a staff member of the President's Council of Economic Advisers. He also has served as a consultant to the United Nations, the U.S. Treasury Department, the Agency for International Development, and the Rand Corporation.